Revolutions in Verse

SRLT

Northwestern University Press
Studies in Russian Literature and Theory

Revolutions in Verse

Isobel Palmer

NORTHWESTERN UNIVERSITY PRESS / EVANSTON, ILLINOIS

Northwestern University Press
www.nupress.northwestern.edu

Printed in the United States of America

10 9 8 7 6 5 4 3 2 1

Library of Congress Cataloging-in-Publication Data

Names: Palmer, Isobel M. J., author.
Title: Revolutions in verse : the medium of Russian modernism / Isobel Palmer.
Other titles: Studies in Russian literature and theory.
Description: Evanston, Illinois : Northwestern University Press, 2024. | Series: Northwestern University Press studies in Russian literature and theory | Includes bibliographical references and index.
Identifiers: LCCN 2024021225 | ISBN 9780810147669 (paperback) | ISBN 9780810147676 (cloth) | ISBN 9780810147683 (ebook)
Subjects: LCSH: Russian poetry—20th century—History and criticism. | Modernism (Literature)—Russia—History.
Classification: LCC PG3020.5.M6 P35 2024 | DDC 891.71409112—dc23
LC record available at https://lccn.loc.gov/2024021225

For Joel

Contents

Acknowledgments

This book began its life in the Department of Slavic Languages and Literatures at the University of California at Berkeley. I am deeply grateful to all those who made life in that community so rich, intellectually and otherwise. I am particularly indebted to Harsha Ram and Luba Golburt, without whose expert guidance, insight, and kind mentorship this project would not have taken shape. Special thanks also to Anna Muza, for all that she taught me about the Russian language, poetry, and performance; to Olga Matich, for sharing her knowledge of Russian modernism and for encouraging me at an early stage; and to Emma Widdis, who got me there in the first place.

I am lucky to know Joseph Albernaz, Alex Bush, and Emily Laskin, who were among the earliest readers of versions of this book. Their collective brilliance and tireless enthusiasm helped me to bring one iteration of this project to a close, and inspired me to see it through to the next. Caroline Lemak Brickman, Matthew Kendall, Luba Golburt, Anna Muza, and Emma Wagstaff also read drafts of portions of the book, and I thank them for their thoughtful comments and suggestions. I am also grateful to Maria Roca Lizarazu, who lent much-needed friendship and encouragement as I revised the book and found a home for it, and to all other colleagues at the University of Birmingham who have offered advice and support along the way. My thanks also to Faith Wilson Stein, to my reviewers, and to everyone else at Northwestern who has helped to make this book a reality.

A large portion of this book was drafted in 2020, and I am indebted to all the staff in the Slavic Reference Service at the University of Illinois for their help in accessing vital materials during this time. Thanks also to all my virtual companions during this period, and especially to Chris Tomlinson, Daniel Jenkins-Smith, Andrew Kulik, and Mike Tucker, for their weekly companionship and good humor. Many other dear friends have been sources of inspiration and welcome distraction over the years; beyond those already mentioned, thanks especially to Dan Brooks, Thomas Dyne, Lily Scott, and Piper Wheeler. Finally, my thanks to Jill and David, to my family, and to Joel, for all their endless patience and love.

Note on the Text

Names and Russian words are transliterated using a modified Library of Congress system, except where a standard English form exists (such as "Shklovsky" or "Yury"). For readability, first and last names ending in -ii have been changed to -y (such as "Valery" rather than "Valerii"). Bibliographic references, including notes, follow the Library of Congress transliteration system. Unless otherwise noted, translations are my own.

Revolutions in Verse

Introduction

MARCH 1913 saw the publication of what remains one of Russian literature's most notorious works: Aleksei Kruchenykh's "Dyr bul shchyl" (fig. 1). Included in *Pomade*, a book created by Kruchenykh in collaboration with the artist Mikhail Larionov, this was the first text to be written entirely in *zaum'*, the "transrational" language invented by Kruchenykh and Velimir Khlebnikov as part of their larger bid to revitalize speech and revolutionize the spirit.[1] The poem—for this is how Kruchenykh labeled his creation—was met with outrage. As the Symbolist poet Valery Briusov wrote: "we can in no way sympathize with reducing speech . . . to interjections and meaningless combinations of sounds . . . besides the fact that they are absolutely 'not expressive,' [these sounds] are in addition extremely unpleasant to the ear."[2] This view was widely shared. What was distressing was not so much the meaninglessness of this new language as the claim that these distorted fragments of sound were enough to make a poem. In making this claim, as the Ego-Futurist poet Vadim Shershenevich observed, the group of Cubo-Futurists to which Kruchenykh belonged "contradict their own initial principle that poetry is a combination of words."[3] "The Cubo-Futurists . . . are turning poetry into nothing," another critic complained.[4] Much the same sentiment has been expressed in recent scholarship, though here in a positive key. "The poetry of the past . . . must be scrapped," as Marjorie Perloff paraphrases what she understands to be the poem's core message—neatly summarizing the pathos of avant-garde art as she does so.[5]

Still, for a text allegedly intent upon exploding poetry as we know it, "Dyr bul shchyl" remains quite legible as a poem. Broken into lines that form definite syllabic units and presented as part of a trio that recalls the poetic cycles so common at that time, the text, for all that it spurns recognizable language, does not dispense with poetic convention entirely. On the contrary, the absence of ordinary language only heightens our awareness of and dependence upon these conventions for understanding, as the numerous detailed accounts of the poem's visual and sonic structure make clear.[6] These studies identify patterns of repetition, symmetry, and contrast that are not

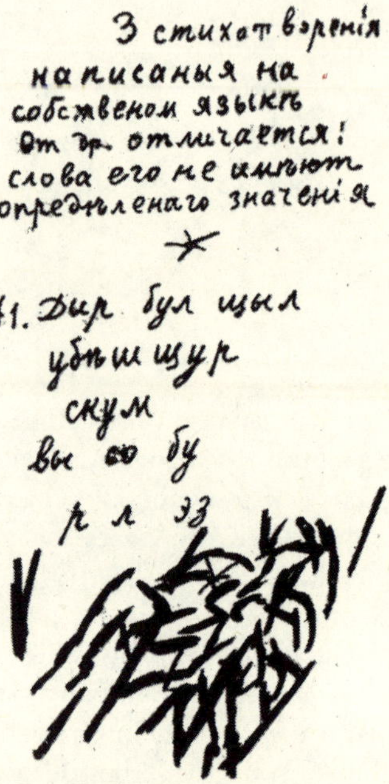

Figure 1. Aleksei Kruchenykh, "Dyr bul shchyl," *Pomade*, 1913.

only little different from those ordinarily encountered in poetry but which also point to further, less immediately apparent formal structures. Nils Åke Nilsson, for example, discovers that the five lines of Kruchenykh's poem have a symmetrically arranged syllable count that recalls the kind of short Chinese or Japanese poems then popular in Russia, as throughout Europe.[7] As Gerald Janecek concludes: "the poem appears as a highly structured composition, more so than the majority of poems, which have to contend with semantics and syntax, and therefore almost inevitably with compromises in the sonic sphere."[8]

In this sense, Kruchenykh's poem is not quite as novel as its transrational clothing might make it appear. Almost twenty years earlier, in 1895, Briusov had caused a similar furor with the publication of his now-infamous monostich in the third (and final) issue of *Russian Symbolists*, a series of publications of Symbolist verse put together and largely penned by Briusov in an effort to bring its titular movement into being. "O cover your pale legs" (O zakroi svoi blednye nogi) (see fig. 2), the text reads in its entirety. By contrast with Kruchenykh's poem, the meaning of this poem appears to be all too readily available. Yet critics and the public alike still declared

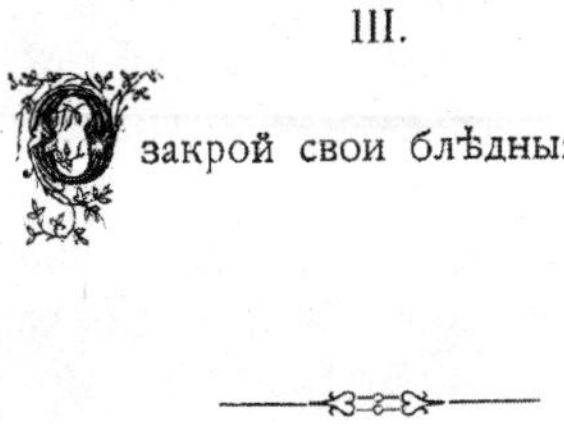
III.

О закрой свои блѣдныя ноги.

Figure 2. Valery Briusov, "O cover your pale legs," *Russian Symbolists*, 1895.

themselves perplexed, and for much the same reason as Kruchenykh's readers: as Yury Tynianov recalled, the most pressing question for many was not "whose legs?" but "why only one line?"[9] Written in regular anapestic trimeter, a relatively common meter in late nineteenth-century verse, the poem adheres to prosodic convention even as it breaks with it in a formal echo of its ambivalent content, at once prudish and lewd. This tension is further heightened by the full page given over to the poem in the issue of *Russian Symbolists* in which it was published, as well as the ornate decoration of its first word: this was a text that looked like a poem, sounded like a poem, and wanted to be read like one—and yet it was not acting like a poem, or at least not quite.

Like "Dyr bul shchyl," Briusov's poem was scandalous not only because of its suggestive content but also because it stripped poetry itself bare, drawing attention to and exaggerating the basic components of its language and structure. The problem with both these poems, I would suggest, was not that they "[turned] poetry into nothing" so much as that they rendered it too much a *thing*: in accentuating the shape and sound of the text, its underlying structures and performative effects, modernist formal experimentation brought readers face-to-face with the perplexing matter of what poetry actually *is*.

While this book concerns modernist debates about and experimentation with poetic form, its chief interest is not the rejection or (re)invention of this or that formal convention. Instead, it asks what these experiments tell us about broader shifts in thinking about the nature of poetry during the first decades of the twentieth century. As I hope to demonstrate, modernist formal experiments are most revealing when understood as a series of efforts to isolate and define the qualities of what I call the poetic medium.

If modernists understood the medium of poetry to be language, the exact status of language in poetry was less clear, and its material basis even less so.[10] The three devices at the heart of this book—rhythm, image, and voice—moved to the center of attention during this period precisely for this reason. These devices name the strange material of poetry without quite defining it: poetry is *like* music, painting, and speech, the modernists remind us, but is not identical with any of them. What did it mean that poetry shared characteristics with these other artistic media? How could the material qualities of *poetic* rhythm, the *poetic* image, and *poetic* voice be defined? And what was the relationship between these material qualities and poetry's less tangible, but no less definite effects? Modernist debates about and experiments with poetic form were an attempt to get to grips with these questions, as well as with the larger issue at their heart: what is specific about poetry as a medium?

I use the term "medium" with an intentional nod to the idea that modernism is defined by its interest in media specificity. This definition of modernism, first proposed by Clement Greenberg, positions the movement as one that is concerned above all with questions of artistic technique.[11] More recent scholarship on modernism has problematized the narrowness of this view, as well as its failure to place aesthetic innovation in its sociohistorical context, a blind spot that, it is argued, perpetuates the damaging indifference to historical conditions with which modernist aestheticism itself is charged. Instead, the field of new modernist studies thinks about modernism in relation to historical and cultural context, broadly conceived, expanding its field of interest both vertically (to take in various forms of "low" and "middlebrow" culture) and horizontally (moving beyond the western European confines previously regarded as the origin point of high modernism) to reposition modernism as the label for a wide array of responses to the experience of modernity rather than a distinct aesthetic position.[12]

My aim in this book is to show that—in the Russian case, at least—these two approaches to modernism are not opposed. Modernist debates about poetry and form cannot be understood in isolation from the multiple, overlapping contexts that shaped them, just as the broader cultural significance of Russian modernism comes into clear view only with these aesthetic debates in mind. This is the basic contention of a number of recent studies of Russian Formalism, which emphasize the close connections between Formalist theoretical approaches and their insistence that literature is a "full-fledged participant in [historical change]."[13] However, the implications of this nexus for our understanding of Russian modernist poetic culture as a whole have yet to be explored at length. Why did poetry come into view as a medium at this moment in literary history, and how did its new visibility as part of a dynamic and rapidly changing media landscape shape the perception of its particular qualities as an art form, a means of communication, and a tool for social change?

Bringing the work of modernist poets into dialogue with that of the Formalist theorists who were their close contemporaries, the organization of this book harnesses the energy of "ruptures and recouplings" (*razryvy i stsepleniia*) that was a central principle of the OPOIAZ Formalists' own approach in order to open up new perspectives on the activities of these figures as individuals and within modernist culture as a whole.[14] Tracing encounters with and debates about rhythm, image, and voice in the work of the poets and theorists gathered here, my goal is not just to uncover the deep affinities between Formalism and artistic modernism, which are so often treated as opposed factions with incompatible aims and ideas; as I hope to demonstrate, these commonalities help to shed new light on the relationship, so crucial for modernist aesthetics more broadly, between formal experimentation and the experience of historical rupture.

REMEDIATING MODERNISM

Viewing modernism's engagement with form through the lens of medium helps to resolve the apparent contradiction between the modernists' rhetoric of novelty, on the one hand, and their continued engagement with established norms, on the other. This was, those involved repeatedly declared, "new art" (*novoe iskusstvo*), "contemporary art" (*sovremennoe iskusstvo*), "the very newest" (*noveishee*)—in short, "modernism" (*modernizm*), a label that Russian modernists were the first among European modernist movements to apply to their own activities.[15] These claims to newness were historically rather unoriginal, as modernists themselves were aware.[16] More pressingly, they obscure important aspects of modernist poetic practice. As often as modernist poets dispensed with syllabotonic convention, for example, they worked within existing rules, reviving syllabotonic meters less commonly encountered in nineteenth-century verse and expanding the range of acceptable rhythmic variations for all metrical schemes. Even the most radical instances of modernist innovation did not dispense with poetic convention entirely, as we have begun to see. (Indeed, Ewa M. Thompson comments wryly, *zaum'* experiments such as Kruchenykh's in some sense simply represent "a new way to say that literary content is conveyed not by means of logical statement but otherwise.")[17]

Despite its reputation as the antithesis of tradition, modernism is thus perhaps better understood in terms of its creative engagement with the past. If there is no doubt that modernist poetry transformed Russian verse, these transformations should be understood as the result of a complex set of negotiations between convention and innovation, "high" and "low" culture, local and imported forms. This was a period that saw both an explosion of interest in fixed verse forms such as the sonnet—a genre that entered its "golden age" in Russia only during the modernist era, much later than in most western European lyric traditions—and the literary adoption of accentual meters common in Russian folk verse; when poets both looked toward the "world culture" of classical antiquity and constructed a variety of myths about Russia's own history.[18] As more recent scholarship emphasizes, such negotiations demonstrate that modernism did not so much reject tradition as *invent* it, as a necessary foil to its own claims to novelty.

In this view, modernism is best defined in what Susan Stanford Friedman identifies as an "adjectival" mode. Whereas definitions of modernism in the "nominal" mode seek to establish some fixed and universal meaning for the term, modernism understood adjectivally "acquires meaning only in relation to its implied opposite."[19] My use of the term "medium" is intended in part to highlight this relational dynamic. In so doing, I aim to make visible the degree to which the heightened interest in poetic form during the modernist period was tied up with the experience of historical change more broadly, which involves not only linear progress through time (from past to present to future), but also the myriad qualitative shifts in point of view and perception that result.

Media scholars talk about the process of "remediation," a concept that highlights the diachronic, historical relationships in which all media are involved and by which they are to an important extent defined. This argument builds on Marshall McLuhan's famous dictum, "the 'content' of any medium is always another medium."[20] New media establish themselves, Jay David Bolter and Richard Grusin contend, by "enter[ing] into relationships of respect and rivalry with other media."[21] Often, this means that new media "refashion" older media, drawing on and "updating" older means of representation in order to "[present] themselves as . . . improved versions of other media."[22] Photography, for example, remediated painting, while film remediated both photography and stage production.

Bolter and Grusin are interested primarily in digital media, but the set of processes they describe applies to media more broadly, including artistic media. Remediation need not always imply competition *between* media, moreover, but may be the result of changes internal to an individual medium. In both cases, the process of remediation follows a similar pattern, one characterized by a pair of contradictory impulses. The new medium strives to become transparent, claiming to provide more immediate access to reality than its predecessors (what Bolter and Grusin term "immediacy"); at the same time, it makes itself opaque, drawing attention to its own (superior) qualities as a medium ("hypermediacy").[23] Often, immediacy actually leads to hypermediacy; "although each medium promises to reform its predecessors by offering a more immediate or authentic experience, the promise of reform inevitably leads us to become aware of the new medium *as* a medium."[24] As John Guillory writes, "it is much easier to see what a medium does—the possibilities inherent in the material form of an art—when the expressive or communicative contents are transposed from one medium to another. Remediation makes the medium as such *visible*."[25]

The development of modernist painting is frequently described in similar terms: under pressure from the rise of photography and film, visual artists turned away from figurative representation and instead embraced abstraction. Greenberg acknowledges this dynamic in "On Abstract Painting" (1944), where he writes, "Let painting confine itself to the disposition pure and simple of color and line, and not intrigue us by associations with things we can experience more authentically elsewhere."[26] Notoriously, however, Greenberg describes this shift not in terms of the dynamic relationships between different media but as the natural progression of all arts toward media purity. According to this account, modernism simply realized most fully the essential truth that Gotthold Ephraim Lessing first identified in *Laocoön* (1766), the modern origin of discussions of medium specificity—namely, that "the unique and proper area of competence of each art coincided with all that was unique in the nature of its medium."[27]

It is essentialism of just this kind that Bolter and Grusin challenge. In their diachronic, media-historical telling, the modernist turn to abstraction is a story of remediation. In this version, the "hyperconscious recognition or acknowledgment of the medium" that we find in abstract art or modernist collage disrupts the transparency of traditional figurative painting or photography, exposing the apparent immediacy of these media as mere convention while at the same time establishing a new set of conventions underpinned by their own claims to truthfulness.[28] Modernist painting reveals not "the irreducible essence of *all* painting," as Greenberg wants to claim, but simply highlights "those conventions which, at a given moment, alone are capable of establishing [a] work's identity as a painting."[29] To put it another way, media are defined not by their fixed and constant qualities but, rather, in relative terms. "A medium is that which remediates," as Bolter and Grusin contend.[30] Contrary to what Greenberg claims, media cannot exist in isolation; any medium needs other media—other "nodes along a signifying chain"—in order to function as a medium at all.[31]

In this connection, the relational, historical frame adopted in many modernist studies of poetic rhythm is striking, as the series of essays examined in chapter 1 begin to demonstrate. Written by Andrei Bely, a Symbolist poet and theorist who pioneered the statistical analysis of rhythm in the Russian context, these essays were an important touchstone for the young Formalists, introducing them to quantitative methods for the study of versification that several of them went on to employ extensively in their own research and which continue to play an influential role in studies of Slavic versification to this day.[32] Direct influence aside, these essays are important for what they tell us about the more general shift that occurred at this time.

Tabulating statistical data from his studies of rhythmic variations in Russian iambic tetrameter verse from the eighteenth century to the present day, Bely uncovered the dynamic, relational quality of prosodic norms; he disrupted the transparency of poetry as a medium, drawing attention to the conventions by which it is underpinned.

Of course, Bely did not make his discovery in isolation, as the chapters in the first part of the book will go on to demonstrate; the relational, historicized view of poetic rhythm outlined in his work was as much the product of processes of remediation as it was one catalyst for them. These processes were set in motion by a number of factors, including, on the one hand, the adoption of new meters and verse forms, and, on the other, the invention of new media technologies. The debates about the nature and correct means of analyzing poetic rhythm that run throughout the modernist period illustrate the hypermediacy to which these circumstances gave rise as, fueled by the emergence of new instruments for recording and measuring sound, theorists sought to describe the components of rhythm in ever more granular detail. At the same time, the very precision of these technologies appeared to confirm the essential immediacy of poetic rhythm as a sonic phenomenon that could only fully be grasped as it was experienced. Despite their claims to scientific exactitude, there is thus less that separates Formalist debates about rhythm (chapter 2) from the highly emotive terms in which poets such as Alexander Blok conceived of this device (chapter 3). In both cases, rhythm is understood in historicized terms as the defining feature of poetry and the particular way in which it mediates between novelty and tradition, continuity and change.

TOWARD A POETIC MEDIUM

The term "medium" is not just a means of repositioning modernism and its interest in formal experimentation and analysis. It is also central to this book's other ambition: namely, to include poetry in media-theoretical discussions from which it has long been excluded. Accounts of artistic media and medium specificity focus largely on visual art, film, and photography.[33] This is striking given the prominence of poetry (a term admittedly used rather broadly) in Lessing's *Laocoön*. Lessing's study was a polemical response to Johann Joachim Winckelmann, who saw the surprising tranquility of the sculpture depicting the agony of Laocoön and his sons as evidence of the fundamental harmoniousness of Greek art.[34] Lessing argued, on the contrary, that this merely reflects the specific requirements of its medium: spatial arts, such as sculpture, cannot depict dynamic events or emotions in the same manner as temporal arts, such as poetry.

Discussion of the material qualities of poetry as medium tends to end here, despite general consensus that the distinction between spatial and temporal art forms is neither particularly accurate nor especially useful. To take a simple example, poetry relies as much upon its spatial layout on the page as upon linear sequence for its effect, just as there is inevitably a degree of temporality and sequential perception involved in the experience of moving one's eyes around a painting.[35] As some have observed, moreover, Lessing is concerned not with the material limits of poetry or painting so much as with their effect on the viewer or reader: whereas painting and sculpture "seek above all to affect the spectator physically," poetry sparks the imagination.[36] That is, poetry is defined for Lessing precisely by its *im*materiality. Similarly, although Greenberg is clear that "the unique and proper area of competence" for painting is the surface of the canvas and the color of paint, he struggles to articulate what the equivalent might be in the case of poetry. In the end, he finds, the fault lies with the medium itself: "if it were easier to define poetry, modern poetry would be much more 'pure' and 'abstract.'"[37]

The difficulty of identifying the material components of poetry has led to the exclusion of this artistic medium from discussions of medium specificity. As the poems and theoretical debates discussed in this book variously demonstrate, however, it is perhaps our definition of medium that needs to be expanded or revised. In challenging the division of material reality into tidy categories and raising questions about the relationship between real and imagined sensory experience, sense perception and material trace, poetry pushes us to refine our analytic tools and to think again about the nature of media, what they communicate, and how.

Interest in the specific qualities of individual media does not necessarily imply media purity, in other words. Modernist conceptions of poetry as a medium were fundamentally shaped by the broader context of inter-artistic experimentation, which was regularly identified as one of the defining features of Russian modernist aesthetics.[38] All of the writers and theorists considered in this book worked in genres and media other than poetry. Boris Eikhenbaum and Boris Pasternak both had an early passion for music, while Vladimir Mayakovsky made a name for himself as a visual artist and actor as well as a poet; we might also think of Alexander Blok's work as a dramatist or the fiction penned by Andrei Bely, Yury Tynianov, and Viktor Shklovsky. They were not unusual in this regard. From Symbolist poetry's fascination with the musical qualities of the word to collaborative avant-garde book projects and productions such as the 1913 opera *Victory Over the Sun*, creative undertakings during this period frequently straddled multiple genres and mixed artistic media. These bold and wide-ranging efforts to expand and diversify modes of artistic expression simultaneously prompted reflection on the specific qualities of each of the individual art forms, making differences between these media perceptible by dint of bringing them into contact.

We see this at play in Kruchenykh's poem, which challenges us to articulate the relationship between the striking and unconventional look of the poem and its equally striking and unconventional sound, a relationship that its unorthodox orthography—which flouts the Russian spelling rules that limit the type of vowel that can follow certain consonants—places at the center of attention. The influence of intermediality on modernist poetry can only be fully appreciated, however, if we think about the questions that such explicit instances of intermediality raised about the material qualities of poetry itself as medium.

One place where such questions were articulated was in debates about the poetic image (*obraz*), the ubiquity of which during this period reflected both a widespread desire to isolate and describe the essential qualities of poetry as a medium and persistent disagreement as to what these qualities might be (discussed in part 2). Such debates were part of a broader effort to rearticulate the nature of the relationship between poetic language and the world beyond it, which poetic images were traditionally understood to mimic or reproduce. Modernists focused instead on the manner in which poetry shuttles between different material strata and spheres of experience—its continual "translat[ion of] one kind of experience of one sense into all the senses," as the media theorist Marshall McLuhan has it—and the processes of translation and transformation in which, as a result, they understood the poetic image to participate.[39] Indeed, this book seeks to demonstrate that if there is anything that unites the highly varied poetic experiments and theoretical ideas about poetry so characteristic of the modernist period in Russia, it was a shared sense of what Thomas H. Ford terms its "translative movement *between*" different material strata and spheres of experience.[40] In moving back and forth across media boundaries and between multiple material strata, from print to sound to embodied performance and more, modernists arrived at a dynamic understanding of poetry as fundamentally *im*pure, always shifting between its multiple possible material forms.

FORMALISM'S CONTEXTS

This mobile, relational understanding of poetry as medium is quite different from that commonly found in Anglo-American scholarship, where form remains the dominant conceptual frame. Static, immutable, unchanging, form in this context has often come to stand for all that is most hermetic, even morally suspect about modernism and the slow drift toward fascism that its "aesthetic of pristine self-regard and hypertrophied opacity" appears to have made inevitable.[41] "Formalism" in this context refers to the critical counterpart to this tendency: the idea, championed by scholars associated with the New Criticism, that the poem is a "well-wrought urn," a self-contained structure to be interpreted in terms of its own internal "pattern of resolutions and balances and harmonizations."[42]

Wary of the insularity associated with such an approach and influenced by the rise of deconstruction and other types of critique, later scholars have increasingly come to favor "fragmentation, unmaking, decomposition" over the oppressive restrictions of form thus defined—to valorize openness over closure, destruction over construction, formlessness over form.[43] This view has itself been criticized in recent years, as a number of studies have sought to rehabilitate form by looking to those places where it gives shape and structure.[44] The latter stance is articulated most forcefully in Caroline Levine's 2015 study, *Forms*, which argues that literary form should be seen as one of the wide array of formal structures that arrange, pattern, and order the social and political world.[45] Even here, however, as Anna Kornbluh notes, the central gesture is ultimately a destructive one: formalism is defended on the basis of its ability to recognize and so to dismantle these "conventional, rigid social and conceptual forms," to "refus[e] . . . hierarchies" and to "escap[e] from enclosing shapes."[46] For her own part, Kornbluh emphasizes instead "the work of building" that she identifies as the central achievement of literary form, where the very solidity and structure that is the object of criticism elsewhere become the source of its political potential, and abstraction is celebrated as a heuristic tool.[47]

Debates about form have thus tended to move along dichotomous lines, arguing in favor of either destruction *or* construction, containment *or* necessary structure, with form regarded as some "whole" that must be either celebrated or dismantled. To these we might add the dichotomy that Austin Warren and René Wellek identify between "extrinsic" and "intrinsic" approaches to the study of text, considered either in relation to its context or as a self-contained aesthetic structure.[48] Much of the debate around form and formalism in recent years has concerned whether formal analysis is more aligned with the former or the latter, as well as the related question of whether such analysis remains cut off from larger social issues or can be said to play an active role in bringing about what Levine identifies as "radical social change."[49]

Russian Formalism has sometimes been bracketed together with New Criticism on the basis that its proponents adopted an intrinsic approach to the study of literature, seeking to understand how the work was "made," as the title of several early essays had it.[50] In parallel, early studies of the movement focused on its own internal logic, emphasizing in particular its insistence on the "autonomy of literature."[51] As Jessica Merrill observes, however, care should be taken to distinguish between different discourses of autonomy.[52] Certainly, the desire for disciplinary autonomy was an important starting point for the scholars active in the Moscow Linguistic Circle and the Petrograd-based Society for the Study of Poetic Language (OPOIAZ) in the 1910s and 1920s. The young researchers involved in these groups sought to differentiate themselves from the academic establishment and to identify "scientific" parameters for the study of literature, noting with scorn the tendency of literary scholars, in Roman Jakobson's memorable description, "to act like the policeman who, intending to arrest a certain person, would, at any opportunity, seize any and all persons who chanced into the apartment, as well as those who passed along the street."[53] But this did not imply a fully autonomous concept of form as a self-contained system.

Rather than interpreting individual texts as self-contained wholes, Formalists such as Jakobson and Viktor Shklovsky understood form as something that travels across a wide range of cultural texts, giving rise to any "perceivable regularity in discourse, such as a particular simile (e.g., arrows falling like rain)."[54] This understanding of form was derived from comparative historical philology, which "described the history of forms as a reservoir of cultural knowledge."[55] Form is deeply imbricated with its social context, in this sense. When the Formalists insisted that literature should be studied as an autonomous field, therefore, this was far from claiming it was an isolated one; indeed, as Serguei Oushakine points out, "insisting on the 'specificity' of this or that sphere of creativity, the authors of this generation saw in narrow professional knowledge not an obstacle to but the basis for active intellectual interventions in neighboring and distant areas of culture."[56]

More recent studies of Russian Formalism have sought to contextualize the movement itself, asking why it emerged where and when it did. Galin Tihanov proposes that Russia and eastern Europe proved fertile ground for literary theory partly as a result of the status with which the Romantic era had endowed national literature in these countries. This gives rise to what he terms the movement's "foundational paradox," the situation whereby it became possible to conceive of transnational and transhistorical qualities such as "literariness" (what Jakobson defined as "that which makes a given work a work of literature") thanks only to a historically specific set of local conditions.[57] A similar dynamic is at play in the work of scholars such as Merrill, Ilona Svetlikova, Ian Levchenko, Igor Pil'shchikov, and others, who provide thorough accounts of Formalism's diverse intellectual sources, from the work of Slavic philologists such as Alexander Potebnya and Alexander Veselovsky to Romantic philosophies of language such as those outlined by Johann Gottfried Herder and Wilhelm von Humboldt, from the activities of nineteenth-century Russian folklorists to the work of William James and contemporary developments in associationist psychology, and beyond.[58] Identifying Formalism as the "product of a historical moment and milieu," these studies illustrate vividly the variety of overlapping historical and national contexts that shaped this particular moment and milieu and the literary theory to which these gave rise.[59]

Despite the range and depth of such studies, extended discussions of the relationship between Russian Formalism and modernist poetic practice remain relatively rare or limited in scope.[60] While few studies fail to note Formalism's objections to Symbolist diffuseness and what they saw as the dilettantish efforts of poet-theorists such as Briusov and Bely, in-depth discussions are limited to those that focus on Formalism's links with Futurism and the idea that the movement emerged as a "scholarly rationalization" of the transrational experiments of poets such as Kruchenykh.[61] This idea has been justifiably criticized as too simplistic.[62] However, an alternative account of the relationship between Formalist theory and this poetic milieu has yet to be produced.

Certainly, Russian Formalism's efforts to systematize the study of the literary text as a system defined by discoverable general principles differentiate this approach starkly from earlier views of the artwork as the unique creation of the artist-genius or as an expression of his interior life. Whereas modernists such as Andrei Bely saw rhythm as the primary "creative impulse," a key to understanding the individual genius of the poet, the Formalists insisted that "the individual creator is only a geometric locus of intersecting lines, of forces born outside himself."[63] This stance represents a qualitatively new understanding of human agency, one that ran parallel with contemporary developments in psychoanalysis (for instance, as Tihanov notes, Freud's conviction that "our psychic life is governed by rules that are independent of us").[64] Yet if this is the case, we must acknowledge that this is the same conclusion to which Bely's studies of Russian iambic tetrameter verse point, as I discuss in chapter 1. Setting off in search of artistic genius, Bely succeeded in undermining this very concept; instead of the source of Pushkin's brilliance, he uncovered his indebtedness to his predecessors and the systemic forces at play in the evolution of rhythm more broadly.

If this is not quite the same as claiming (in Osip Brik's now infamous quip) that *Eugene Onegin* would have been written even without Pushkin, the two arguments are not unrelated.[65] Both view poetry not as a self-contained whole, but as an art form that is inextricable from the historical context and processes in which it is embedded; in the terms I am suggesting, they viewed it as a medium. It was this that Bely's studies of rhythm brought into new focus. The quantitative approach upon which these studies were based was not abstract, as its critics sometimes complain, but, on the contrary, treated the poetic text as something radically concrete: counting stressed positions by reciting poetry aloud and representing graphically the changing metrical profile of iambic pentameter verse from the eighteenth century to his own day, Bely made a claim about the tangible reality of metrical convention in the present, on the one hand, and its inherent historicity, on the other.[66]

The importance of this interplay between concrete instance and theoretical abstraction for conceptions of poetry during this period was particularly evident in debates around poetic voice, the focus of the final part of this book. The boom in popularity of poetry evenings in Russia, as elsewhere, went hand-in-hand with a surge of enthusiasm for sound-based analysis or "Ohrenphilologie," as it was known. Unlike traditional "Augenphilologie," this new method based its analysis on study not of the printed text but of the "sounding" text, poetry as recited. But what exactly was the relationship between the printed poetic text and its recited counterpart? How should concrete instances of recitation feature in analysis of the poem and theoretical accounts? And where was the line to be drawn between poetics and linguistics? In debating methodological issues such as these, Boris Eikhenbaum, Sergei Bernshtein, and other researchers at Petrograd's Institute of the Living Word (Institut zhivogo slova) grappled with the larger questions posed by the new technological age: what was the status of the poetic text? Was there a single authoritative way to read, or multiple ways? These are much the same questions that run through the early work of Vladimir Mayakovsky, whose frequent public appearances and involvement in the theater formed part of a wide-ranging exploration of the shifting role of the poet in the new media landscape of his time.

One of my goals in writing this book has been to find new ways to think about the relationship between modernist poetry and Formalist theory. The latter did not emerge simply as an explanation of modernist experimentation or as a corrective to its more outlandish ideas about how poetic language works; rather, both were the product of a shared cultural milieu. By placing the work of these poets and theorists side-by-side, this book also seeks to recalibrate the relationship between poetry and theory more generally, bringing the two spheres into a conversation in which both participate equally. As such, I treat the poetic texts discussed here not as concrete illustrations of particular theoretical concepts or postulates but as efforts to theorize in their own right. Though it is common to speak of theory "lagging behind" poetry (or vice versa), as though these were two entirely separate endeavors, what I aim to demonstrate here is that these two activities developed symbiotically, as poetic practice became a way of working through theoretical questions regarding the nature and functioning of poetry and theory became a kind of practice in turn, alive to its embedded position within the literary process and with it, history.

Building on the Formalist method of productive *neviazka* (divergence), each part of the book pairs a canonical modernist poet with a Formalist theorist in order to provide a snapshot or cross-section of contemporary debates and practices about these devices seen through the lens provided by each figure and their work. These accounts are by no means exhaustive; on the contrary, by situating these figures and poetic devices in modernist culture conceived as a "field of artistic possibilities," my hope is to find a way to account for the "baffling heterogeneity" of modernist poetry and Formalist theory without lapsing into a list of shared traits.[67] Reading poetic and theoretical texts side-by-side, my aim is not just to demonstrate the common threads running through the diverse artistic and intellectual output of this era. By describing the qualitatively new conception of poetry and form to which the historical and cultural conditions of late imperial and early Soviet Russia gave rise, I also lay the groundwork for a revised account of modernism in this space. This account follows its protagonists in finding in poetry a means to think across multiple contexts and scales, from the broad sweep of literary history to the narrower confines of the stanza, the individual line, or the metrical foot, and the variety of situational and relational contexts that mediate attention, emotion, and everyday action in between. This approach does not look to overturn binaries between novelty and tradition or history and form so much as to trace how modernists came to view poetry as a means of negotiating between them.

Chapter One

Andrei Bely's Science of Verse

ANDREI BELY was the first in Russia to identify rhythm and meter as distinct elements of poetic form, and the first to suggest that rhythmic deviation from the metrical scheme could be tracked using statistical methods, an approach that continues to dominate Russian prosody today. Yet his groundbreaking work in this area is seldom acknowledged without simultaneous mention of its eccentricity and numerous errors.[1] Contemporary reviewers were skeptical of *Symbolism* (*Simvolizm*, 1910), the collection of essays in which Bely's work on rhythm first appeared in print, questioning its claims to scientific precision.[2] The copious notes with which Bely furnished this assorted collection of essays were criticized for their lack of rigor, and were felt by many to typify the renegade approach and cumbersome style of the collection as a whole.[3] A source of more general consternation was the book's apparent indecision between the lyrical or idealist mode of articles such as "The Future of Art" ("Budushchee iskusstva," 1909) and the analytical, scientific position adopted in the "formalistic" articles on meter and rhythm. Not only did these articles directly contradict one another in places, but their polarized attitudes and styles appeared to betray a fundamental dissonance in both Bely's theoretical approach and his understanding of art.[4] Later scholars, too, have questioned the ultimate coherence of a system that combines the religious impulse with rigorous rationalism, and a highly metaphorical style with mathematical equations; even such sympathetic commentators as Steven Cassedy have suggested that, ultimately, the two approaches must be regarded as "conflicting temptations that [Bely] never entirely resolved."[5]

Bely, born Boris Bugaev, was certainly a man of diverse and eclectic interests. As the son of a prominent Moscow mathematician, Nikolai Bugaev, and his artistic society wife, Alexandra Bugaeva, the conflict between science and art had deep roots in his biography. Bely's interests ranged widely, however, from mathematics, biology, and chemistry to music, philosophy, literature, Buddhism, the occult, and beyond. After graduating with a first-class degree from the Faculty of Physics and Mathematics at Moscow University in 1903, he promptly enrolled in the Faculty of History and Philology. Meanwhile, he had become acquainted with the mystical philosophy of Vladimir Solov'ev and established himself as a prominent Symbolist, publishing a series of literary "symphonies," articles on Symbolist aesthetics, and, in 1904, a book of poetry, *Gold in Azure* (*Zoloto v lazuri*). This was just the beginning of a long career during which Bely published incessantly across a wide range of genres, at times changing his philosophical outlook and political position at almost the same rate. He could be both tender and irascible; emotionally volatile and devoted; an "eccentric" (*chudak*) by his own admission, yet a central figure in the lives and work of many of his contemporaries and successors. Despite these idiosyncrasies—and perhaps even thanks to some of them—this book can begin nowhere but with Bely, whose work in the period from 1907 to 1912 helped to shape the conception of poetry described in this book.[6]

Bely's work on meter and rhythm was characteristically ambitious, pursuing a rigorously formalistic approach that had few precedents in Russia at that time. Published as a cluster in the second part of *Simvolizm*, the resulting essays—namely, "Lyric and Experiment" ("Lirika i eksperiment"), "Attempt to Characterize the Russian Iambic Tetrameter" ("Opyt kharakteristiki russkogo chetyrekhstopnogo iamba"), "Comparative Morphology of the Rhythm of Russian Lyricists in Iambic Dimeter" ("Sravnitel'naia morfologiia ritma russkikh lirikov v iambicheskom dimetre"), and "A. S. Pushkin's 'My beauty, do not sing for me . . .' (An Attempt at Description)" ("'Ne poi, krasavitsa, pri mne . . .' A.S. Pushkina (Opyt opisaniia)")—do seem at first to be starkly at odds with the remainder of the volume, in which Bely attempts to theorize Symbolism, often in overtly idealist terms, not simply as an artistic movement but as an entire worldview.[7]

Approaching the matter from the other direction, however, Bely's inclusion of the "formalistic" essays on meter and rhythm in his grand theory of Symbolism is telling. As I will contend, it was precisely Bely's desire to theorize Symbolism as a metaphysical system that drove him to engage so intently with scientific prosody during this period. Form, Bely believed, was the means to the spiritual end he desired, and was the engine of art's religious significance. Science and metaphysics were thus in his eyes far from contrary impulses. The apparent muddle of Bely's work on poetic form—which considers the interactions between rhythm and meter in poetry, poetry's interstitial position between sound and shape, and its movement between dynamic life and "crystallized" death—represents, I will argue, an effort to account for formally structured poetry's constitutive position *in the middle*. The tension between science and lyricism in Bely's account of poetic form provides an early and vivid illustration of what I am suggesting we regard as modernism's heightened sensitivity to poetry as medium.

Bely wrote several essays devoted to differentiating between artistic media, to which I will return at more length below. His critical writing frequently refers to the "means" (*sredstvo*) by which poetry achieves its goal, as well as its function as a "mediator" (*posrednik*), both potential translations of the English "medium." These cognates demonstrate that Bely's interest in the material qualities of poetry was also an interest in the way that poetry mediates. In the language of contemporary media theory, he treats poetry not simply as an artifact or technology but also as "a perspective for understanding."[8]

The term "medium" is also useful because it highlights some of the sources of this new way of thinking about poetry. Bely's was a generation in the middle, in many senses. Though Symbolism strove for organic unity and dreamed of a harmonious future to come, the most salient characteristic of early twentieth-century modernist culture in Russia was its almost compulsive binarism. Symbolism was built upon a dualist belief in the divide between this world and a transcendent "beyond" toward which its practitioners strove, a division variously expressed as the conflict between the real and the ideal, between spatiotemporal reality and eternity, between the visible world and "essence," or between the surface of consciousness and the depths of the spirit. This overarching divide, a version of the Kantian gap between the phenomenal and noumenal realms, was buttressed by the further binary oppositions that structured Symbolist culture and thought, including the Nietzschean duo, Apollo and Dionysus, then a frequent point of reference in literary-artistic discussions, as well as pairs such as chaos and cosmos, cognition and creativity, reason and emotion, or contemplation and action.

Beyond philosophical dualism, the Symbolist obsession with binary thinking had its roots in historical circumstances. While they could not have known that they were an inter-revolutionary generation, modernist artists were nonetheless highly aware of their precarious position "on the border between centuries," as the title of Bely's later memoir puts it (*Na rubezhe dvukh stoletii*, 1930). The increasingly rapid pace of industrialization and the growth of the urban population intensified their sense that the previous era was at an end.[9] The arrival of a capitalist ethos of materialism and utilitarianism in Russia seemed to pose a direct threat to the pursuit of art and beauty that the Symbolists held so dear. The surge of interest in stylized representations of past epochs in Symbolist art represented one effort to resist these trends and, as Irina Shevelenko has demonstrated, to carve out an alternative path for modern Russia.[10] Others looked ahead to the apocalyptic reckoning toward which they felt modern life was rapidly careening, a sentiment that became particularly widespread in the wake of the Russo-Japanese War and the 1905 Revolution. The failed 1905 Revolution also intensified Symbolist artists' awareness of the gulf between the intelligentsia and the people, a divide that is at the center of Alexander Blok's work, to which we will return.

All of the above begins to explain the incongruity of Bely's sudden turn to the study of rhythm in 1907, which came amidst a period of intense personal, artistic, and social crisis. Cast into despair by the failure of the 1905 Revolution, a thwarted love affair, and a year of vicious polemics with the so-called "mystical anarchists," a breakaway Symbolist group based in St. Petersburg, Bely experienced a "crisis of consciousness," as the title of an essay from that period has it, and fits of serious depression.[11] If there is something slightly manic about the long days and nights Bely spent in frenzied calculations of metrical deviation during this period (as he writes in *Between Two Revolutions*, "I worked in a frenzy, giving up whole days and nights to calculating rhythms and working on my article, 'Crisis of Consciousness and Henrik Ibsen'"), it is also first proof that, for Bely, one key to his generation's predicament lay in poetry and form.[12] Recognizing the difference between meter and rhythm and characterizing this difference as one of diametric opposition, Bely draws poetry into the more general crisis of contradiction to which modern life had given rise. Poetry could not resolve these contradictions. On the contrary, its usefulness, Bely came to argue, lay precisely in its own conflicted position, always between old and new; dynamism and fixity; one subjectivity and the next.

RHYTHM AND METER

Bely worked assiduously on the study of prosody during the summer of 1908. This work immediately bore fruit. Arriving at Bely's summer residence that summer, the poet Vladislav Khodasevich recalls, he was ushered to a table stacked with papers, as Bely gleefully announced his "Archimedean" discovery: poems written in the same meter have different rhythmic profiles. Although this distinction, still at the center of Russian metrics, would soon become "common knowledge" (*obshchee mesto*), as Khodasevich notes, "on that day it was a discovery truly as simple and sudden as that of Archimedes. The law in poetics that meter and rhythm do not correspond should be named for Bely."[13]

Bely's distinction between meter and rhythm is typical of the "delirium rhythmicum" that swept through Europe in the latter part of the nineteenth and early twentieth centuries.[14] As modern discourses of progress placed a new emphasis on efficiency and the strict management of time, modernists ostentatiously broke with meter and its association with calculation, constraint, and arbitrary division; "so long as we calculate, we cannot enjoy," as Nietzsche wrote in one early piece on the topic.[15] Instead, they declared their allegiance to rhythm, which became for many modernists, rhetorically at least, the formal means by which to assert their freedom from rational calculation and the standardization of modern life. Russian modernists echoed this rhetoric. "Contemporary verse must be subordinated to the vibrations of the poet's soul and not to the count of syllables," as Briusov declared.[16]

Much the same sentiment is expressed throughout "Lyric and Experiment" and the other essays in *Simvolizm* dealing with metrics. Whereas rhythm is the "natural expression" of the "spirit of music," he writes, meter is an imported, artificial set of conventions that "crystallizes" rhythm, robbing it of dynamism and life.[17] Meter falls firmly on the side of abstraction, rational cognition, and theory, tendencies that are judged negatively both here and throughout *Simvolizm*. Rhythm, meanwhile, is the manifestation of man's creative powers, the epitome of creative practice. It is thus not meter but rhythm, Bely makes clear, that imparts to poetry its special status, and hence it is rhythm that is "the most immediate task [*blizhaishaia zadacha*] facing researchers in the area of Russian poetry" (*SS* 5:192/245; translation modified).

Yet though Bely may have felt that a greater number of deviations from meter led to a "richer" rhythm and heightened "musicality," he does not, in fact, question the existence of meter as such, as his own commitment to counting syllables already indicates.[18] On the contrary, he states explicitly that a thorough understanding of poetic meter is a necessary prerequisite for any theory of rhythm. In the discussion of Nikolai Nekrasov that opens "Lyric and Experiment" ("Lirika i eksperiment"), the theoretical center of the essays on rhythm in *Simvolizm*, Bely accepts without question not only Nekrasov's use of amphibrachic trimeter, but also the foundational role that this meter plays in determining the structure and content of the poem's language (*SS* 5:185/236). As the closing paragraphs of this article continue to insist, "a carefully elaborated notion of meter" must be the basis of any adequate understanding of poetry (*SS* 5:213/270).

This position is also reflected in Bely's own poetic practice. The poems he wrote during that summer of 1908, when he was absorbed by the study of German and Russian prosody and his work on the Russian iambic tetrameter, constitute something of a study in meter; the overwhelming majority of these poems, collected in *Urn* (*Urna*, 1909), are written in iambic tetrameter or other iambic meters, albeit with a range of experimental rhythmic variations.[19] In line with Bely's declaration, at the end of "Lyric and Experiment," that the goal of experimental criticism was to discover the "laws" of rhythm, his "Rhythm Circle" produced a textbook on rhythm, the introduction to which reiterates the importance of meter for the study of rhythm.[20]

Bely was far from unique in this regard. While there was unquestionably a rise of interest in free verse and other forms of nonclassical meter in the first decades of the twentieth century, metrical structure was far from abandoned entirely.[21] On the contrary, such experimentation drove a growing interest in meter and prosodic convention, which became the subject of intensive study and fierce theoretical debate. Bely probably first encountered the new enthusiasm for metrical analysis in the early 1900s at Briusov's weekly gatherings (the so-called "Wednesdays"), where poetics was a regular subject of discussion.[22] This gathering was typical for the period, which saw a resurgence of *kruzhok* culture, small "circles" dedicated to the discussion and study of shared interests, which played a significant role in promoting the study of verse. Bely himself would briefly convene a group devoted to rhythmical analysis, to which I will return below; there were many others besides.[23] These groups addressed the urgent questions that modernist experimentation with meter and rhythm were raising about the nature of poetry and its conventions. Why was verse that was not divided into equal feet or even lines of equal length nonetheless perceived as rhythmic? How did such verse remain perceptible *as verse*?[24]

Bely approached the question methodically via a method he referred to as "enumeration" (*ischislenie*). Analyzing 596 lines of verse written in iambic tetrameter (the most common meter in Russian literary verse) from the work of twenty-six different poets (including his own), he compared the ideal pattern of stresses projected by meter with the actual pattern of stressed syllables in a given line by noting those lines that omitted stress in the first foot, the second and so on. He then produced tables in which the total numbers for each poet, based on the 596 lines analyzed, were placed side by side (see fig. 3). This revealed the most common rhythmic variations of iambic tetrameter in the work of individual poets, giving a picture of which variations were acceptable—that is, perceived as rhythmic—during the different periods under study.

The results of these experiments were presented in four essays gathered in *Simvolizm*. As Khodasevich reminds us, the most significant discovery contained in these essays was held to be that of the diametrical opposition of meter and rhythm, variously expressed as a contest between stagnation and creativity, abstraction and life. Nonetheless, the essays do not dispense with meter. Rather, the combined effect of these articles and the abstractions of Bely's quantifying approach is to make meter newly tangible as a dynamic historical phenomenon.

Bely was not, of course, the first to notice that metrical verse does not always correspond to a given metrical scheme. This issue was at the heart of the extended debates regarding metrics when syllabotonic versification first entered Russian verse in the eighteenth century. In his famous "Letter on the Rules of Russian Versification" ("Pis'mo o pravilakh rossiiskogo stikhotvorstva," 1739), Mikhail Lomonosov insisted not only that existing tonic meters—hitherto the backbone of Russian versification—be jettisoned

Сумма ускорений ямбического диметра (на 596 строках):	Ломоносов	Державин	Богданович	Дмитриев
На первой стопе	13	46	24	25
« второй стопе	139	139	114	100
« третьей стопе	272	263	271	251
« первой и третьей	5	26	9	14
« второй и третьей	11	1	5	5
« первой и второй	«	«	«	«

	Капнист	Батюшков	Жуковский	Пушкин
На первой	35	28	90	110
« второй	112	33	52	33
« третьей	230	313	280	341
« первой и третьей	7	7	44	60
« второй и третьей	9	5	2	1

	Лермонтов	Языков	Баратынский	Тютчев	Бенедиктов	Павлова
На первой	101	126	164	115	59	107
« второй	47	13	4	62	24	72
« третьей	321	388	325	342	343	271
« первой и третьей	58	85	62	76	30	44
« второй и третьей	«	2	1	2	«	3
« первой и второй	«	«	«	«	«	1

	Полонский	Фет	Майков	Мей	Некрасов	А. Толстой
На первой	96	139	77	123	81	83
« второй	43	34	24	17	42	13
« третьей	284	330	299	352	347	323
« первой и третьей	40	62	36	65	44	41
« второй и третьей	2	«	«	2	«	«

	Мережковский	Сологуб	Брюсов	Блок	Городецкий	
На первой	86	146	73	13	77	
« второй	16	27	48	173	11	
« третьей	359	313	286	282	274	
« первой и третьей	55	74	36	55	29	
« второй и третьей	«	«	«	4	«	

Figure 3. The results of Bely's "enumeration" of Russian iambic tetrameter verse. From Belyi, *Sobranie sochinenii* 5, no. 216.

entirely, but, moreover, that every foot in the verse line should bear a stress and thus comply with the pattern of stressed syllables projected by any given syllabotonic metrical scheme. This position proved untenable, not least since Russian, in which the average word length is three syllables, permits only one stress per word. Lomonosov was quickly forced to acknowledge the necessity of "pyrrhic" (unstressed) feet. Nonetheless, the legacy of his initial view of the matter was felt in the nineteenth-century view of pyrrhic feet, which continued to be regarded as a lamentable, if unavoidable compromise between the demands of the syllabotonic system and the structure of the Russian language. In this light, the modernist position exemplified by Bely, which viewed deviation from the ideal metrical scheme as a positive phenomenon, might be regarded as less a revolution in attitudes toward meter than an evolution, a further step toward accepting the inevitable gap between metrical scheme and the Russian language by naming the result of their interaction ("rhythm").

The detail of Bely's analysis clearly demonstrates, moreover, that rhythmic variation in iambic tetrameter verse is achieved not simply by omitting ever greater numbers of stressed syllables in each line, but through different combinations of stressed feet in isolated and successive lines. Comparing numerical data for poets working in each era—from Lomonosov in the eighteenth century to Alexander Blok in the twentieth—he finds that, though the total number of omitted stressed syllables does, on average, increase, the numbers are by no means consistent enough to point to an ongoing decline in adherence to the metrical scheme. In fact, the difference between the modernist verse of Sergei Gorodetsky (1884–1967), which contains the fewest feet without stress (362 of a possible 2,384 in 596 lines of iambic tetrameter, or 15.18 percent), and, at the other extreme, the Romantic poetry of Nikolai Iazykov (1803–1846), which contains the most, is relatively small (165 feet, or 6.92 percent of the possible 2,384).[25] More striking, and the focus of Bely's discussion, is the *position* of these unstressed feet, as well as the increasing variety in the range of their possible combinations within a given poem. If, during Lomonosov's time, the overwhelming majority of omitted stresses fell on the second and third feet of any given iambic tetrameter line, Pushkin was more likely to omit stresses on the first and third feet; poems written in the latter half of the nineteenth or early twentieth century, meanwhile, show no clear preference. Other findings were more surprising. One of Bely's most shocking revelations here, given Pushkin's cultural status, was to refute his reputation as a metrical innovator; as Bely shows, it was in fact Pushkin's fellow Romantic, Vasily Zhukovsky, who initiated the turn from eighteenth-century patterns of stress to the preferred early nineteenth-century omission of stress on the first and third feet.

As a whole, then, and despite Bely's preference for certain rhythmic deviations over others, the study does not advocate rejection of the metrical scheme but, rather, identifies the shifting possibilities available to poets for "acceptable" deviation from the metrical scheme at different times. This was the first time that the metrical structure of Russian verse had been analyzed in historical perspective, and the results were truly a revelation: where formerly readers had felt intuitively that some poets were metrically more innovative than others, such intuitions were now revealed to have a firm basis in historical and metrical fact.

Bely's account does not, moreover, reveal a gradual retreat from metrical structure in the modern day. Rather, he describes the development of rhythmic variations as a cumulative process, where each successive generation of poets adds further to the growing store of rhythmic possibilities for iambic tetrameter verse; so Briusov, writing in the early twentieth century, omits almost as few stressed positions as Lomonosov, while the work of his contemporary Blok follows more closely in Tiutchev's (omitted) footsteps. Bely's main emphasis is on the specific manner in which poets employ meter, which they work with rather than against; his central discovery was that rhythm, rather than entirely free, conforms to evolving poetic norms.

Despite the emphasis that Bely himself placed on the opposition between meter and rhythm, therefore, what is most significant about his study is that it makes perceptible the role of convention in structuring poetic language. This is true in a quite literal sense: tabulating stressed syllables and diagramming rhythmic variations, Bely gives prosodic convention tangible weight and shape. The result is a diachronic view of rhythm that overrides his own subjective claims regarding the rhythmical richness of this or that poet and instead reveals the dynamic and fundamentally historical reality of metrical structure in use. Bringing poetry into focus through this media-historical lens was the first step toward defining its specificity.

RHYTHM AND MATTER

Bely's essays on rhythm also propose suitable instruments for the analysis of poetic language. Beyond the use of statistical analysis, the most important such instrument is his method of graphic notation (*zapis'*). This system of grids and geometric figures is designed to replace conventional systems for the notation of metrical schemes and to capture the dynamic motion of the rhythm unique to each individual poem. Bely went on to develop this system in collaboration with his *ritmisty* ("rhythmists"), a group of students and enthusiasts with whom he met in his "Rhythm Circle" on a semi-regular basis between 1910 and 1912 under the aegis of the newly founded Musaget "academy."[26] The circle presented an opportunity to put the experimental method outlined in *Simvolizm* into practice. The graphic method has been called both the least and the most excessively scientific element of Bely's analysis. In this section, I put such criticisms aside and consider instead what this method tells us about Bely's conception of the specific nature of the poetic medium and its material qualities.

Bely addresses the question of medium specificity directly in "Forms of Art" ("Formy iskusstva," 1902), an essay he included in *Simvolizm* and placed at the beginning of the section containing the essays on rhythm.[27] The essay is essentially an account of Schopenhauer's hierarchy of the arts, which explicitly ranked temporal arts such as poetry and music above plastic ("spatial") arts such as painting, sculpture, and architecture.[28] Music, according to this scheme, is the highest art form since it most closely approximates pure temporality. This view was widespread among the Symbolists. Consequently, if somewhat paradoxically, given the origins of this idea in an assertion of the specificity of music as an artistic medium,, the Symbolists sought to infuse literature with the "spirit of music" and to erase the boundaries between the arts more generally.[29] Bely himself returned repeatedly to this theme in his theoretical writing and his artistic practice, even inventing a new genre, the literary "symphony," a kind of novel in which plot is subordinate to musical structures such as theme and variation. While such experiments appear to push against a notion of medium specificity, they might equally be viewed as extended investigations of just this issue, a means of testing the particular qualities and material limitations of both music and literature. Bely's "musical aesthetic" is characteristic of an intermedial approach to the question of medium specificity that directly informs his conceptualization of the poetic medium.

In "Forms of Art" and other critical essays, Bely explicitly locates the specificity of poetry in its boundary position *between* musical and visual art forms. Bely's formal experiments also frequently place this boundary at the center of attention. His pioneering use of staggered lines and other graphic techniques, for example, explored the relationship between poetry's shape on the page and its intonational contours in performance.[30] Conversely, Bely wrote his poetry in complete silence and without moving at all; as his wife, Klavdia Nikolaevna Bugaeva, recalls, "he said that until the poem was written down and the eye passed over the lines like a kind of musical notation, one could say nothing. First it was necessary to *see* them and then check by ear how the voice would fit into them."[31] All of this indicates that Bely viewed poetry's position at the intersection of visual/spatial and verbal/temporal art forms quite literally, in terms of the material qualities of poetic language, as well as in the more diffuse, theoretical terms suggested by his philosophical interests.

This conception of poetic materiality fundamentally informs the system for the graphic notation of rhythm that Bely devised in these essays. This system is the part of his work on prosody that attracted the sternest criticism from theorists who followed him; it is, according to Zhirmunsky, "the least successful aspect" of the method and the one most urgently requiring correction, from the point of view of metrics.[32] Certainly, the system has its eccentricities (see fig. 4). It consists of three columns. In the first is the poem itself. The second consists of a grid in which each square represents a foot; each square shows the combination of stressed and unstressed syllables in each foot. The final column is another grid, in which points are placed in squares corresponding to feet in which stressed syllables have been omitted. Points in consecutive lines are then joined by straight lines to form a variety of shapes. Bely gives the resulting "figures"—of which there are forty-three

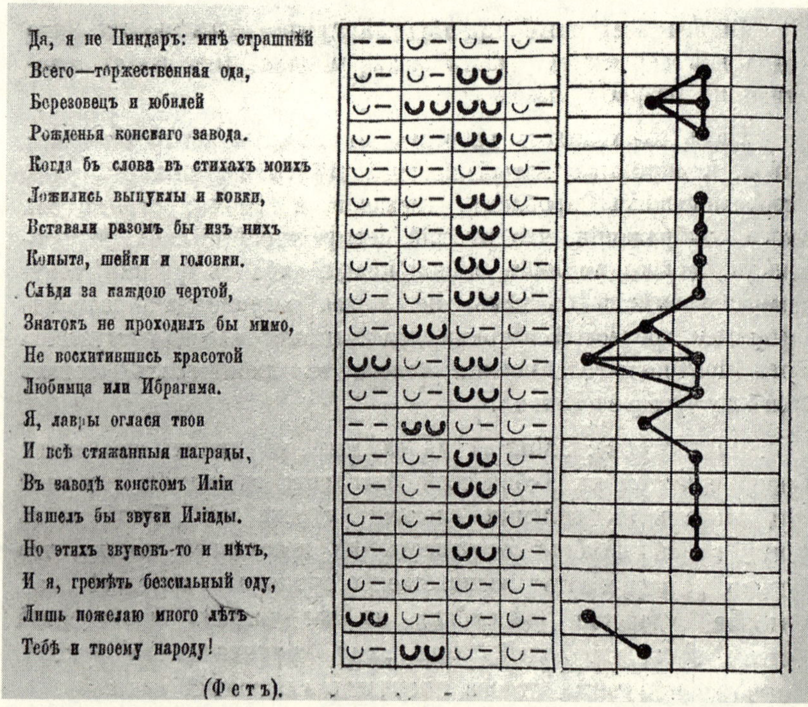

Figure 4. Bely's system for graphic notation of rhythm, based on an example by the nineteenth-century poet Afanasii Fet. Each square stands for one metrical foot. The central column depicts stressed and unstressed syllables using standard notation. The column on the far right depicts these patterns using the geometric method proposed by Bely. From Andrei Belyi, *Simvolizm: Kniga statei* (Moscow: Musaget, 1910), 260.

in total—names that range from the straightforwardly geometric ("angles, rectangles, rhombuses, squares") to the more fanciful (the "roof" and the "inverted roof," the "ladder," the "cross" [the product of a roof followed by an inverted roof]); and these are further subdivided into "basic" (*osnovnye*) and "derived" (*proizvodnye*) figures (*SS* 5:200/255). It is not just the quantity or variety of figures that produces rhythmically "rich" verse:

> A great many figures are formed by [patterns of] half-accents. They can be classified as simple, complex, symmetrical (longitudinally or transversally). The most effective rhythmic figures are those whose graphic designs are symmetrical: the "roof," the square, and their combinations in the rhombus and "cross" are examples of symmetrical figures. As far as the rhythmic line itself is concerned, a broken, zigzag shape is an indication of rhythmic richness, while a simple line is an expression of rhythmic poverty. (*SS* 5:202/257–58)

Where dots are not joined together by lines (i.e., where they do not occur on consecutive lines) or where there is an "accumulation of empty spaces," "a true rhythm has not yet emerged" (*eshche ne vyrazivshiisia ritm*) (*SS* 5:202/258). All of the above effects can be seen in figures 4 and 5.

Despite its eccentricity, Bely's system of graphic notation represented a significant theoretical advance, acknowledging, for the first time, the importance of the interplay of metrical dispersions between verse lines in addition to the stress pattern of individual lines. Nonetheless, Bely's successors found plenty to criticize. Zhirmunsky identified two particular issues, both relating to much-debated details of scansion. First, the system only marks *omitted* stresses, thus failing to register "the 'supplementary stressing' of weak syllables, which is no less essential from the point of view of rhythm."[33] Even more problematic, Zhirmunsky argues, is the system's neglect of strophic boundaries: Bely's rhythmic figures happily straddle two stanzas, whereas, in fact, the strophic boundary "considerably weaken[s] the connection between consecutive lines." The system, in Zhirmunsky's view, thus fails to reflect "any rhythmic reality accessible to perception" (*ne otrazhaiushchii nikakoi dostupnoi vospriiatiiu ritmicheskoi real'nosti*).[34]

For Steven Cassedy, by contrast, the proximity of Bely's graphic figures to perceptual "reality" is less important than their extra-perceptual significance.[35] According to Cassedy, the concrete aesthetic object—in the manner of an Orthodox icon—becomes for Bely "a front for something that lies *behind* it, that is to be retrieved, and which then effectively replaces the concrete object." The geometric figures are, Cassedy argues, another example of the iconic act, "wherein the subject, through experience of a concrete perceptum strives to approximate (but can never actually attain) direct experience of the transcendent."[36] Viewed from this angle, the three columns of Bely's

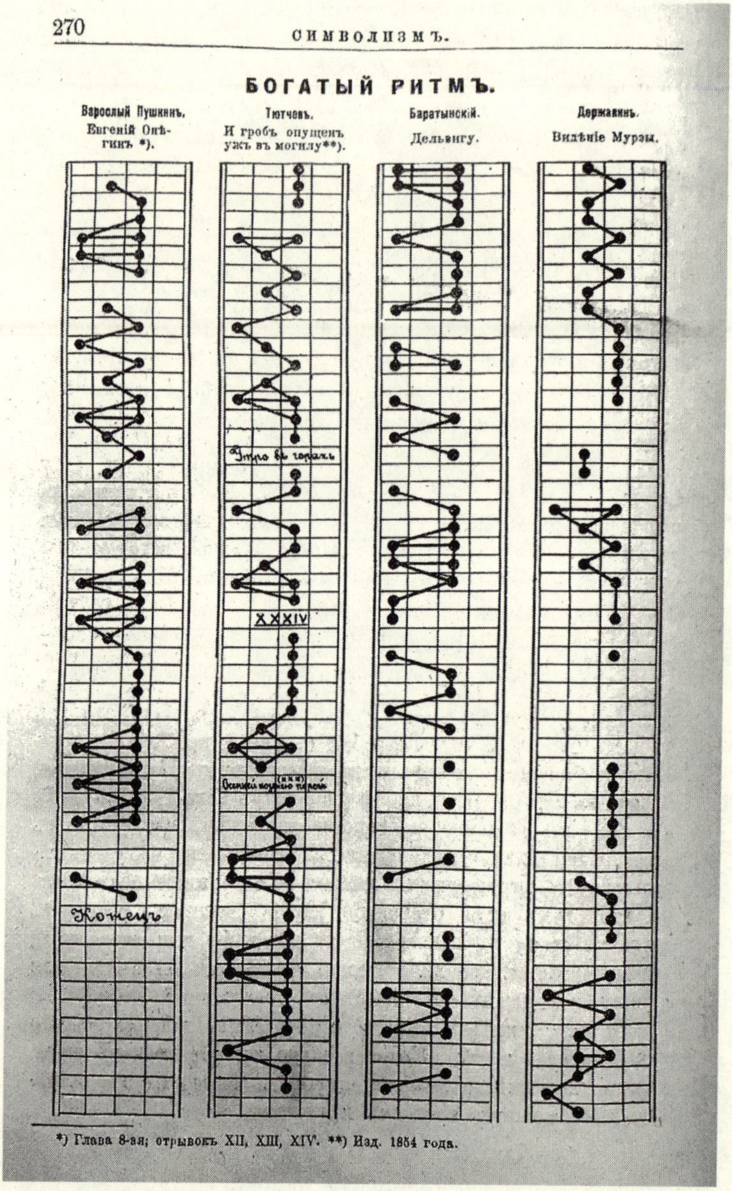

Figure 5. Graphic figures illustrating "rich rhythm" in four texts (from left to right): three stanzas from chapter 8 of Pushkin's *Eugene Onegin* (1830); Fyodor Tiutchev's "And the coffin has already been lowered into the grave . . ." (1835); Evgenii Baratynsky's "To Delvig" (1821); and Gavrila Derzhavin's "A Mirza's Vision" (1783). From Belyi, *Simvolizm,* 270.

system do not record metrical variation so much as the process of striving for a direct experience of transcendence, and even of gradually approaching it; simultaneously, they testify to the inevitable failure of this pursuit.

Zhirmunsky refers to Bely's graphic method as a graphic *priem*, a "device" or "method." The term used by Bely to refer to his efforts to record rhythm, however, is *zapis'*, a word with multiple uses but which generally indicates a recording or notation of something seen or heard. Bely's use of this term suggests an alternative interpretation of the graphic figures, one that foregrounds their status as an inscriptive medium. In an important sense, of course, a *zapis'* of poetic rhythm is a somewhat defunct mechanism: it records something that is already "recorded" by the words of the poem. It is perhaps this that represents the main role of the graphic figures in the essays, however, which function precisely to draw attention to the poem's own status as an inscriptive medium of sorts. Emphasizing poetry's materiality, the *zapis'* reminds us that, as Lisa Gitelman notes of inscriptive media more generally, "the representations they entail and circulate are crucially material as well as semiotic."[37] Like many verbal nouns in Russian, moreover, *zapis'* can refer both to the product (record/transcript) and the action (recording/transcription); it refers both to medium as artifact and to medium as a process of mediation. Bely's determination to devise an appropriate *zapis'* for rhythm represents an effort to better define the connection between the material limitations of poetry as a medium and the manner in which this poetic medium intervenes in its environment.

Nowadays, the word *zapis'* most commonly refers to audio or video recordings, both analog and digital, but its root is *pisat'*, which in Russian means both "to write" and "to draw." Bely's graphic figures straddle these two spheres (perhaps not coincidentally, given the rapid rise and spread of sound recording technologies in Russia at the turn of the century).[38] Although the figures are usually treated as visual representations of rhythm, the first stage in producing them was sonic: the pattern of stressed syllables in a given poem needed to be *heard* before it could be recorded. When Bely convened his "Rhythm Circle" in 1910,[39] the first order of business was to assess its members' "hearing" (*slukh*).[40] This was not a health check, but a test to ensure that all the so-called *ritmisty* had an accurate sense of which syllables in a given line bore stress. (The group planned to build on Bely's work in *Simvolizm*, using their increased numbers to apply his method to an even larger body of iambic tetrameter verse.)[41] The ability to *hear* rhythm correctly was identified as a necessary prerequisite for the correct *depiction* of rhythm on the grids at the center of Bely's study.

The graphic figures thus encode a series of discrete operations: first, the visual processing involved in correctly identifying the intonation of a given line; then, the articulation of this intonation when the poem is read

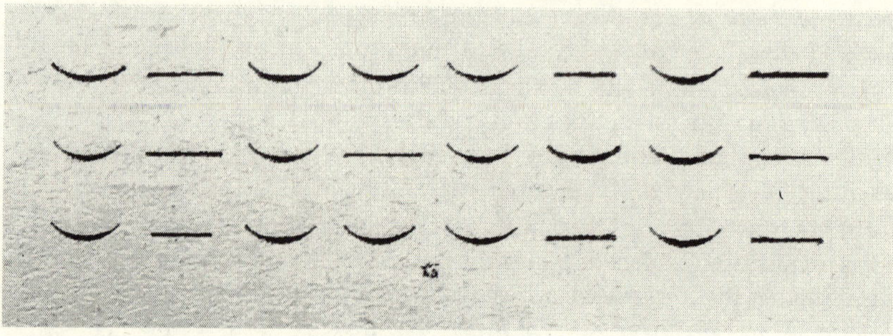

Figure 6. The reader is left to identify the geometric shapes created by stress patterns. From Belyi, *Simvolizm,* 313.

aloud; finally, the aural recognition of which syllables bear stress. In this sense, the figures constitute a kind of reverse ekphrasis, a visual description not only of the poem's verbal fabric but also of the listener's encounter with it. Like ekphrasis proper—which performs, in W. J. T. Mitchell's formulation, "a form of nesting without touching or suturing, a kind of action-at-distance between two rigorously separated sensory and semiotic tracts"—the graphic figures require completion in the mind of the reader.[42] This is literally the case in the section of "Attempt to Characterize . . ." which provides examples of geometric figures as they feature in the work of selected poets (see fig. 6): here, the arrangement of stressed and unstressed syllables in each poem is represented using conventional metrical scansion, leaving it to the reader's mind's eye to trace the lines necessary to form these shapes, which are referred to by their geometrical name in the text (e.g. "triangle," "rhombus," and so on) (*SS* 5:225–37).[43] The absent figures draw our attention to the intersection between the visual and aural instantiations of verse by insisting on their separateness, thereby both exposing the inherent intermediality of poetry, and also demanding that the reader confront this intermediality by traversing the boundaries between them.

John Elsworth calls Bely's work on rhythm "a method of learning to perceive differently."[44] Certainly, the graphic figures with which the studies are furnished amount to an emphatic assertion of the materiality of the poem, which includes not only its sonic (temporal) and graphic (spatial) elements but also a third thing, an indexical trace of its "fore-history and after-history," the poet's creative forces and each reader's encounter with the same.[45] The figures highlight not only the materiality of the text, but also our encounter with the text as interface. This material aspect of the poetic text only stands out more starkly if we consider, as Cassedy and others suggest, that Bely's graphic figures gesture beyond themselves to the abstract or idealized Forms that they represent; for the transcendent is reached precisely through the moment of contact that the poem's material makes possible. The specificity of the poetic medium lies both in its intermediality, its permanent suspension between verbal and visual, and the fact that this intermediality only becomes fully apparent when we interact with it.

Like so many of his fellow Symbolists, Bely dreamed of penetrating the "veil of phenomena" to access a higher state of consciousness and divine redemption. Far from precluding an interest in the materiality of the artistic medium, this aspiration focused his attention on the unique combination of material qualities that rendered poetry the interface between the phenomenal and the noumenal realms. Bely's repeated attempts to devise an appropriate method of *zapis'* for poetic rhythm foreground poetry's status as a space of transition and transformation, the nexus between temporal and spatial form.

RHYTHM AND MAGIC

Thus far, I have argued that Bely's studies of meter and rhythm bring him up against the material specificity of poetry. As we have seen, he regards the poetic medium not as an immutable object with given, self-defining properties, but as an inherently historical artifact involved in continual processes of obsolescence, innovation, and renovation. His rhythmic "recording device" highlights the mixed quality of the poetic medium, whose specificity lies in its insistently interstitial position between visual and auditory, spatial and temporal forms. The final section of this chapter turns to the next essay in *Simvolizm*, "The Magic of Words" ("Magiia slov"). Also written in October 1909, this text is seldom placed in direct dialogue with "Lyric and Experiment" and its companion essays, despite its proximity to them in the volume itself. It is often treated completely separately from these "formalistic" essays, seeming to signal the complete abandonment of science in favor of mystically inclined metaphysics. In fact, the essay follows quite logically from the formal discussions that precede it, moving from their analysis of the material qualities of poetry to an assertion of the agency of the poetic medium—a theory that defines poetic form in terms of what it does, and how. This becomes clear when we focus not on the comparison between dead and living words that the essay is now best known for but its lengthier, and arguably more significant consideration of the tension between form and formlessness and the differences between the mediated and the unmediated world.

"The Magic of Words" is usually quoted with a wry smile, as evidence of Bely's semi-mystical, somewhat outlandish ideas about the power of the poetic word, here accorded magical properties. This was not an unusual claim for a Symbolist poet (Alexander Blok had published an essay on a similar topic just the year before).[46] The younger generation of Symbolists had inherited the image of the poet as theurgist from the mystical philosopher Vladimir Solov'ev. The real purpose of art, so this generation believed, was to transform life. And language, in the hands of the artist-demiurge, was the means by which this new world would be conjured.

Its more fanciful aspects aside, this belief formed the basis of a serious, if not entirely original theory of language as a fundamentally creative phenomenon. Bely and other Symbolists inherited this view of language from Alexander Potebnya, who was influenced in turn by Wilhelm von Humboldt.[47] In broad terms, this theory regards language as an energetic phenomenon (*energeia*, in Humboldt's terms) rather than a made thing (*ergon*)—as a creative process that is, or should be, constant and ongoing.[48] In "The Magic of Words," this is posed in terms of the distinction between the "living word" (*zhivoe slovo*) of poetry and its decaying counterparts. All language is originally poetic (that is, metaphorical), Bely argues, since it is born of the creative act of naming a thing. This act not only asserts the existence of things, he writes, but actually brings them into being. Since the creative word is "living," however, it can also die. The product is either the crystallized "word-term" (something like a preserved fossil of the original metaphor, inert but bearing witness to its creative origins) or the prosaic word, the "stinking corpse" that is produced when common usage drains a poetic word of its creative life and makes it rot. Such "zombified words" (*khodiachie slova*)—dead, but feigning life—make "a mockery of man's creative striving."[49] It is poetry's task to stem the tide of such words by returning to language its role as "a creative medium, forging new realities rather than mechanically reproducing preexistent ones."[50]

Once again, Bely introduces contradiction in this essay rather than seeking to overcome it. As in the essays on rhythm, however, the opposition between the "living word" and the crystallized "word-term" (as opposed to the half-living, half-dead "zombies") is a dynamic, cyclical one between interdependent poles. This is an important point of divergence from Potebnya. The latter placed the act of creation in a mythical linguistic past when, he argued, there still existed an intimate connection between signifier and signified. Bely was critical of the resulting "static" view of language's creativity.[51] "The Magic of Words" returns instead to Humboldt's initial conception of linguistic creativity as taking place in the continuous present tense:

> The eviscerated word is an abstract concept; the abstract concept completes the process of subjugating nature to man; it is in this sense that humanity, at certain stages of its development, erects temples of knowledge from living speech; then comes a new need for creativity; the seed-word, which has retreated into the depths of the unconscious, swells and bursts through its dry

> shell (the concept), sprouting a new shoot; this revival of the word signifies a new organic period of culture; the old men of yesterday's culture, under the sway of new words, leave their temples and go out into the woods and fields, again begin to enchant nature for new conquests; the word tears off from itself the shell of concepts; it glitters and sparkles with a virginal, barbaric display of colors. (*SS* 5: 319).

This paragraph blends two different visions of the natural world. On the one hand, this is a world that functions according to predictable cycles—one in which the green shoots of new, creative words, provided with the right conditions, break through the hardened shells of word-terms with the coming of each spring. On the other, it is a world prey to the unpredictable natural elements, those forces against which humans must repeatedly defend themselves by means of poetic language. The passage thus repeats in allegorical terms much the same argument as that made in the essays on rhythm, which emphasize poetry's perpetual movement between old and new, control and abandon, text and sound; at the same time, it adds its own opposition, that between nature and culture. The poetic word mediates between these two spheres: both the tool by means of which wild nature is tamed and the wild seed that forces its way through culture's cracks, it plays the role of agriculturalist, harnessing the power of the elements and channeling it into new growth and sustenance.

In this sense, the essay resonates directly with the turn in media theory to the concept of "cultural techniques"—a concept that broadens the typical definition of media to take in actions as well as materials, the intersection of a tool and the "operative chains that precede the media object they generate."[52] One commonly cited example of a cultural technique concerns the use of a plow to draw a line in the ground that marks out city limits, an action that "generates the distinctions between inside and outside, culture and nature, 'us' and 'them,' considered necessary to the creation of a new order."[53] Bely is quite explicit that this is the role played by poetic language in his theory. "Every word is an incantation," he writes; "the combination of words, regardless of their logical sense, is the means [*sredstvo*] by which man protects himself from the inrush of the unknown" (*SS* 5:321). The poetic medium gives shape and meaning to what would otherwise have been "formless and void," its activity situated in the threshold moment when the poetic word is leveraged against the formless chaos of untamed nature, on the one hand, or the calcified forms of reified knowledge, on the other; the result is a temporary poetic cosmos.[54] In Bely's essay, this is a fight between life and death, where the danger comes both from nature (the fear induced by thunder) and from culture (the poisonous, rotting word); the poet-sorcerer must defend both these fronts, each of which becomes more threatening in proportion to the defeat of the other. The note of real fear that sounds in parts of the essay, as "man, in horror, begins to enchant dangers unknown to himself by means of the word," fighting to preserve life, which is "sustained [only] by the living power of speech," reveals the urgency of the task in front of poetry, but also a real faith in the ability of the poet, like the sorcerer, to transmute word into act and to bridge the gap between the external world of phenomena and the internal world of experience and perception (*SS* 5:320). The medium of poetry is its message, to borrow Marshall McLuhan's seminal formulation; the significance of the poetic word lies in its formative role, its ability to frame our experience and to define its grounds.

This emphasis on poetic activity and the living, sounding word positions poetry as a question of means, rather than end. The essay itself makes the same claim for theory, which it casts not in terms of teleological progress toward a "final answer" but as a cyclical process. As soon as knowledge (*poznanie*) is attained, it becomes ignorance (*neznanie*); the end is but cause for a new beginning, the renewed pursuit of knowledge through action. There is no knowledge, as it asserts, "only the creation of a new world in sound" (*SS* 5:317). To criticize the essay for its failure to provide a full-fledged theory of language or cognition is, therefore, to neglect one of its central arguments, namely, that such a theory can only ever be unfinished. Like the poetry and language it describes, the theoretical approach proposed by the essay is an ongoing, incantatory activity, where meaning is secondary to form and its effects.[55] And indeed, the essay—which repeats key words and mirrors whole phrases—hypnotizes as much as it convinces. In so doing, it enacts one of its central assertions, namely, that epochs that see a resurgence of "living speech" are also eras during which "poetry invades the sphere of terminology" (*SS* 5:319).

The essay is a manifesto for a new kind of theory, a *living* theory that is dynamic and responsive, eschewing the temples of knowledge in favor of the exhilaration of the thunderstorm. It is this living theory that is the subject of the pages to follow, in which I trace each of the three ideas outlined here—the historicization of the poetic medium and its subsequent visibility; the particular material qualities of this medium; and the manner in which it intervenes in the world and our experience of it—as they appear in the poetry and theoretical debates of the modernist era. As in the case of Bely, it will often be my suggestion that it is where the various theories that emerged from this work seem to wander furthest from scientific rigor that the era's most characteristic attitude toward form is located. "We are alive," as the concluding line of Bely's essay declares, its final incantation.

PART I

Rhythm

Prosody was an early focus of Formalist attempts to define a scientific methodology for the study of literature that was free of the conceptual imprecision of Symbolist theory and academic scholarship. Their first target was the wide range of metaphorical senses in which the term "rhythm" was used in both popular and scholarly writing at the time. As the Formalist scholar Osip Brik observed in 1919:

> Rhythm is typically understood as everything that alternates "regularly," regardless of what precisely is alternating. Musical rhythm is the alternation of sounds in time. Poetic rhythm is the alternation of syllables in time . . . you hear talk of the rhythmic alternation of buttons on a vest, the rhythmic alternation of chairs in the living room, and even . . . the rhythmic alternation of day and night, winter and summer. In short, wherever you find some kind of periodic repetition of elements in time or space, you get talk of rhythm.[1]

The view of rhythm described here appears to be quite distinct from that of Bely and his modernist contemporaries, for whom rhythm was defined above all by its *ir*regularity. As we saw in the previous chapter, however, regularity also played an important role in this definition, which took as its basis rhythm's negative relationship to a regular metrical norm. The result, in any case, is the same: in equating poetic rhythm with rhythmic experience more generally, Brik complains, both camps reduce rhythm to a single dimension, that of periodic repetition; in so doing, they fail to account for what it is that makes poetic rhythm particular. As he writes, "it is jumping itself that is rhythmically designed, while the tracks left by the jumps are only data for assessing this jumping."[2]

The fact that Brik himself turns to a metaphor at this juncture in his argument speaks to the difficulty of the task he sets himself. The relationship between different kinds of rhythmic experience continues to be much disputed. Rhythm is "a highly extensible concept," Alexander Freer observes, an effect that can be observed in a multiplicity of "musical, corporeal, chronological, and philosophical" phenomena; as such, "an analysis of rhythm can be . . . a question of aesthetics, political economy, geography, media theory," and more.[3] Precisely for this reason, Peter Dayan and David Evans contend, a "general theory of rhythm" is both impracticable and unproductive. "There is nothing one can say about rhythm that engages with everything that we hold rhythm to be; depending on your point of view, it is either too broad a concept (perhaps, indeed, it is not a single concept at all), or too elusive."[4] In this view, which is much the same as that expressed by Brik, rhythm can only satisfactorily be analyzed in context: poetic rhythm must be treated *as poetic rhythm* if it is to be understood at all. Even when the issue is thus delimited, however, a number of questions remain open. Should a theory of poetic rhythm limit itself to structures observable in the text, or should it include reflections on the perception of poetic rhythm?[5] What is the connection between the two?[6] And what role does rhythm play in the creation of poetic meaning?

The chapters in this part of the book do not advocate for any one of these positions. Rather, they aim to nuance accounts of the relationship between modernist and Formalist theorizing about poetry by showing how similar arguments played out during the decades under study here. Brik and other Formalists were keen to point out the differences between their own understanding of rhythm and what they regarded as the dilettantish approach found in studies by modernist poets such as Bely. These young scholars were trying to establish themselves and to shore up the credibility of their approach; one means of doing so was to reclaim the science of poetic language from modernist poets and establish it as their own realm.[7] While there is no doubt that the Formalists introduced a degree of rigor to the study of versification, it should be remembered that there was significant disagreement even in their own ranks regarding "concrete solutions and methods."[8] These disagreements were both narrowly technical (debates regarding the status of the metrical foot, for example) and more broadly methodological, with different approaches reflecting what Merrill identifies as the division within Formalism between research in comparative poetics, or the study of patterns across a historical corpus of texts, and that concerning the psychology of poetic perception. In other words, they reprised many of the same issues that had arisen in the course of modernist debates about rhythm, as was seen in chapter 1 in relation to Bely's studies of iambic tetrameter.

My purpose in highlighting these parallels is not to minimize the achievement of Formalism in systematizing and refining theoretical approaches to and understanding of poetic rhythm. (Indeed, acknowledging the themes that recur in debates about rhythm during this period is an important step toward appreciating the specific interventions that Formalists made in this area.) Instead, placing debates about the correctness of this or that approach to the study of versification to one side, my aim in this part of the book is to ask what the terms of these debates reveal about the shifting set of emotions and ideologies with which rhythm as a concept was invested during the early decades of the twentieth century.[9]

As recent studies in historical poetics argue convincingly, meter and rhythm cannot be regarded as aesthetic terms distinct from the cultural or political sphere but must be recognized as "imaginary, constructed" categories; they never operate merely as "the measure of the line" but always also as a powerful discourse that interacts with discourses about culture more broadly.[10] For modernism, which simultaneously "invent[ed] tradition, suppresse[d] its own continuities with the past, and . . . produce[d] nostalgia for what has been seemingly lost," rhythm was a particularly loaded concept, becoming a byword for resistance to positivistic rationality and industrial modernity and the epitome of their much-touted rebellion against convention and the past.[11] Brik and other Formalists rejected this view. Poetic rhythm should be treated *as* rhythm, they contended, and not as a mimetic reflection of seismic historical changes or the contradictions of modernity at large. Nonetheless, the determinedly empirical terms in which Formalists approached rhythm were no less shaped by historical conditions and broader cultural discourses than the studies of their modernist predecessors.

One place where this interplay becomes particularly visible is in the reflections on media change that were embedded in these studies and which played a central role in the theories of rhythm that emerged. Remediation, as I discussed in the introduction to this book, refers to the dynamic whereby new media "refashion" older media, presenting themselves as "improved," more "transparent" versions of those media.[12] This emphasis on immediacy is accompanied by heightened awareness of the medium, or what Bolter and Grusin term "hypermediacy." Processes of remediation thus provide a useful lens through which to understand conflicting accounts of rhythm during this period, when rebellion against existing norms went hand-in-hand with a heightened interest in describing and transforming these norms.[13]

The Formalists were to some degree conscious of these processes: as Tynianov writes in *Problem of Verse Language* (*Problema stikhotvornogo ia-*

zyka, 1924), "the period of literary revolutions we have been experiencing over the past decades has raised with extraordinary force the question of the constructive principle of poetry."[14] This study is the subject of chapter 2, where it is considered alongside several other Formalist studies of rhythm. As I show, while the Formalists broke significantly with modernist accounts of rhythm, adopting new methods and reaching quite different conclusions, their approach was shaped by much the same dynamic, historicized understanding of poetry as medium as that first articulated by Bely—a view of poetry that was, I contend, inflected by ideas about rhythm in turn.

Chapter 3 turns back to read the modernist poetry of Alexander Blok through this media-historical frame. The highly emotive key in which rhythm is discussed in Blok's critical writing appears to represent an extreme example of the modernist tendency to blur the lines between poetic rhythm and rhythmic experience more broadly, with rhythm often used as a synonym for immediacy and authentic, unmediated access to the real. By the same token, however, his work demonstrates heightened sensitivity to and careful engagement with the particular qualities of rhythm as a poetic device. My aim in this chapter is to show that his work should therefore be included in accounts of modernist debates about rhythm as a formal device; indeed, it is its apparent imprecision that illustrates most clearly the emerging conception of poetry as a medium, central to the vision of poetry as an active participant in historical change that was shared by modernist poets and Formalist theorists alike.

Chapter Two

Yury Tynianov and Rhythm as Remediation

FORMALIST STUDIES of rhythm were conscious of their origins in the "crisis" provoked by modernism's challenge to established prosodic convention. During periods of innovation, Boris Tomashevsky observes in his 1923 study, "Problem of Verse Rhythm" ("Problema stikhotvornogo ritma"), the "authority of traditional forms" falters and "it becomes clear that there is something in the poetic system that needs to be resolved."[1] If a resolution to the similar crisis in eighteenth-century verse was reached relatively quickly, with syllabotonic verse ultimately displacing the still-nascent syllabic tradition, the twentieth-century crisis was more serious and extended. Shored up by the work of Pushkin, Lermontov, and the rest of the nineteenth-century canon, syllabotonic verse was less easily dislodged by the nonclassical verse forms then gaining popularity. Instead, the two systems came to coexist, and the range of metrical forms and acceptable rhythmic variations continued to expand. This situation revealed a seemingly paradoxical truth: the greater the weight of established tradition, the greater the uncertainty this produced.

As was shown in chapter 1, the dependence of rhythmic innovation upon established convention was one of Bely's central discoveries. "The idea that successful innovation requires a deep knowledge of the past" was also, Merrill reminds us, "a basic tenet of OPOIAZ Formalism."[2] According to recent scholarship on modernism, this tendency was characteristic of the period more broadly; indeed, these studies argue, the modernist pursuit of novelty entailed the invention of tradition as counterweight and foil. As Friedman writes, modernism "establishes a cult of the new that constructs retrospectively a sense of tradition from which it declares independence. Paradoxically, such a tradition—or, the awareness of it as 'tradition'—might come into existence only at the moment of rebellion against it."[3]

The concept of tradition had, of course, existed prior to modernism. It played a particularly important role in the work of Alexander Veselovsky, whose "historical poetics" provided one starting point for Formalist theory.[4] This approach looked beyond the individual work to the "broader domain of popular verbal tradition," with the goal of literary studies understood to be the identification, "through comparison, [of] the repeating elements in literary history."[5] Rule-bound and accretive, the relative stability of tradition in this framework (the word Veselovsky uses is *predanie*, from the verb *peredat'*, meaning "to pass on") was contrasted to the "individual" element of creativity, which Veselovsky left to one side.

This dichotomy between accumulated tradition and innovation was taken up in modernist debates, where it received a characteristic twist. Tradition was not so much stable as static, Bely and others contended. This stasis could be combated only through individual creativity, of which rhythm was the most direct expression. The paradoxical result of this stance, as we saw in chapter 1, was to recast tradition as something inherently unstable. In defining rhythm in terms of its resistance to metrical stasis, Bely's studies showed that convention is in fact subject to continual modification. This "relationship between the general rules, or accumulated traditions, and the individual act of creativity" was precisely what the Formalists also sought to explain.[6] Though these theorists moved away from the linear modernist narrative of innovation "overcoming" the dead weight of tradition and sought to understand the act of creativity from a psychological, rather than spiritual, point of view, they, too, identified rhythm as the key to understanding the interplay between the two.

These points of overlap between modernist conceptions of rhythm and Formalist approaches demonstrate lines of continuity that are obscured by familiar oppositions between modernist vagueness and Formalist precision. Acknowledging these continuities not only reveals previously unexplored aspects of modernist approaches to rhythm (to which I will return at more length in the next chapter, where I consider the poetry of Alexander Blok); it also alerts us to those places where Formalist theorizing exhibits distinctively modernist traits. This goes beyond established links between Bely's statistical work on rhythmical variations and directions taken in Formalist studies of versification to consider the emerging conceptions of poetry as medium toward which such connections point.[7]

This shared view of poetry as medium is particularly apparent when it comes to the very point that appears most to distinguish Formalism from its modernist predecessors, the use of empirical methods. As will be described at more length below, the availability of new tools for study of the poetic text intensified processes of remediation, both heightening interest in the material components of rhythm (hypermediacy) and amplifying discourses of immediacy. Despite and perhaps even because of their claims to greater objectivity, that is, Formalist theories of rhythm often reproduce modernist claims regarding the inherent vitality of rhythm, albeit in modified form. This dynamic brings into new focus the importance that Formalist theorists attached to certain features of verse, particularly its sonic properties, and makes visible the media-historical framework within which the characteristic qualities of poetry were articulated during this period.

This framework provides important context for Yury Tynianov's 1924 study, *Problem of Verse Language*. Critical accounts of this study often treat it separately from his work on literary-historical issues, viewing it as a "purely theoretical work" that aims "to illuminate not the mechanisms of literary-historical movement but certain constant characteristics of poetic language."[8] Reading *Problem of Verse Language* in dialogue with the technical debates around prosody that proliferated during this period makes clear that Tynianov's interest in the "constant characteristics" of poetic language did not run counter to his interest in literary history. On the contrary, these two poles existed in a state of dynamic tension and mutual influence. Indeed, as I will contend, it was precisely in their interaction that Tynianov located the specificity of poetic rhythm, which he understood, via the perspective made available by processes of remediation, in terms of its embeddedness in historical processes.

REMEDIATING TRADITION

Formalist theorists moved away from static conceptions of meter as a set of abstract rules against which the concrete rhythm of a given line rebelled. Where Bely and others conceived of meter and rhythm as opposed forces, with metrical regularity as the restrictive fetters against which rhythmic irregularity strained, these figures emphasized instead the productive interaction of these two tendencies. They aimed to describe rhythm as a complex, multidimensional phenomenon that emerged in process—to turn their attention, in Brik's formulation, from the static traces of rhythmic movement to the "jumping" itself.

First presented at meetings of the Moscow Linguistic Circle and OPOIAZ in 1919–20, though not published until 1927, Brik's "Rhythm and Syntax" dispenses with the metrical foot to take a more holistic view of the verse line as a "metrical unit" (*metricheskoe edinstvo*) within which particular forms of movement—indexed by stress and periodicity (*udarnost' i preryvnost'*)—productively interact with syntax. Enumerating stress and pauses is not sufficient to account for poetic rhythm, Brik argues, since conversational speech is also organized according to such patterns. In order to understand what lends poetic rhythm its special quality, we must locate the "rhythmic impulse," that is, the specific principle according to which stress and periodicity are determined in verse.[9] "Rhythm is not the result of movement but movement itself," as he remarks.[10]

The concept of the "rhythmic impulse"—which would gain traction among some Formalists, and particularly Tomashevsky—is offered as an alternative to the view that meter precedes rhythm (i.e., that rhythm amounts to a series of "deviations" from the norms dictated by the metrical scheme).[11] Instead, Brik views both meter and rhythm as tendencies, latent potentials that take on concrete dimensions within the context of the linguistic material of a given poem and as dictated by the rhythmic impulse. Rejecting the terms "stressed and unstressed" (*udarnye i neudarnye*), Brik thinks in terms of syllables that "have been stressed" or "have not been stressed" (*udarennye i neudarennye*). As he writes, "theoretically, every syllable can be stressed or can *not* be stressed—everything depends on the rhythmic impulse."[12]

This shift entailed a change of temporal orientation. The linear modernist narrative of rhythmic innovation overcoming metrical inertia was replaced by one that foregrounded the interplay of convention and novelty in the present. "Nobody would ever dream of saying that a person dancing the waltz combines some definite, periodically recurring movements, [though] clearly a person dancing the waltz is performing a certain pre-given formula," as Brik remarks.[13] Tomashevsky makes this still more explicit when he speaks of the interplay of "canonized" and "non-canonized" elements in producing our sense of a poem's rhythmicity, where "canonized" refers to established metrical norms and "non-canonized" refers to other aspects of the poem's sonic organization, including rhythmic variations that have not yet been assimilated into the metrical canon. These categories are, by definition, in flux; what is canonized today may fall out of use tomorrow, and vice versa. Innovation and convention are two sides of the same coin.

To some degree, these accounts of rhythm reprise earlier modernist studies and even go further than them. Like Bely, the Formalists emphasized the unpredictability of rhythm, its openness to chance and change. For the Formalists, however, rhythmic unpredictability comes not from outside the poem, from the poet's special feel for rhythm, but is built into its fabric. If the Formalists disagreed considerably as to how this rhythmic effect is produced, they agreed in broad terms that it could not be analyzed on the basis of isolated units such as the foot but could be analyzed only as a process—as the product of the "alternation" (*smena*) between elements in the verse line and the poem as a whole.[14]

Rhythm, in this view, is a contingent phenomenon that is to an important degree determined by its immediate context. This is one reason why these accounts emphasize the quality of stressed syllables rather than their quantity, and find that even the quality of a given stress is not constant but dependent on a number of variables. This last matter was frequently discussed in debates about issues such as half-stresses. As Roman Jakobson argued, half-stresses must be viewed as mobile. The same line could receive differing stress depending on the metrical context in which it appears and the rhythmic role that unstressed syllables are called upon to perform: for instance, "The line 'kochuiushchie karavany' is pronounced differently depending on whether it is positioned among iambic or amphibrachic lines (1. kochUiushchIé kAravAny. 2. kochUiushchiE karavAny)."[15] Numerous studies sought not only to determine different degrees of stress, but to account for the rhythmic significance of the position of stress in relation to word, phrase, and line boundaries; issues such as intonation also began to be studied in more detail. In all these ways, the Formalists sought to account for rhythm as a phenomenon that arises from the interaction between established conventions and the individual instance.

Formalist criticisms of concepts such as the metrical foot are often understood as part of their broader effort to devise more accurate, objective means for the study of poetic form. Without disputing this view, it is important to note that there was also a historical dimension to the theories of rhythm they were developing. Uncovering this historical dimension makes clear that these theories constituted not so much a departure from modernist approaches to rhythm as their logical extension. Bely's studies of iambic tetrameter verse had led him to the insight that innovation relies upon a knowledge of tradition; however, he continued to speak of the two in the binary terms upon which modernism was founded. In moving beyond simplistic dichotomies between meter and rhythm or regularity and irregularity, Formalist scholars began not only to derive a fuller understanding of the multiple, competing factors that contribute to the emergence of rhythm, but also to articulate in more detail what Bely had identified as the crucial role played by the interaction between innovation and tradition in this process. This point is not trivial. As the next section will describe, Formalist theories of rhythm and the methods they employed to analyze it continued to be shaped by a distinctively modernist opposition between present and past.

REMEDIATING RHYTHM

Where Bely's studies of rhythm were based on careful listening to verse as it was recited and the study of the graphic "recordings" (*zapisi*) that he created on the basis of this listening, the Formalists took advantage of the enormous and growing body of experimental data being produced in Europe, the United States, and, increasingly, Russia. Such studies emphasized the importance of empirical research methods, and particularly sound-based analysis, which came to be viewed as the most scientific and comprehensive approach for the study of rhythm.[16] These advances merely intensified those processes of remediation that color modernist accounts of rhythm, however. As sound recording and reproduction technologies made possible ever more granular study of the components of the poetic text, heightening interest in the distinctive qualities of poetic rhythm, assertions regarding rhythmic immediacy grew correspondingly insistent. These were now couched in media-historical terms rather than the emotive or spiritual framework typical in Symbolist theory, but similar binaries persisted.

New methodologies for studying rhythm emerged thanks to growing interest in experimental phonetics. The development of tools for measuring, recording, and visualizing the traces of speech opened avenues for research into the "physical substrate of speech production and perception," which these tools made available for detailed scrutiny. The possibility of applying these methods and tools to the study of poetics was recognized early on. E. W. Scripture, for example, a pioneer in experimental phonetics, saw the study of the nature of verse as one goal of his research into "speech curves," graphic representations of the flow of speech made by tracing as a continuous line the grooves produced by the gramophone stylus as it recorded speech.[17] This kind of empirical research promised to make the study of rhythm ever more precise, enabling theorists to move beyond the counting of stressed positions to consider "the whole range of sonic phenomena subject to systematic organization in poetic speech."[18]

Particularly influential for debates about rhythm in Russia was "Ohrenphilologie," an acoustic approach to verse analysis developed by the German researcher Edward Sievers, which took the "pronounced" (*proiznesennyi*) text, rather than the printed page, as its main object of study.[19] Proponents of Ohrenphilologie (so called to distinguish it from the visual bias of traditional text-based "Augenphilologie") argued that poetry could be analyzed only on the basis of sound, that is, through the analysis of a specific instance of the poem being read aloud (whether recorded or "live"). As Tomashevsky writes in "Problem of Verse Rhythm," "the classification of rhythmic phenomena must be based on phonetic analysis of speech."[20] This shift was understood to have significant consequences for the study of rhythm, which could now be analyzed in its full complexity: "before," when poetry was studied on paper, metrics dominated conceptions of verse rhythm; "now," when recitals and sound recordings had become widespread, a more complex picture of the factors contributing to rhythm had emerged.[21]

Tynianov devotes several chapters at the beginning of *Problem of Verse Language* to a discussion of Ohrenphilologie.[22] While he acknowledges the "decisive role" (*PVL* 38) played by Ohrenphilologie in changing conceptualizations of rhythm and the study of it, he is cautious about the note of technological determinism that can be heard in accounts such as that of Tomashevsky, which he had reviewed the year before.[23] If the emergence of

Ohrenphilologie was facilitated by the new availability of recording devices, the existence of these devices did not make the non-acoustic elements of poetry defunct. On the contrary, Tynianov asserts, the history of poetry is cyclical: during some periods, its acoustic aspect is more tangible; at other times, other elements take precedence (*PVL* 38). Moreover, many of the new technical instruments that were being used for the analysis of rhythm failed to distinguish between sound with stylistic significance and purely incidental sound. Thus, although sound-based analysis did indeed allow for more nuanced description of the sonic qualities of verse rhythm, this did not necessarily amount to more direct or fuller access to rhythm than traditional text-based analysis.

Tomashevsky is in fact similarly cautious about reducing poetry wholly to its acoustic side. As he observes, audio recordings tell us no more about which aspects of the poem appeal most to the listener than a printed text. In practical terms, then, the properties of the printed text must be considered alongside the poem's acoustic and motor-articulatory aspects, "since the work of poets gets to audience mostly in printed form." Still, he eventually concludes, "you have to bear in mind that the printed text is just an artificial, conventional sign of living speech."[24] Comparison of different media again becomes a means of asserting the greater immediacy of "pronounced" poetry, the natural form of which is taken to be "living speech."

Tynianov takes the opposite view. If the printed text cannot capture the sound and cadence of the spoken word, he reasons, the same applies in reverse: not all elements of a printed poem can be articulated or heard. Since any theory of poetic rhythm must be able to account for all those instances where a text is perceived as both poetic and rhythmic, such moments must also be accounted for. Tynianov takes the example of the "equivalent" (*ekvivalent*), a term he uses to refer to "anything which substitutes extra-verbal features for the text, above all its partial omissions, such as a partial substitution with graphic features, etc." (*PVL* 43). His first example is the original publication of Pushkin's "To the Sea" ("K moriu," 1824), where all but the first two words of the eighth stanza are replaced by dots to produce the "equivalent of a stanza" (*ekvivalent strofy*):

> The world grew empty. . . . .
>
> . . . .
>
> . . . .
>
> . . . .

Scholarship typically regards such texts as unfinished, Tynianov tells us, whether simply never completed or purposefully left blank in an effort to preempt censorship. Tynianov counters that such omissions should be treated as aesthetic facts. Stanzas such as the above carry the "sign" of meter, its potential. In the absence of verbal text, it is this "constructive factor" alone that is perceptible. This demonstrates the strength of this constructive factor, which not only continues to exert itself in the absence of any words, but actually does so more forcefully. This additional "pressure" (*nazhim*), as Tynianov terms it, is in part due to our heightened sense of the *potential* dynamism of those elements so tantalizingly obscured by the lines of dots (*PVL* 47). It also has to do with the way the missing stanza interrupts the poem's metrical flow, making us simultaneously aware of the sudden absence of meter and the strength of the precedent it has set, as the metrical energy of preceding stanzas carries over and seems to animate the omitted lines. Thanks to the equivalent, the strength of the "learned behavior" (*navyk*) that the poem and its meter have instilled in us becomes perceptible; the automatism of meter is thereby overcome (*PVL* 48).

If Ohrenphilologie expanded and complicated researchers' understanding of verse rhythm in some respects, Tynianov's conclusion implies that it ultimately remained too concerned with the empirically measurable traces of rhythm. In this sense, Ohrenphilologie made much the same methodological error as studies of rhythm based on the enumeration of metrical stress. In both cases, there is some "thing" called rhythm, which it is the task of the researcher to isolate and describe. To correct this imbalance, Tynianov looks to those moments where the empirically measurable traces of rhythm are completely lacking. Even at such moments, Tynianov wants to show, rhythm remains the *dominanta*, the constructive factor that subordinates every other element and gives poetic language its special quality.

Ohrenphilologie and its shortcomings thus helped Tynianov to begin to articulate the relationship between poetry's constant characteristics and historical change. What Ohrenphilologie and the processes of remediation it set in motion made most apparent for Tynianov was not the sonic basis of poetic language, but poetry's status as what media scholars term a "qualified" medium. Qualified media—which include specific media genres, such as newspapers, movies, radio programs, and so on, as well as artistic media like painting, sculpture, and photography—are the product of cultural practices, which produce a conventional understanding of how a medium is used, what it looks like, and how it has developed through history; they "appear and (perhaps eventually) disappear and . . . are intelligible only in certain cultural and social contexts."[25] Poetry, likewise, Tynianov points out, is culturally constructed: what appear to be its innate qualities are in fact the result of cultural consensus. The emphasis that proponents of sound-based analysis placed on poetry's acoustic qualities is a case in point.[26]

The consensus as to what constituted rhythmic poetry was repeatedly challenged during the modernist era, as we have seen. The rate of innovation made the mechanisms whereby new metrical forms and rhythmic variations were assimilated into the canon newly perceptible. Even as this process highlighted the historicity of verse, it raised questions about poetry's inherent qualities—those basic medial constraints that are not solely the result of convention. As Irina O. Rajewsky points out, "dance theatre cannot truly become painting—just as painting itself can never become genuinely photographic, even though this is suggested at times by photorealistic painting . . . What can be achieved in this respect is only an illusion, an 'as if' of the other medium."[27] We will turn to consider the basic medial constraints of poetry (as compared with, say, painting) at more length in the next part of the book, which looks at the image. For now, what is important is that Ohrenphilologie mistakenly took sound as one such innate quality of poetry. As Tynianov points out, however, the preference for sound over print was simply the result of a particular set of historically specific cultural circumstances.

Still, it was thanks to Ohrenphilologie and its bias toward sound that Tynianov reached his own conclusion about poetry's basic material constraint. This lies not in the material sound of poetry as "living speech," but in the way that poetry organizes its material—what he describes as the "unity" (*edinstvo*) and "density" (*tesnota*) of the verse line, on the one hand, and the "dynamization" (*dinamizatsiia*) and the "successivity" (*suktsessivnost'*) produced by these characteristics of the verse line, on the other (*PVL* 73–76). I discuss these terms at more length below. For now, what is important is that these terms describe material *conditions*, rather than the material itself. What Tynianov is interested in is not isolating rhythm itself, but understanding how rhythm as a constructive principle interacts with the material of the poem, whether this is sonic, textual—or, as in the Pushkin poem just discussed, neither of these things. The theory of rhythm that the first part of *Problem of Verse Language* goes on to develop tries to account for the manner in which verse rhythm both makes this material perceptible and simultaneously imbues it with special dynamism; that is, it begins to argue that processes of remediation are generated by the poetic text itself.

ANACHRONIZING RHYTHM

As Svetlikova has convincingly demonstrated, the emerging field of semantics was an important influence for Tynianov at the time of writing *Prob-*

lem of Verse Language. His study relies extensively on contemporary developments in psychology concerning the perception of meaning; indeed, its original title (rejected by the publisher as too abstract) was *Problem of Verse Semantics* (*Problema stikhovoi semantiki*).[28] In focusing on the role of rhythm in determining verse semantics, *Problem of Verse Language* departed significantly from the studies of versification that had preceded it. Tynianov's approach was directly opposed to those who viewed periodicity or "the recurrence of 'comparable phenomena' in time" as the defining feature of rhythm—a principle, as we saw, that underpinned even those theoretical approaches which moved away from concepts such as the metrical foot and sought less static models for the description of rhythm.[29] On the contrary, Tynianov asserts at the end of his study that "in poetry, time is completely imperceptible" (*v stikhe vremia sovsem neoshchutimo*) (*PVL* 170). Rhythm is not simply a sequence of sounds in time but the *dominanta*, the central organizing principle of verse language; its primary significance lies in its implications for meaning.[30]

Tynianov's rejection of linear temporal descriptions of rhythm did not mean that his own theory was completely ahistorical, however; indeed, as his discussion of the equivalent begins to make clear, one reason why he resists such descriptions is that they obscure the true nature of poetry as a historical medium. Further consideration of the claim that "time is completely imperceptible" will help to illuminate his own view of this matter.

Tynianov makes his assertion regarding the "imperceptibility" of time in the context of a comparison with prose. Our awareness of the excessive time devoted to the description of Ivan Iakovlevich eating bread with onion in Nikolai Gogol's short story "The Nose" ("Nos," 1836) is the source of this scene's comic effect; this awareness, he writes, has to do with the "simultaneity" of prosaic speech, in contrast to the "successivity" of the verse line. Svetlikova locates one potential source for this pair of terms in associationist psychology, and particularly Wilhelm Wundt's work on perception.[31] Like Wundt, upon whose work he draws, Tynianov is interested above all in the temporality of each individual moment of perception. As Svetlikova summarizes, "either we instantly recognize that which we perceive, so that the moment of perception and recognition . . . coincides in time, or some time passes between [perception and recognition]."[32] In the former case, we are dealing with simultaneity; in the latter, with successivity. The effect of successivity is to "make the word difficult" (*slovo okazyvaetsia zatrudnennym*) (*PVL* 68).

Tynianov acknowledges this source, citing Wundt directly as well as the linguist Lev Shcherba, whose *Russian Vowels in Qualitative and Quantitative Terms* (*Russkie glasnye v kachestvennom i kolichestvennom otnoshenii*, 1912) also draws on Wundt's work. Nonetheless, the concept does not enter Tynianov's work unchanged. As Svetlikova notes, Wundt speaks of simultaneous and successive *associations*, whereas Tynianov deals with "successivity *of the verse line*" (my emphasis). He is quite clear, moreover, that poetic language must be considered a special case and should not be categorized alongside other types of speech in which the semantic element is not primary (as, for instance, Lev Iakubinskii does in his discussion of children's babbling).[33] Whereas Wundt is interested in the perception of meaning in general, Tynianov's concern is the perception of meaning in the light of

> the objective conditions of verse as a construction, among which are included the dynamization of speech as a result of the application of the basic principles of verse—unity and density of the verse series—to the unfolding [*razvertyvanie*] of the verse material. (*PVL* 69)

For Tynianov, that is, successivity relates not to sequence in time, however delimited, so much as to the movement of the verse line conceived as a spatiotemporal "construction." The perception of meaning is crucially inflected by this context.

Merrill makes a similar point in her discussion of *Problem of Verse Language*, which she situates in relation to the Formalists' interest in "similarity associations." This idea was taken from Veselovsky, who conceived of the history of language and thought in terms of "the continual, gradual evolution of ideas, developing in complexity and abstraction through a cumulative process of associative connections."[34] For Veselovsky, these associations were initially conceptual; Merrill cites the example of the "convergence" between the noise of thunder and the noise of battle, which Veselovsky argued "becomes the basis for an expanding, collectively shared network of associations," or tradition.[35] Over time, he contended, such associations "degrade" into formal "similarity associations," that is, musical or rhythmic effects. The Formalists, by contrast, argued that both types of association operate at the same time. Tynianov's interest in semantic associations should thus not distract us from his concern with the formal structure of the text, Merrill writes. "Rhythm for Tynianov is a property of language that emerges when it is very densely patterned; that is, when there are many repetitions of sound or stress in close succession. This creates a 'boundary' around this series, which 'transforms' and 'isolates' it. Within this boundary, associations based on sonic similarity override existing contiguity relations . . . a word's 'prosaic' meaning is weakened, and it takes on new secondary meanings as a result of its association by similarity with other words in the series."[36]

As Merrill demonstrates convincingly, Tynianov's theoretical approach reflects his efforts to bridge the gap between the universal laws that comparative philology sought to describe (in this case, parallelism) and the perception of the individual text (as governed by psychological laws). This entailed a quite specific view of rhythmic temporality, which her description implies without addressing directly.

A key term here is "unfolding" (*razvertyvanie*), which appears alongside "successivity" and related concepts throughout the study.[37] As Tynianov states, "the concept of flow, of 'unfolding' [*razvertyvanie*] by no means necessarily implies temporality. Flow, dynamism can be taken on their own terms, outside time, as pure movement" (*PVL* 28). The notion of "pure movement" is probably traceable to the philosopher Henri Bergson, whose work was an important touchstone for the OPOIAZ Formalists.[38] Bergson criticized the quantitative view of time dominant in much of Western thought, arguing that multiplicity in time can only be understood in qualitative terms. Four chimes of a clock are experienced not as four equivalent but distinct sensations but "[melt] into one another in such a way as to give the whole a peculiar quality, to make a kind of musical phrase out of it."[39] Perhaps more surprisingly, Bergson also conceives of matter in durational terms. We think that objects have fixed, static shapes, Bergson argues, when in fact, as Marta Braun summarizes, "the shapes of material objects are not properties of the objects but are 'snapshots taken by the mind of the continuity of becoming.'"[40] As Bergson himself writes, "All division of matter into independent bodies with absolutely determined outlines is an artificial division."[41]

With Bergson in mind, an additional interpretation of Tynianov's terminology might be ventured whereby the definition of each term taken individually is less important than the way in which these terms are combined. Referring, on the one hand, to the "unity" and "density" of the verse line (its spatial existence) and, on the other, to the "successivity" and "dynamism" that result (its temporal qualities), Tynianov makes emphatic the idea of *shape in motion* that is at the heart of his theory, as the frequent use of spatial terms in the study—including "volume" (*ob"em*) and "breadth" (*shirota*) as well as the verse "construction"—further confirms. These terms are combined with an emphasis on the movement and dynamism of the verse line, in which individual units act "progressively" and "regressively" to establish networks of interactions that reach backwards and project forwards, constantly modifying the range of semantic possibilities associated with each word (*PVL* 60–61).[42] As Tynianov writes early on in the study, "we have just recently overcome the celebrated analogy: form-content = glass-wine . . . Instead of this, one should recognize even spatial form as dynamic *sui generis*" (*PVL* 27).

In other words, rather than contrasting the static traces of rhythm to "jumping" in the present, Tynianov conceives of the line as simultaneously fixed and in motion. "Boundaries" are established, creating rhythmic "units" in turn, as Merrill describes; but equally important are the shifting constellations into which these units are drawn as the poem unfolds. This idea anticipates recent discussions of rhythm, which argue that rhythm challenges us "to reconceive of structure along dynamic lines," as one study remarks, requiring us to rethink both time and space in order to grasp them as a "dynamic configuration."[43] Tynianov's descriptions of shape in movement also recall the strange status of the "interval," the central image of an essay by him on contemporary poetry written just a few months after his completion of *Problem of Verse Language*. In Dragan Kujundzic's description, the interval represents "a moment of constitution and erasure" that is defined both by its relation to the past and its anticipation of the future even as it itself exists "outside time."[44]

There is an analogy to be drawn here with the dual action of remediation, which simultaneously brings the particular qualities of a given medium into focus via comparison with other media and renders the medium transparent. This analogy is justified in light of the historical framework within which theories of rhythm took shape during this period, particularly given Tynianov's own engagement with the explicitly media-historical accounts that these produced. The step that Tynianov takes is to locate the work of remediation within the poem itself, which continually draws attention to its own material and, *in so doing*, produces the sense of dynamic movement that appears to transcend these limits. As he writes, "*it is precisely the unity and compactness of the series which is the objective sign of rhythm*" (*PVL* 66; emphasis in original).

In closing, a few words about the relationship between this view of rhythm and Tynianov's literary-historical concerns. On a quite straightforward level, Tynianov's description of rhythm as a "dynamic configuration" is alert to the role played by the interaction between the concrete instance and established convention. If the limits of the verse line (its "unity" and "density") are necessary for both the emergence of dynamic movement and the semantic transformation or change in perception that results, these limits must make themselves felt. When metrical structures become fixed, too closely associated with one or another syntactic structure or lexical sphere, the tension between rhythm and semantics is weakened, and the dynamism of the verbal material becomes imperceptible, relying as it does upon the felt interaction of all these elements. To be effective, a new element—whether a completely new metrical pattern or a "hackneyed" (*stertyi*) one used in a new context, whether a neologism or a familiar word in new circumstances—must be introduced in order to make this interaction newly tangible (*PVL* 29).

This is the same principle as that found in Tynianov's theory of parody, which he first elaborated in the 1921 article "Dostoevskii and Gogol: Towards a Theory of Parody" ("Dostoevskii i Gogol: K teorii parodii"). According to Tynianov, parody operates according to a combination of the new and the old: an old form (in this case, metrical structure) may be renewed via the introduction of new material (non-typical lexicon, for example), or a new form may be employed to renew old material. In *Problem of Verse Language*, he calls this the "dialectical" development of form. The act of parodic reproduction is premised upon the inevitable routinization of form—its steady tendency, over time, toward fixity. It works to forestall this fixity precisely by exploiting it, relying upon "this mechanized routine," as Oushakine notes, in order "to smuggle in . . . a new substance. To be effective parody has to introduce new material through the constraints of the old form."[45]

The rhythmic fabric of a given poem does not simply produce variations of established metrical forms; it *parodies* these previous uses.[46] Rhythm in this conception is a historical device in the sense that it exists only in relation to old forms, but one that simultaneously always relies on the "anachronism" that is a central mechanism of parody. What is important here is that anachronism is a feature not only of a rhythm's relationship to metrical convention but also *of the verse line itself*, in which each word is anachronistic in the sense that it never belongs solely to its own present context but is always inflected by its interaction with earlier words and the expectation it sets up for ensuing ones (the "progressive" and "regressive" dynamic discussed above).

Despite its apparent neglect of historical issues in favor of a narrow focus on prosody, *Problem of Verse Language* is thus fundamentally informed by literary historical concerns. While treating rhythm as the defining and most constant characteristic of verse language, Tynianov simultaneously insists on its inherent historicity. This quality consists not merely in meter's function as a mechanism of historical memory, a topic that has been widely discussed in studies of Russian versification, but also, and perhaps more counterintuitively, in its present and future effects: the capacity of rhythm to rupture temporal continuity, to bring about innovation by making tangible the many different layers of pastness from which it emerges. As such, Tynianov's theory represents a distinctive refraction of the discourse of immediacy so common in early twentieth-century discussions of rhythm, one that locates the source of this immediacy not in rhythm's purported contiguity with poetic creativity or in its apparent basis in sound, but within verse structure itself and the interplay of convention and novelty that both makes this structure perceptible and dynamizes it.

As Oushakine contends, "'anachronizing' form, taking it out of context" is an essential step toward perceiving discursive structures as *formal*, rather than in psychological or expressive terms (the rhythm of my soul, and so on).[47] Yet Tynianov also shows that taking form out of time is the surest way to reveal its embeddedness in time. This is consistent with the emphasis among OPOIAZ Formalists on the ongoing struggle between old and new as the defining feature of literary history, a position that extracted history itself from time to render it one long "present-as-such" (*aktual'nost' kak takovaia*).[48] Tradition becomes a kind of dynamic cross-section that is revealed in the work of each poem—like rhythm, a mobile phenomenon that evolves and changes with each poem, and which is at the heart of the broader "ebb and flow of succession and transformation" that drives literary evolution.[49]

Despite the Formalists' reputation for what Leon Trotsky called "semi-statistical" methods involving "the counting of repetitive vowels and consonants, of syllables and epithets," many of them did not in fact take a quantitative approach to the study of rhythm.[50] In looking beyond specific methods or conclusions to consider the media-historical framework within which these theorists conceived of the characteristic qualities of rhythm during this period, this chapter has, moreover, demonstrated that even apparently technical debates about prosody were shaped by broader historical concerns. The next chapter reverses this lens to look at rhythm in the work of Alexander Blok, a figure whose impressionistic, often emotive assertions about the contradictions of modernity belie his own careful reflections on the nature of rhythm and of poetry as historical medium.

Chapter Three

Alexander Blok and the Rhythms of History

ALEXANDER BLOK made his poetic debut during an era of rapid and dramatic change in Russian prosody, but he was not part of the first generation to push for such change. By the time his first published collection, *Verses on the Most Beautiful Lady* (*Stikhi o prekrasnoi dame*), appeared in 1905, older poets such as Briusov, Konstantin Bal'mont, Zinaida Gippius, Dmitrii Merezhkovsky, and others had been at work for ten years or more, goading the literary establishment with bold experiments and self-conscious challenges to established metrical norms. Briusov, in particular, had experimented extensively with nonclassical meters such as the *dol'nik*, an accentual verse form in which stressed syllables are separated by unstressed intervals of varying length.[1] It was probably Blok's encounter with Briusov's *Tertia Vigilia* (1900), which contains numerous poems in this vein, that precipitated his own first foray into nonclassical meters at the end of 1901. Nonetheless, Blok's use of nonclassical meters differed from that of his elder contemporaries in one crucial regard: whereas poets such as Briusov sought to emphasize the novelty of accentual verse forms, Blok's poetry helped to assimilate them into the Russian poetic tradition.[2]

As Mikhail Gasparov has shown, poets such as Briusov used accentual verse forms sporadically and according to no particular system. This meant that readers were less likely to recognize or grow accustomed to such forms, instead perceiving them as "new" each time they encountered them.[3] This sense of unpredictability was amplified by the fact that the intervals between stressed syllables in Briusov's accentual verse remained highly variable, displaying little consistency from poem to poem. All these effects ensured that Briusov's use of nonclassical meters remained marked as a departure from established prosodic convention. In this manner, he flaunted his freedom from the rules and restrictions of traditional syllabotonic verse and simultaneously drew fresh attention to the role of prosodic organization in poetic speech; to put it in terms of remediation, his claim to more immediate expression went hand-in-hand with "hyperconscious recognition or acknowledgment of the medium."[4]

By contrast, Blok's experiments in accentual verse were informed from the start by a conscious search for connection with the Russian poetic tradition. He based his *dol'nik* on Romantic translations or imitations of German verse by poets such as Vasily Zhukovsky, Mikhail Lermontov, Afanasy Fet, and Apollon Grigor'ev, where the tendency is to limit intervals between stressed positions to one or two syllables. Those poems in *Verses on the Most Beautiful Lady* that are written in accentual verse mimic this style, adopting three-stress lines with intervals of one or two syllables. This is the characteristic pattern that became known as "Blokian verse." Blok also thought carefully about the metrical structure of the book as a whole. Rather than placing *dol'nik* poems randomly, as Briusov had done, he carefully dispersed them throughout the book, interspersing them with poems written in more familiar syllabotonic meters. This arrangement helped to highlight the similarities between *dol'nik* verse and its syllabotonic counterparts, lessening the sense of difference between them, while at the same time ensuring that readers remained alert to the possibility that any given poem might be written in *dol'nik*.[5] In this manner, *Verses on the Most Beautiful Lady* "trained" the reading public, helping them to acquire an ear for the new meter and rendering it newly transparent, while at the same time making them more consciously aware of "its link with past poetry" and its own status as "a particular variety of verse, distinct from other accentual meters."[6]

The previous chapter argued that modernism invented tradition not simply because it needed a foil, something against which to rebel; on the contrary, this process was part of a broader shift in thinking about the contemporary moment and its dialectical relationship with both past and future. Innovation was understood as not only a challenge to established norms, but also a process that generates new conventions. Whether or not Blok thought explicitly in these terms, the careful orchestration of meter in *Verses on the Most Beautiful Lady* suggests that he shared this view, seeing rhythm as reliant upon existing patterns as much as upon disruption of these patterns and the new patterns that this latter act establishes in turn.

Approaching Blok's work from this angle allows us to better understand his position in relation to technical modernist debates about versification, to which, despite his status as one of modernism's most innovative practitioners, he is not generally held to have contributed. This is hardly surprising. Blok did not typically engage in such debates, except to express his distaste for them. As Bely recalls, he "considered detailed study of the anatomy and physiology of creativity to be dangerous for a poet . . . a particular kind of suicide."[7] Similarly, in "Soul of the Writer" ("Dusha pisatelia," 1909)—penned around the same time that Bely's scientific work on meter and rhythm was getting under way—he cautions that "the most dangerous thing" for a writer is the loss of his "inner . . . rhythm."[8] This inner rhythm was what connected the writer to the Russian people (*narod*) and the larger historical forces that moved them.

It is this view of rhythm as an elemental force (*stikhiia*) that appears to most distance Blok from those, such as Bely and the Formalists, who sought to understand rhythm as a formal component of the verse line (*stikh*). The relationship between modernist assertions regarding the immediacy of rhythm and theoretical interest in its technical qualities was by no means one of straightforward opposition, however, as we have already begun to see. In order to prove the vitality and freedom of poetic language, Bely quantified it; and the Formalists frequently referenced qualities such as immediacy in their efforts to devise objective methods for the acoustic analysis of rhythm. Like the work of these figures, Blok's emotive assertions about rhythm must be read with an eye to media-historical processes and the contradictions of the age more broadly.

Blok's concerns about the potential loss of rhythm, a term that he used as shorthand for both his own creative life and the vitality of the Russian nation as a whole, heightened his sensitivity to the inevitable artifice implied by modern lyric poetry—the "hatred" of which, he writes in an essay of 1908, "is the source of at least half my work" (*PSS* 8:8). This antipathy stemmed at least in part from his mounting sense of despair regarding what he saw as the fatal aimlessness and "endless circling" of modern existence (*PSS* 7:25). Blok expressed these concerns in terms of the opposition between nature and culture (or, as he later labeled these same poles, culture and civilization) that was becoming important for him during the same period, as well as with reference to another binary opposition, that between "fate" (*sud'ba*) and "contingency" (*sluchai*).[9] According to this scheme, lyric poetry and its individualist, aimless circling belonged to the degenerate, urban domain of contemporary culture and the intelligentsia; nature, by contrast, was associated with the harmonious rhythms of the folk and the idealized, stable past these evoked. "The closer man stands to the elements . . . the more rhythmic his words will be," he writes in "Poetry of Spells and Incantations" ("Poeziia zagovorov i zaklinanii," 1906).[10]

Regularity is both a negative quality and a positive one in these essays, whose author detests the unpredictability of modern existence but fears stasis; who longs for the constancy of tradition, but desires change. If the period between 1905 and 1910 saw significant shifts in the specific terms in which Blok articulated these concerns and the relative importance he attached to them, his thinking remained within the orbit of this relatively stable set of binary positions and the insistent contradictions that prevented their resolution.

While such concerns might be dismissed as largely metaphorical, of little direct relevance for understanding Blok's versification, the degree to which the binary structure of Blok's thought echoes oppositions already encountered in debates about rhythm, as well as the dual logic of immediacy and hypermediacy that underpins remediation, should not be ignored. These parallels confirm the close connection between these technical debates and the historical concerns to which Blok's essays give voice. This proximity is further demonstrated by Blok's own sensitivity to the interaction in poetic rhythm between regularity or established norms and irregularity or metrical novelty, between the transparency of the medium and heightened awareness of it. This is not to claim that the rhythm of Blok's poetry directly reflects the historical concerns described in his critical prose. Indeed, part of my argument in this chapter is that Blok's poetic practice provided a different set of tools for engaging with the historical conditions in which his generation found themselves. As in the case of Tynianov, the particular conception of rhythm that emerges is a distinctively modernist one.

To develop this claim, this chapter looks at several of the poems eventually gathered in *City* (*Gorod*, 1904–08), a section (*razdel*) that appears halfway through the second volume of Blok's trilogy, which was first published in its final form in 1916. As the first section of the trilogy that is devoted wholly to an urban setting, *City* lends itself to a discussion of how modern themes enter Blok's poetry and thought. The rise of modernist aesthetics coincided with the rapid expansion of urban populations throughout Europe. Frightening and exhilarating in equal measure, the city gave spatial form to the precipitous changes brought about by industrial modernity and the many tensions to which it gave rise. These problems were not new. Blok's urban poetry draws extensively on nineteenth-century literary depictions of the city, both as it features in the work of Charles Baudelaire and as it is portrayed in the texts belonging to what has become known as the "Petersburg text" of Russian literature. While Blok's ability to capture the fleeting, chaotic nature of modern urban experience drew particular praise, he was not alone among his contemporaries in drawing on this stock of literary depictions of Russia's newest capital, founded in 1703 by Peter I as the "window" through which Russia was to enter modernity and regarded by modernist poets as the abyss into which contemporary society was about to fall once again.[11]

These themes remain common in scholarship on Blok's work during the period covered by *City*, which comprises the 1905–07 Revolution, including the period of the most severe government repressions that followed. These were, we learn, years when Blok grew increasingly disillusioned with the mysticism of his earlier work and turned instead toward contemporary sociopolitical reality and civic concerns (*obshchestvennost'*).[12] *City* is concerned precisely with this shift, one that is expressed as much through the rhythms of the poetry as in its content. While the reading I offer here is historical, it will not be concerned with the ways in which Blok's rhythms mimetically reflect material historical conditions. On the contrary, what I am interested in here are the questions that these conditions raise about the material qualities of poetry and poetic rhythm, which the modern city made tangible in new and quite specific ways.

My discussion of individual poems reads across form and content, considering rhythm both in its technical, prosodic sense and in relation to Blok's larger historical concerns. As such, I follow Blok in using the term "rhythm" loosely to describe not only the arrangement of stressed syllables, but also a range of other repetitive patterns and themes. If this sometimes leads my discussion into the territory of metaphor, it is my contention that it is only by considering Blok's metrical practice as an extension of his broader concerns that we can fully understand the nature of his modernism and the degree to which these concerns overlap with those of Tynianov and his Formalist peers.

RHYTHM IN/AS HISTORY

City begins at an end. "The Last Day," its first poem, introduces an urban space that is defined by its eschatological temporality, from the biblical reference contained in its title to the mysterious gash that is rent in the sky in its final stanza. The poem is hardly unusual in this regard. Fear of the end runs through the literary myth of St. Petersburg, and was stoked further by the apocalypticism that was widespread during this period.[13] These myths mingle in the contemporary urban scene depicted in Blok's poem. Yet if disaster beckons, it never quite arrives; the poem, the city, and history resolutely fail to align.

The poem begins cautiously, undermining the finality of its title via a series of false starts:

Последний день

Ранним утром, когда люди ленились шевелиться
Серый сон предчувствуя последних дней зимы,
Пробудились в комнате мужчина и блудница,
Медленно очнулись среди угарной тьмы.

Утро копошилось. Безнадежно догорели свечи,
Оплывший огарок маячил в оплывших глазах.
За холодным окном дрожали женские плечи,
Мужчина перед зеркалом расчёсывал пробор в волосах.

Но серое утро уже не обмануло:
Сегодня была она, как смерть, бледна.
Ещё вечером у фонаря её лицо блеснуло,
В этой самой комнате была влюблена.

Сегодня безобразно повисли складки рубашки,
На всём был серый постылый налёт.
Углами торчала мебель, валялись окурки, бумажки,
Всех ужасней в комнате был красный комод.

И вдруг влетели звуки. Верба, раздувшая почки,
Раскачнулась под ветром, осыпая снег.
В церкви ударил колокол. Распахнулись форточки,
И внизу стал слышен торопливый бег.

Люди суетливо выбегали за ворота
(Улицу скрывал дощатый забор).
Мальчишки, женщины, дворники заметили что-то,
Махали руками, чертя незнакомый узор.

Бился колокол. Гудели крики, лай и ржанье.
Там, на грязной улице, где люди собрались,
Женщина-блудница—от ложа пьяного желанья—
На коленях, в рубашке, поднимала руки ввысь . . .

Высоко—над домами—в тумане снежной бури,
На месте полуденных туч и полунощных звезд,
Розовым зигзагом в разверстой лазури
Тонкая рука распластала тонкий крест.

3 февраля 1904[14]

The Last Day

Early in the morning, when people were too lazy to shift,
Anticipating the grey dream of the last winter days,
A man and a harlot awoke in a room,
Slowly came to their senses in the choking gloom.

Morning stirred itself. Hopelessly candles burned their last,
A guttering stub loomed in guttering eyes.
Behind the cold window female shoulders shuddered,
The man before the mirror combed the part in his hair.

But the grey morning no longer deceived:
Today she was, like death, pale.
The evening before her face had shone under the street lamp,
In this same room she had been in love.

Today the folds of his shirt hung shapelessly,
Everything had a grey, repellent patina.
Furniture stuck out its corners, cigarette butts and papers were
strewn all about,
Most terrible of all was the red commode.

And suddenly sounds flew in. A willow, swelling its buds,
Set swaying in the wind, shedding snow.
In the church, a bell struck. Ventilation windows flew open.
And down below a hurried running became audible.

People hurriedly ran out beyond the gates
(The street was hidden by a wooden fence),
Boys, women, janitors noticed something,
They waved their hands, tracing an unknown pattern.

A bell thrashed about. Shouts boomed out, barking and roaring,
There, on the dirty street, where people had gathered,
A woman-harlot—from the bed of drunken desire—
On her knees, in a shirt, raised her hands up high . . .

Up high—above the houses—in the fog of a snowstorm,
In the place of midday clouds and midnight stars,
A pink zigzag in the gaping azure,
A delicate hand spread out a delicate cross.

February 3, 1904

It is morning, the first line of each of the three opening stanzas insists; yet each proceeds only to recede further into memories of the evening just passed. Turning in the fourth to look at the room in which the man and woman have woken up, the poem seems to cast about for direction: should it move forward or back, or stay in the room to gather dust along with the commode?

This aimlessness is compounded by the poem's meter, an example of strict accentual verse (what some scholars term *taktovik*).[15] Rarely encountered in nineteenth-century literary verse and employed for the first time in Blok's oeuvre here, in this type of accentual verse the number of stressed syllables per line varies, as does the interval between them. In "The Last Day," each line has between four and six stressed syllables, with intervals of between one and three syllables; there is considerable variation between each line. The unfamiliarity of this meter is compounded by the poem's opening lines, each of which follows a different pattern. This metrical irregularity is thrown into further relief by the regular caesura and rhyme scheme and the rising and falling cadence that results; we are lulled into the same fitful slumber as the poem's drowsy inhabitants.

It is only with the intrusion of the outside world that the poem revives. "Suddenly" sounds from the street enter through the window and, suddenly, in its fifth stanza, the poem is filled with action: a church bell rings, windows are flung open, and a proliferation of "ras-" verbs, which signal the start of (dispersive) action, declares decisively that the poem has begun again. Shorter sentences and parenthetical statements establish a new, restless norm that reenergizes the poem. We set off running with the crowd. Even now, though, we are in a strange relation to beginnings and ends: something seems to have happened to cause the excitement, a beginning we do not discover until the very end of the poem—which, reintroducing the figure of the prostitute, prompts us to return to its start. This is a Möbius poem, in which the woman who is shaken out of her stupor by noise on the street seems to be the same woman who causes that noise; the decisive, if mysterious action with which the poem ends is thus the harbinger of a disaster that is perpetually delayed by the strange loop of its own action.

The competition between poetic repetition and narrative progression is a constant feature of Blok's early poetic output and particularly in *Verses on the Most Beautiful Lady*. Here, the repeated use of the pattern that became known as the Blokian *dol'nik* not only helps to familiarize readers with this new metrical form, as briefly described at the beginning of this chapter, but also contributes to the sense of suspension that is so crucial on the level of narrative, as the lyric hero wanders through a mystical landscape in search of an enigmatic female figure (the embodiment, according to the mystical philosophy Blok inherited from the Russian philosopher Vladimir Solov'ev, of the Divine Sophia). On the level of the individual poem, the formal repetition of the "ring" (*kol'tso*) structure adopted in many of them—whereby the end of the poem returns to and reprises its opening lines—further thwarts narrative progression; these are, as Clare Cavanagh notes, "courtship poems marked by a resistance to consummation."[16] In "The Last Day," by contrast, consummation, far from resisted, is all too readily available. The prostitute, wooed beneath a street lamp that is the urban cousin of the candles which light the temples of Blok's early verse, is a fallen version of the Beautiful Lady, much as the poem's unusual accentual meter is a distorted echo of the mellifluous *dol'nik* characteristic of that earlier collection.

Scholars tend to regard such refractions of Blok's earlier poetry in his later, urban poetry as evidence of his view of the city, typical of the modernist era, as a morally corrupt space—a "terrible world" (*strashnyi mir*), as the title of a later cycle declares outright, that deals a fatal blow to the idealist worldview of the poet's youth and the lyricism of the poetry with which it is associated. The repetition that in Blok's earlier verse keeps the lyric hero on the threshold of transcendence and attainment of his ideal here becomes a feature of the debased world, trapping the poem and its inhabitants in the grey reality of modern urban life.

To focus solely on repetition is to miss an important aspect of this poem, however, in which this sense of entrapment collides with the mysterious event that "suddenly" sends its inhabitants running for the street. This event—lying at the center of the poem yet oddly hard to place temporally, cataclysmic yet also anticlimactic—differs starkly from those that animate Blok's earlier work, which attaches profound significance to what he saw as the interconnections between "the facts and phenomena of 'earthly' life [and] specific events in the life of the poet" and the Events of non-phenomenal, noumenal time.[17] Zara Mints gives one example, citing the occasion when Blok appeared alongside Lyubov Mendeleeva in several scenes from *Hamlet*, staged in the village of Boblovo in August 1898. Returning home after the performance, Blok saw a meteor in the sky. This meteor made its way into the poems inspired by this and other encounters with his future wife and muse, where it serves as both objective proof of the poems' basis in real events and as a symbol of the spiritual Events set in motion by these meetings.[18]

In "The Last Day," by contrast, it is precisely the disjuncture between earthly events and non-phenomenal Events that is at stake. This lack of synchronicity is felt in the insistent contradictions that define both form and content: the predictability of rhyme and strophic form against the poem's unpredictable meter; the inevitability of the coming End at odds with the uncertainty of the poem's own beginning(s) and end(s). The lightning that flashes at the end of the poem (a type of *stikhiia* in the ordinary sense of "natural element") seems to be the Event that might finally unite these disparate tempos, but even this does not bring the poem to its expected apocalyptic end. Instead, it becomes emblematic of the contingency (*sluchainost'*) that characterizes modern life and the rest of the poems in *City*, in which the repeated singularity of the Event so characteristic of the *Beautiful Lady* poems gives way to the random encounter and a persistent sense that the main event—what actually *happens*—has just slid out of view.

This feeling that something is missing is reflected on the level of rhythm, where it is the random distribution of clusters of three *un*stressed syllables that contributes most to our sense of metrical unpredictability in the first half of the poem. In the first stanza, such clusters (underlined in the example below) are distributed evenly, with one or two in each line, reinforcing the relative regularity in the number of stressed syllables per line (5-6-4-5):

> Ранним утром, когда люди ленились шевелиться
> Серый сон предчувствуя последних дней зимы,
> Пробудились в комнате мужчина и блудница,
> Медленно очнулись среди угарной тьмы.

In line five, however, all sense of predictability is lost: three of these clusters appear in quick succession, followed by none in lines six and seven (in which intervals range between one and two syllables) and a further three in line eight:

> Утро копошилось. Безнадежно догорели свечи,
> Оплывший огарок маячил в оплывших глазах.
> За холодным окном дрожали женские плечи,
> Мужчина перед зеркалом расчёсывал пробор в волосах.

As a result, the rhythm of the second stanza feels markedly less regular than that of the first, despite the fact that the number of stressed syllables in each line is more consistent (5-5-4-5).[19] These clusters of three unstressed syllables become less frequent in the second half of the poem, with none occurring in either stanza five or six (starting with the words "And suddenly . . ."). When they reappear in the seventh stanza, where we encounter the woman on her knees in the street, this sudden absence of stress again knocks us off balance, drawing our attention to the information that we lack, the missed event.

As scholars have observed, Blok's poem was probably inspired by Briusov's "The Pale Horse" ("Kon' bled," 1903), which Blok had heard Briusov reading only a few weeks before composing his own poem.[20] Briusov's poem and its apocalyptic street scene provides rhythmic as well as thematic material for Blok's poem, with at least one contemporary mistaking Blok's unusual accentual meter for the trochaic heptameter used by Briusov.[21] There are important differences between the two poems, however. In stark contrast to the lethargic opening stanzas of Blok's poem, Briusov's first lines plunge the reader into the midst of a crowd of people, omnibuses, cabs, and cars all "racing" along a city street lined with towering buildings:

> 1 Улица была—как буря. Толпы проходили,
> Словно их преследовал неотвратимый Рок.
> Мчались омнибусы, кебы и автомобили,
> Был неисчерпаем яростный людской поток.

Вывески, вертясь, сверкали переменным оком
С неба, с страшной высоты тридцатых этажей;
В гордый гимн сливались с рокотом колес и скоком
Выкрики газетчиков и щелканье бичей . . .[22]

The street was like a storm. Crowds passing,
As if pursued by an inescapable Fate.
Omnibuses, cabs and cars racing,
Endless was the furious flow of folk.
Signboards, twisting, winked from both sides of their face,
Gleaming from a terrifying thirty-floor height;
The din of wheels and hooves, cracking whips
And newsboys shouting, all united in a proud hymn . . .

Filled with the noise of vehicles, machinery, people, and newspaper headlines, this chaotic urban scene is emphatically modern—a quality that is only thrown into further relief in the second verse by the sudden invasion into this scene of a "fiery horseman" (*vsadnik ognelikii*), come to mete out divine justice to the sinners of the city (as the cries of one "madman" in the crowd make explicit).[23] No sooner has the horseman disappeared than all the citizens (except the madman and a woman) dismiss this visitation as an "empty dream" (*pustoi son*); they continue to stream down the street, the final lines of the poem repeating the final quatrain of its first stanza.

The deep ambivalence of "The Last Day" is due in part to its lack of this kind of explicit eschatological imagery and plot. As a comparison of the two poems makes clear, however, it also stems from the absence, in Blok's poem, of any easily identifiable historical backdrop at all. This is a modern city, to be sure, but one that lacks the seething crowds and motor vehicles that place Briusov's city so squarely in the early twentieth-century imaginary. If the date appended to the end of the poem suggests a possible link with the Russo-Japanese War, which began on January 27 (February 9), 1904, current events are not evoked in the poem even obliquely (compare the newspaper boys that shout on Briusov's street). Rather, the sense of foreboding that runs through Blok's text is pointedly ambiguous, refusing to take on clear shape. As in the case of its metrical uncertainty, it is the product as much of what is missing as of what is there.

On one level, then, Briusov's poem helps to decode "The Last Day," clarifying the reason for the state of suspension in which its inhabitants find themselves: modern existence condemns the city crowds to apocalyptic reckoning but simultaneously renders them incapable of engaging with it, immune to the moral cleansing that this day of judgment might bring. On another level, however, it is precisely the differences between these two poems that holds the key to understanding "The Last Day." Echoing the trochaic heptameter of its predecessor but significantly distorting it, the accentual meter used in Blok's poem subverts its own narrative of unchanging repetition. Stumbling over this rhythm that is *almost* familiar, but not quite, readers are forced into the kind of active engagement with their surroundings that is so lacking in the world of the poem itself. Whereas Briusov's poem ends its unambiguous narrative by reproducing wholesale its opening lines, sweeping its reader onward with its crowds, the mysterious final lines of Blok's poem send us back to its start in an effort to fill the gaps in its narrative. Repetition contains the potential to break its own cycle.

Even as Blok's poem laments the state of suspension to which modern life condemns its inhabitants, it prompts a reexamination of the present and its relationship to past and future much like that described in the previous chapter. The rhythm of the poem does not reflect the disordered rhythms of the modern city so much as offer a means for thinking through the contradictions inherent to modern historical experience more broadly.

A brief reading of one of the next poems in *City* will help to illustrate this point further. Eschewing modern urban reality in favor of a mystically infused landscape that recalls *Verses on the Most Beautiful Lady*, "The Duel" ("Poedinok") reprises the circular structure typical of these earlier poems much more explicitly than "The Last Day." Unusually, however, the poem contains not one but two such cycles. While seeming to revert to the mode of frustrated consummation that is such a common feature of the *Beautiful Lady* poems, that is, "The Duel" articulates a conception of rhythm that is also crucially inflected by modern experience:

Поединок

Дни и ночи я безволен,
Жду чудес, дремлю без сна.
В песнях дальних колоколен
Пробуждается весна.

Чутко веет над столицей
Угнетённого Петра.
Вечерница льнёт к деннице,
Несказáнней вечера.

И зарёй—очам усталым
Предстоит, озарена,
За прозрачным покрывалом
Лучезарная Жена . . .

Вдруг летит с отвагой ратной—
В бранном шлеме голова—
Ясный, Кроткий, Златолатный,
Кем возвысилась Москва!

Ангел, Мученик, Посланец
Поднял звонкую трубу . . .
Слышу ко́ней тяжкий танец,
Вижу смертную борьбу . . .

Светлый Муж ударил Деда!
Белый—чёрного коня! . .
Пусть последняя победа
Довершится без меня! . .

Я бегу на воздух вольный,
Жаром битвы утомлён . . .
Бейся, колокол раздольный,
Разглашай весенний звон!

Чуждый спорам, верный взорам
Девы алых вечеров,
Я опять иду дозором
В тень узорных теремов:

Не мелькнёт ли луч в светлице?
Не зажгутся ль терема?
Не сойдёт ли от божницы
Лучезарная Сама?

22 февраля 1904[24]

The Duel

Days and nights I lack will
Wait for miracles, doze without sleep,
In the songs of distant church towers
Spring awakens.

It breezes delicately above the capital
Of oppressed Peter.
Evening star clings to morning,
Each evening more ineffable.

And at sunrise—to tired eyes
Appears, sun-bright,
Behind a translucent shawl,
The Sun-radiant Wife . . .

Suddenly flies with martial boldness—
Head in battle helmet—
The Bright One, the Meek, the Golden-armored,
He who Moscow's glory raised!

Angel, Martyr, Envoy
Lifted a sonorous pipe . . .
I hear the heavy dance of horses,
I see the mortal struggle . . .

The Light Man struck the Old!
The white—the black horse! . . .
Let the final victory
Be won without me!

I run out into the free air,
Exhausted by the heat of battle . . .
Strike, carefree clock,
Ring out the spring chime!

Stranger to arguments, true to the gazes
Of the maiden of scarlet evenings,
I go to keep watch again
In the shadow of decorated palace towers:

Won't a light flicker in the parlor?
Won't the towers blaze with light?
Won't there descend from the sanctuary
The Sun-radiant Herself?

February 22, 1904

The lyric hero wanders through the first three stanzas in a state of suspended expectation ("I wait," "I dream") until he approaches a vision of the "Sun-radiant Wife" (*Luchezarnaia zhena*). His union with this woman is prevented by the abrupt intrusion of a different encounter, the duel of the poem's title, in which the rider of a white horse (the patron saint of Moscow, Saint George, associated in the folk imaginary with goodness and light) does battle with the rider of a black one (the founder of Petersburg, Peter the Great, associated, particularly in the modernist imaginary, with demonic forces). Eventually, the hero flees this overstimulating scene to return to the reveries of the poem's start. The use of trochaic tetrameter in this poem, a meter most often encountered in the nineteenth century in poetic fairy tales (*skazki*) and ballads, heightens the sense that the hero of this poem moves through a space that has more in common with the mystical landscapes of the *Beautiful Lady* era than the modern city.[25]

What about the rhythm of Blok's poem? The stanzas devoted to the duel largely conform to nineteenth-century rhythmical convention for trochaic tetrameter, omitting stress on the first and third feet of the line.[26] The six stanzas that frame this scene follow a more unusual pattern, however. In the first and seventh stanzas, the first two lines are fully stressed; in the second and eighth, only the first line is fully stressed; in the third and ninth stanzas, none are.[27] This progressive reduction in the number of realized stresses parallels the speaker's progress from his initial position of earthly entrapment (fourteen of sixteen syllables in the quatrain bear full stress) to his vision of the "Sun-radiant Wife" (nine of sixteen). Do light feet function here as a form of "rhythmic italics," to borrow a term from linguistic-statistical prosody, marking out the first and final sections of the poem from the central section? If this is the case, it leaves the duel announced by the poem's title in an odd position. At the center of the poem, in more ways than one, but taking place in its most metrically regular section (stanzas four, five, and six), it becomes mere metrical background for the third and ninth stanzas and the thematic counterpart to the spiritual quest these depict.

The poem comes into clearer focus when we consider its rhythm as the product not only of patterns of stress in individual lines, but also the sequence of the poem as a whole. As Maksim Shapir points out, following the Formalists, rhythm is determined not only by quantity and distribution of stress but also its quality. Exactly the same sequence of stressed and unstressed syllables can have a different "real" (*real'nyi*) rhythm in different contexts, Shapir notes, whether these contexts are entirely distinct poems with different metrical schemes or different stanzas within a single poem.[28] This may be because the abstract sequence of stressed and unstressed syllables is realized by different words or syntax; but it may also be due simply to their differing positions within the artistic whole. In Yury Lotman's words, the repetitive patterns of meter and rhythm not only "reveal similarity in difference" but also "establish difference in the similar."[29] A line at the end of the poem sounds different from a line at its start. If the final stanza in Blok's poem reprises the metrical pattern of the third stanza, that is, this repetition only emphasizes the difference in its rhythmic profile. This difference is in part a factor of syntax: where the third stanza consists of a single, enjambed sentence, the ninth instead ends with a series of insistent questions. It is also—simply, though crucially—because this is the second time this exact pattern of metrical deviations has appeared in the poem. The final stanza cannot be a return because it is a repetition, and precisely in this manner marks its difference from the third.

"The Duel" was written after Blok's first visit to Moscow, where he was struck by the affirmative key of the Moscow Symbolists' spiritual hopes: "I feel that something important is beginning for me," he wrote upon his return to Petersburg in a letter that vividly contrasts the bright dreams of the Moscow Symbolists with the gloom of the St. Petersburg circles in which Blok was used to moving.[30] Read in a biographical key, the duel becomes a poetic rendering of this trip and its emotional consequences, combining the conflict between the two Symbolist groups with the long-standing rivalry between Russia's two largest cities, here represented by their founders on horseback, to express the hopefulness reawakened by Moscow, the "mythical and mystical" (*skazochno-misticheskii*) city of ancient legend, and its happy poets (*PSS* 2:730).

The hopeful quality of this poem is communicated by the subtle but distinct shift that has taken place in its temporal orientation by its close. The hero may return to his former reveries, but his perspective has been altered: the state of passive expectation that characterizes the first stanzas—when the speaker, "lack[ing] will" (*bezvolen*), passively awaits "miracles"—has been replaced by a new, active stance in relation to the surrounding world (as the reappearance of the root "-vol-" [will, freedom] here without negation [*vol'nyi*, *privol'nyi*] further indicates). Commanding the spring bell to ring out, the hero moves restively through space and sharpens his focus impatiently on the future.

It is no coincidence that one of the poem's only temporal deictics appears at this juncture, and that it is one that signals repetition: "again." As Roland Greene remarks, "the adverb *again* explicitly insists on the similarity of past and present," but fails to "cancel the present tense's implicit, automatic affirmation of its own distinctiveness."[31] Its purpose, Sharon Cameron claims elsewhere, "is not to chart sameness but disparity."[32] In the context of this poem, "again" emerges from the duel, an event that brings sequential earthly time into contact with cyclical poetic time. When the hero abruptly flees before the duel's conclusion, he flees linear temporality—a temporality that is at odds with the circling motion of his quest for the ideal (which, were it ever to be reached, would involve the transcendence of time, not the completion of a trajectory *in* time), but which, it turns out, provides this poetic pursuit with new purpose.

If "again" confirms the hero's immersion in time, it also highlights the poem's own trajectory from the first three stanzas to the last, the rhythm of which is perceived in relation to what has come before. The poem's embeddedness in time is further underlined by the series of questions with which it ends. These questions point beyond the limits of the poem on the level of form as well as content, their repeated syntactic structure interacting with the rhythmic variations that they reprise to generate the next in the long series of iterations that make up the poetic tradition. As in "The Last Day," the modernism of this poem is less a factor of metrical innovation than of its dramatization of this tension between novelty and repetition, the predictable and the unexpected.

REMIXING RHYTHM

So far, I have been arguing that rhythm plays a central role in the encounter with modernity staged by the poems in *City*. Rhythm in these poems does not mimetically reflect historical conditions so much as dramatize the tensions to which they give rise and the qualities of poetic rhythm that they make particularly salient. In this section, I extend this argument to consider the qualities of poetic rhythm that the social space of the modern city made more sharply perceptible.

"The Unknown Woman" ("Neznakomka," 1906) was the poem that made Blok famous, extending the reach of his work far beyond the narrow circle of mystically inclined Symbolists who had until then been his sole audience. The poem was frequently recited in the *cafés chantants* then so popular with the urban middle and lower classes, and prostitutes even took to calling themselves after the poem's mysterious heroine.[33] The appeal of the poem across these two spheres echoes the ambiguity at its center: does the cheap, suburban restaurant in which the speaker sits become the setting for a genuine mystical experience, or is the speaker simply drunk? Is the mysterious woman of the poem's title the embodiment of the Beautiful Lady, or just another "Neznakomka," out to make her living for the night? As I will suggest here, this concern with the singularity of the event *in* the poem extends beyond its bounds to raise broader questions about poetry's relationship to tradition and the repetition this implies.

Незнакомка

1 По вечерам над ресторанами
Горячий воздух дик и глух,
И правит окриками пьяными
Весенний и тлетворный дух.

Вдали, над пылью переулочной,
Над скукой загородных дач,
Чуть золотится крендель булочной,
И раздаётся детский плач.

И каждый вечер, за шлагбаумами,
Заламывая котелки,
Среди канав гуляют с дамами
Испытанные остряки.

Над озером скрипят уключины,
И раздаётся женский визг,
А в небе, ко всему приученный,
Бессмысленно кривится диск.

И каждый вечер друг единственный
В моём стакане отражен
И влагой терпкой и таинственной,
Как я, смирён и оглушён.

А рядом у соседних столиков
Лакеи сонные торчат,
И пьяницы с глазами кроликов
«In vino veritas!» кричат.

И каждый вечер, в час назначенный
(Иль это только снится мне?),
Девичий стан, шелками схваченный,
В туманном движется окне.

И медленно, пройдя меж пьяными,
Всегда без спутников, одна,
Дыша духами и туманами,
Она садится у окна.

И веют древними поверьями
Её упругие шелка,
И шляпа с траурными перьями,
И в кольцах узкая рука.

И странной близостью закованный,
Смотрю за тёмную вуаль,

И вижу берег очарованный
И очарованную даль.

Глухие тайны мне поручены,
Мне чьё-то солнце вручено,
И все души моей излучины
Пронзило терпкое вино.

И перья страуса склонённые
В моём качаются мозгу,
И очи синие бездонные
Цветут на дальнем берегу.

В моей душе лежит сокровище,
И ключ поручен только мне!
Ты право, пьяное чудовище!
Я знаю: истина в вине.

24 апреля 1906. Озерки.[34]

The Unknown Woman

Over the restaurants on sultry evenings
the stale hot vapours rise,
and a corrupting spirit born of springtime
sounds in the drunken cries.

Over the boredom of suburban villas,
the alleys dusty-dry,
glimmers the golden sign above the baker's,
and tired children cry.

And every night beyond the level crossings,
with bowler hats askew,
saunter the local wits with girls a-giggle,
to criticize the view.

Over the lake is heard the creak of rowlocks,
and female shrieks resound,
while high above, the moon, surprised at nothing,
grins meaningless and round.

And every night my glass reflects my image,
friend of my solitude,

who by the strange wine's aromatic power,
as I am, is subdued.

The sleepy waiters, stuck beside the tables,
watch for an empty glass,
while drunken men, with eyes like rabbits', bellow:
'In vino veritas!'

But every evening at the fated hour—
or is it just my dream?—
a figure moves across the misted window,
a girl in silks that gleam.

Slowly she passes through the drunken rabble,
companionless and fair,
and by the window sits, a mist of perfume
spread round her in the air.

Her silken waist, her hat of sable feathers,
her narrow hand with rings,
seem to exhale a breath of long-forgotten
and legendary things.

Tranced by the wonder of her nearness, striving
to pierce her shadowy veil,
I look on an enchanted shore, an enchanted distance
beyond some magic pale.

Unspoken mysteries to me are given,
another's sun is mine;
transfused through every corner of my being,
steals the astringent wine.

Within my brain the drooping ostrich feathers
wave languidly and sweep;
blue on that distant shore the eyes that flower,
immeasurably deep.

Safe in my soul there lies a hoarded treasure,
whose key is only mine—
Oh, you were right indeed, you drunken monsters,
the truth is found in wine.

April 24, 1906. Ozerki.[35]

As most readers observe, the poem divides perfectly into two parts of six stanzas each, which correspond to the two worlds between which the hero, the subject of the seventh and central stanza, is suspended: the monstrous banality of suburban St. Petersburg and the "enchanted distance" of his longed-for ideal. This division between two levels of reality is reflected in the imagery of the poem's two parts. Scholars have noted the abundance of mundane, material objects in the first six stanzas (the restaurant, the dust, the dachas, the baker's sign, and so on), associating these with the general air of *poshlost'* that hangs over the first, "earthly" part of the poem. Even nature is deformed, made tawdry by the people and activities that intrude into it.[36] The last six stanzas, by contrast, shift to the more abstract, poetic register typical of Blok's earlier work (the "breath of long-forgotten / and legendary things," the "shadowy veil," the "enchanted distance," the "distant shore"). The poem's metrical structure reinforces this sense of division. Whereas the first, "earthly'" part refuses to settle into a pattern (with light feet irregularly scattered throughout each stanza, producing no fewer than ten rhythmic variations on the iambic tetrameter scheme in which the poem is written), the second, "poetic" part is much more consistent, with twenty one of its twenty-eight lines following the most common variation for iambic tetrameter verse (where the third foot of the line is without stress).[37]

Clearly demarcated by the seventh stanza—in which we find three fully stressed lines in succession for the first and only time in the poem—the two parts of the poem appear as inverted mirror images of each other. Yet the split between the poem's "earthly" and "poetic" parts is not as stark as might first appear. As Zara Mints observes, the first part of the poem includes not only non-poetic lexicon but also words and word-combinations from *Verses on the Most Beautiful Lady*. Evenings in the world of the first volume, for example, are a sacred time when the hero "meets" with his mystical beloved; nature is the sphere of Her presence. Combined with the banal, sometimes even grotesque language of the first part of the poem, these signs of her presence are devalued; nonetheless, they are there. In the second half of the poem, words that are important for the *Verses* . . . do outnumber others, confirming the poetic atmosphere of these stanzas; but other elements are also present and poeticized, elements that would not have been considered aesthetic during the era of the first volume and which belong firmly to the sphere of suburban nightlife (perfume, feathers).[38]

What are we to make of this blurring of the earthly and the poetic, and how does it affect our interpretation of the poem? John Bowlt understands the effect to be a homogenizing one: insistently mingling the earthly and the divine, the poem's symmetrical structure does not so much promise transformation and transcendence as create an overwhelming "sense of having been there before" that "testif[ies] to the ultimate sameness of all levels of consciousness in the poem."[39] However, as Mints's observations imply, repetition does not only imply sameness. Elements from Blok's earlier work are deformed or transformed by the new context in which they appear; the poetic takes on new attributes in an everyday setting and vice versa. This leads Mints to read the poem in a more optimistic key: whether or not the poem depicts a real spiritual experience, it testifies to Blok's growing ability to see poetry in mundane reality.

Just as important as repetition within the poem and Blok's own oeuvre are the echoes between "The Unknown Woman" and its cultural context. While Blok would not have been familiar with the term "semantic aureole," a phenomenon first described by Kirill Taranovsky, this mechanism—whereby particular meters become associated over time with specific themes or motifs—or a version of it, plays an important role in his work.[40] As Gasparov persuasively demonstrates, "The Unknown Woman" employs a distinctive metrical structure—iambic tetrameter with alternating dactylic and masculine rhymes—likely borrowed from Briusov, who had used it frequently for poems about chance encounters on the street.[41] Briusov was a formative influence for Blok; as we have seen, his presence makes itself felt in much of Blok's urban poetry from this period. This influence was perceived quite distinctly by his contemporaries and colored their reception of this poem. As Anna Akhmatova wrote in a 1907 letter, "many of his poems are strikingly reminiscent of V[alery] Briusov. The poem "The Unknown Woman," for example . . . but it's magnificent . . ."[42]

Gasparov's reading of "The Unknown Woman," like the concept of the semantic aureole more generally, is built upon an accretive conception of poetic tradition whereby meters acquire significance over time as they are reused and reimagined in different contexts. Blok's poem makes use of this mechanism and indeed exaggerates it. It is not just Briusov's meter that the poem borrows; upon closer inspection, there is very little in the poem that is wholly original, whether because Blok is borrowing from his own earlier work or from the wider culture. As Magomedova points out, for example, citing several poems by Briusov, Bely, and Innokenty Annensky, the poem repeats a number of tropes and themes already in circulation during the modernist era. In particular, restaurants in Symbolist lyric verse frequently became the site of a "border between worlds," with texts of this kind frequently revolving around a transition between the empirical world and a world beyond it.[43] This is not to mention Blok's own rehearsal of the poem's central themes, whether in other poems ("There ladies flaunt the latest fashions . . ." ["Tam damy shchegoliaiut modami . . . ," 1911], the next poem in *City*, originally titled "The Unknown Woman. Variant"), in the play of the same name, or in his essays (most famously, "On the Current State of Russian Symbolism").[44]

Elsewhere in Blok's work, we find instances that, while not strictly speaking examples of semantic aureole, can be categorized alongside this phenomenon. Blok's use of accentual meters is one such example. Starting in the years around the Revolution of 1905, as Gasparov shows, the use of accentual meters gradually became associated in Blok's oeuvre with revolutionary unrest—a tendency that became fully legible only retrospectively, from the vantage point of *The Twelve* (*Dvenadstat'*, 1918).[45] Describing Blok's turn to the nineteenth-century poetic canon in the latter half of the 1910s, Lydia Ginzburg notes the consonance between this canon and Blok's social concerns during this period. If Blok's turn to common nineteenth-century meters in search of a fitting cadence for twentieth-century civic verse does not necessarily imply the revival of particular semantic aureoles, it serves as further proof of his awareness of a connection between metrical tradition and thematic concerns.[46]

Blok's sensitivity to the broader poetic context in which each individual poem is perceived is most fully illustrated by his "trilogy of becoming human," the three volumes that were "to bridge the distance between self, nation, and history" by organizing the poet's lyrics into a multifaceted expression of the experience of modern man.[47] The project was set in motion in 1910, when the publishing house Musaget commissioned an edition of Blok's collected works. Blok was by no means the only poet of his generation to conceive of the book as an integrated whole. Symbolist poets actively sought to erase the boundaries between individual works by cultivating a poetics of "correspondences" based upon the associative connections inherent to the symbol and nurtured by the lyric cycle.[48] These efforts were designed to create that "resonating network of inter-referentiality" which was a central component of the Symbolist worldview and the interpretive community upon which this resonance relied.[49] Blok took this principle to its logical extreme, arranging all of his pre-1916 poetry into cycles.[50] Here, again, the effect is to exaggerate the dependence of each individual poem on the broader context in which it appears.

In the case of *Verses on the Most Beautiful Lady*, as Jonathan Stone has shown, this process involved physically cutting up the original edition, rearranging its poems, and amending or adding dates. Whereas the first edition of *Verses on the Most Beautiful Lady* uses context to familiarize readers with the *dol'nik*, here the poems are arranged in what appears to be chronological order, an instance of what Stone labels "biographical Symbolism." This term describes the general shift among Symbolists away from esoteric mysticism and toward an approach that would both enable uninitiated readers to understand the development of the movement and encourage them to view Symbolism as central to Russia's recent cultural history.[51] Blok reinforces this shift toward linear narrative when he describes the lyric hero's journey through these three volumes in linear terms, "from a moment of blinding light, through the unavoidable marshy forest . . . to despair, curses, 'retribution' and . . . the rebirth of 'public' man, an artist who courageously looks the world in the face."[52] Dmitrii Maksimov was the first to trace the various permutations of the theme of the "path" (*put'*) in Blok's work and to describe its role in integrating the three volumes of his trilogy, weaving together Blok's own youthful search for the Beautiful Lady with the fate of the nation at large.[53] In this manner, the trilogy as a whole overcomes the rhythmic disjuncture that I identified as a feature of poems such as "The Last Day."

At the same time, as Lydia Ginzburg and others have observed, the complex structure of each volume in the trilogy and the sections and cycles contained within them combine to form a narrative that is far from linear. Instead, "themes and their corresponding styles not only replace each other, but also coexist, intersect and collide."[54] The effect is much like that observed by Tynianov: just as the context of the verse line causes the meaning of each individual word constantly to shift and change, the dynamic set of intersecting contexts constituted by the trilogy renders the meaning of each individual poem radically mutable.

Jacob Edmond has noted the tension between modernism's imperative to "make it new" and its own reliance on the copy.[55] Taking a meter associated with Briusov and using it for his own poem on the same theme, Blok not only copied Briusov's original but created a blueprint for further copies, as key motifs from Blok's poem were repeated, appropriated, and remixed in countless poems written in the same meter over the next decades.[56] While concepts such as the remix might seem anachronistic in relation to modernism, this practice was an intrinsic part of the modernist approach. Briusov himself built a whole career out of translating French poetry and crafting his own versions of this poetry's central themes, motifs, and formal structures. More generally, as we have seen, Russian poetry of this period not only invented (or resurrected) new, nonclassical meters but also revisited existing syllabotonic meters, reinvigorating these meters by combining them with non-poetic lexicon or imprecise rhymes.

"Even the most exact repetition contains differences," Jacob Edmond writes.[57] These differences are at the heart of "The Unknown Woman," a poem in which repetition is both a central thematic concern and a primary formal device. As such, the poem dramatizes what Edmond identifies as the dialectical relationship in modernism between the call to "make it new" and the imperative "make it the same."[58] This is also the dialectic of rhythm, which, as we have seen, modernists and Formalists viewed in terms of the interplay between novelty and tradition, repetition and change. What makes Blok's poem "better" than Briusov's originals, Akhmatova wondered? It may well have to do with the fact that its metrical and rhythmic structure is more finely orchestrated, or that it combines these with a greater abundance of technical devices. But it may also have something to do with the fact that the poem is a repetition: drawing on a meter and motifs already familiar to the reader of Briusov's work, the poem provokes not only the excitement of the new but also the thrill of recognition. (This is much the same ambiguous emotion provoked in the speaker by the Unknown Woman herself.) Similar but different, Blok's poem, its Briusovian forefather, and its own numerous offspring are—despite the contingency that defines them—experienced as part of what Lisa Gitelman identifies as a network of "social experiences of meaning," or what Craig Dworkin calls "nodes of articulation along a signifying chain."[59]

The proliferating arguments about the correct way to define poetic rhythm that were such a feature of the modernist period in Russia were born of a widespread desire to account for its special dynamism—that intangible, diffuse quality upon which modernists based their claims to perpetual innovation. In this sense, rhythm is, like modernity itself, what Friedman identifies as "a term at war with itself, a term that unravels its own definition, a term that codifies the principle of indeterminacy and in so doing opposes its own commitment to perpetual change."[60] Modernists were not unaware of this tension, as my discussion in these chapters has tried to show. The special quality of poetic rhythm came to be understood in terms of its potential to make tangible the complex interactions between present, past, and future via the multiple textual and intertextual contexts that determine the perception of rhythm in any given instance.

PART II

Image

In the previous chapters, I showed that debates around rhythm were closely tied to processes of remediation. Even as rhythm became a byword among modernist poets for the immediacy of poetic expression, their work drew attention to versification as a dynamic system. The study of meter in historical perspective highlighted the role of poetic convention in determining and defining what is perceived as rhythmic. Against this backdrop, rhythm came to be understood as an expression of the inherent historicity of the poetic medium, the most constant feature of which modernists understood to be its ability to register difference and change. In the section that follows, I turn to consider how remediation led not only to awareness of poetry's historicity, but also to heightened sensitivity to its material qualities.

That the physical *stuff* of language matters more in poetry than in everyday speech is neither a historically specific nor a particularly new claim. It is worth returning to here, however, due to the new emphasis that it received during the modernist period. Just what exactly *is* the material of poetry, these poets and scholars asked—and how does this material dimension affect the particular way in which poetry mediates our perception and experience of the world?

In Russia, debates about the relation of poetic material to matter more generally were telescoped through polemics around the image, or *obraz*. Historically, the attraction of the term "image" for literary criticism has been precisely its erasure of the boundary between reality and its representation.[1] The term first entered English-language criticism in the seventeenth century under the influence of empiricism, which regarded knowledge as the product of the impressions left by sensory experience upon the mind. In parallel, poetry came to be regarded as "a process of pictorial production and reproduction."[2] This visual conception of imagery was rejected during the Romantic era, when the notion of vivid illustration was abandoned in favor of the so-called higher image. This pointedly *in*visible image was intellectual and inward; it did not simply store sensory impressions of external reality, but translated or transfigured these impressions to reveal a more profound truth than that available to rational thought and mundane vision. By the late nineteenth century, this debate had been taken up in psychology, which was undergoing a dramatic paradigm shift in relation to the status of the mental image or idea as a component of thought.[3]

These conflicting accounts of the poetic image share a degree of ambiguity regarding the precise nature of the type of sensory experience recorded or provoked by poetic language, on the one hand, and the relation of this experience to the world at large, on the other. Is the poetic image primarily visual or verbal? Does it capture a trace of the outside world or imaginatively reproduce it? What is the relationship between sensory experience and thought, and how is this expressed in language?

These ambiguities point to one reason that the *obraz*/image became such a contested term in the polemics of the modernist era. Referring simultaneously to material form and semantic figuration, the image became a conceptual platform for rethinking poetic representation. For the Symbolists, the potency of the concept lay in its apparent confirmation of poetry's ability to sustain a uniquely intimate and organic relationship between signifier and signified (recall Bely's thunderous *grrrom*). For the Futurists, the term "image" became a kind of scornful shorthand for this Symbolist view; but they themselves merely replaced it with the "word"—which, pointedly unencumbered by referential duties as it may have been, they continued to define in terms of the relationship between its physical aspect and semantics ("the word is wider than meaning!" as Kruchenykh declared). For both groups, the central question remained that of how the material of poetry relates to the material of the world and to the sense we make of it—a broad area of enquiry, to be sure, and one that produced answers as numerous as there were poets, but one that was, more often than not, channeled through the *obraz*/image and its cognate concepts.

The very ambiguity of the term "image" was thus in part responsible for renewed interest in the specificity of poetry as a medium during this period. This ambiguity also helps to explain why it makes sense to talk about heightened interest in medium specificity in a context so committed to intermedial experiment. Such experiments were ubiquitous in modernist circles. Russian Symbolists strove to create synthetic art forms, using sound patterning to bring their poetry as close as possible to music. Later, Futurist poets invented a whole language on the basis of expressive sound, *zaum'*; this was also the main focus of the earliest Formalist publications. Many of these poets were trained in painting and collaborated with artists to create books in which the use of handwritten and lithographed text erased the boundary between picture and text.[4] The limits of the phonological alphabet became a frequent topic of discussion, as poets and theorists looked to Chinese and other ideographic or pictographic scripts in search of a model for a more labile medium for expression.[5]

With all this in mind, it should come as no surprise that the term "intermediality" (*intermedialität*) first appeared in an article about Russian avant-garde poetry, where it describes text-picture relations in concrete poetry.[6] Used in this narrow sense, "intermediality" refers to media combination, where distinct media are co-present. In the much broader sense in which it is now used, however, it serves as an umbrella term that "applies to any transgression of boundaries between conventionally distinct media"—from intermedial references (such as the evocation of filmic techniques in literature) to medial transposition (for instance, a film adaptation of a theatrical play).[7] As we have seen, Bolter and Grusin's concept of remediation goes even further, positing that all media are by definition involved in intermedial relationships; "all mediation is remediation," as they claim.[8] This latter definition echoes Marshall McLuhan's seminal thesis that all media "contain" other media, as well as W. J. T. Mitchell, for whom "all media are mixed media."[9]

These arguments offer a necessary correction to "impossible and utopian" discourses of media purity of the Greenbergian sort usually associated with modernism.[10] Nonetheless, they risk being too broad. As Irina O. Rajewsky cautions, recognizing the "constructedness and historicity of media conceptions" should not blind us to the practical truth that, "[for] concrete intermedial practices in the arts . . . media borders and medial specificities are indeed of crucial importance."[11] The fluid nature of these borders only highlights the need for precision in describing the specific quality of any individual "mixed" medium at any given historical moment. As Lars Elleström writes, "media are both similar and different and one cannot compare media without clarifying which aspects are relevant to the comparison and exactly how these aspects are related to each other."[12] In other words, if "all media are, *from the standpoint of sensory modality*, 'mixed media'"—to cite Mitchell's later, refined version of his claim—what precise kinds of sense-data do different media produce and in what proportion, and what kind of sensations or experienced effects do they provoke?[13]

As I will argue in the chapters in this part of the book, modernist artists and theorists became interested in the specific qualities of individual media such as poetry in part as a result of the modernist penchant for mixing media.

The conclusions they reached were shaped by the ubiquity of intermedial experiment during this period in turn. This context, I contend, made modernist poets and theorists sensitive to the multiple material forms between which poetry can move. As Thomas H. Ford observes, "sound poetry can only be said to exist when it is framed at least implicitly by a text that employs all the semiotic articulations of writing that sound poetry itself has renounced."[14] The same holds true in reverse for visual or "concrete" poetry, which draws at least part of its effect from our awareness of its pointed transposition of sound patterning into typographic play. This mutual framing is repeatedly highlighted in *zaum'* texts and theoretical writing. Kruchenykh's "Dyr bul shchyl," for example, the founding text and manifesto for this new expressive sound language, is prefaced by an introduction that emphasizes graphic mediation ("*written* in my own language," emphasis mine).[15] The graphic form taken by such texts is at least as important as their sonic performance; both guarantee the radical semantic contingency at the heart of the Futurist program. "A word written by one hand or set in one typeface is completely unlike the same word in a different inscription," as Kruchenykh and Khlebnikov declared in one of several joint manifestoes, "The Letter as Such."[16]

The presence of the hand in the statement just quoted is characteristic: like the Futurist interest in vocal performance, it begins to demonstrate the diverse set of medium bearers that *zaum'* texts explored and through which they articulated their meaning—from the sound of individual letters and phonemes to print, handwritten script, voice, and the body.[17] For all that *zaum'* texts appear to foreground one or other material dimension of the poem, that is, their real concern is with what Ford describes as the "felt hesitation or translative movement between" the multiple material strata that they inhabit, on the one hand, and the meaning they thereby convey or create, on the other.[18]

This intermedial conception of poetic materiality shaped the way that modernists talked about and used the image/*obraz* in their work, as is made clear by the apparent contradiction that runs through so much poetic activity and theorizing during this period, from the symbol to the Futurist "word-as-such," from Potebnya's "thinking in images" to Shklovsky's theory of estrangement. These concepts are all based on some notion of the independence of poetic language as an autonomous sphere. At the same time, they insist upon its unique capacity to intervene in and reinvigorate the object world. These contradictory impulses provide further evidence of what Tihanov identifies as the period's prevarication between two opposing "regimes of relevance," an older regime that located the value of literature in its social utility, and an emergent one, embodied most fully by Russian Formalism and the literary theoretical tradition to which it gave birth, that valued literature above all as an autonomous discourse.[19] The prominence of the image in artistic debate during this period demonstrates, I want to show, that the coexistence of these two regimes of relevance gave rise to a third: one that understood the social utility of literature in terms of its specific material qualities and the transformative potential these entailed.

The two figures at the center of this part of the book are the poet Boris Pasternak and the Formalist Viktor Shklovsky. Pasternak more than once expressed his disapproval of Formalism and of the formal study of verse in general, but made an exception for Shklovsky's well-known concept of estrangement (*ostranenie*).[20] This idea was first described by Shklovsky in "Art as Device" ("Iskusstvo kak priem," 1917), an essay that is often regarded as the origin point of, and shorthand for, Formalism as a whole. There are a number of other intriguing parallels between the two figures. Both are regarded as canonical figures in Russian modernism, but both have proven difficult to place. Although Pasternak moved in Futurist circles and even belonged to a Futurist group, Tsentrifuga, the singularity of his poetic style made him something of a "misfit" for his time, to cite the category into which one recent history of Russian literature places him.[21] Shklovsky, too, is caught, in Tihanov's terms, "at the cusp of two . . . conflicting regimes of relevance."[22] These conflicting regimes lend his theoretical work of these years its characteristic duality, insisting upon the autonomy of literature—its independent value—while still valuing it for its instrumental uses. Both figures also embody the more general dynamic described in this book, the tension between innovation and tradition. Perhaps most significant, therefore, is the "attitude in which we see Pasternak throughout, forever amazed and enchanted by his discovery: Spring again!"[23] This attitude mirrors precisely the dynamic of estrangement, where, in Tihanov's apt phrase, "the new is hailed as the savior of the old or the ever extant."[24] Both Pasternak and Shklovsky, in other words, are invested in the renewing force of poetry; and both locate this force in the image.

Chapter Four

Viktor Shklovsky's Stone

IT MAY SEEM somewhat perverse to include Viktor Shklovsky in a chapter on the image. Shklovsky's first forays into print took direct aim at the idea, popularized by the nineteenth-century philologist Alexander Potebnya, that poetry is "thinking in images." The most famous example is "Art as Device," first published in 1917. This essay makes short work of demoting the image. "Thinking in images is not what unites all arts or even literature," Shklovsky declares.[1] The poetic image "has nothing in common" with cognition; it is but one of the wide variety of devices by means of which poetry "create[s] the strongest possible impression" (*naibol'shee vpechatlenie*)."[2] Soon, we arrive at the essay's central claim. Art is not "a way of thinking and understanding," but a way of *seeing* and *perceiving*:

> And so this thing we call art exists in order to restore the sensation of life, in order to make us feel things, in order to make the stone stony. The goal of art is to create the sensation of seeing, and not merely recognizing, things; the device of art is the estrangement of things and the complication of form, which increases the duration and complexity of perception, as the process of perception is, in art, an end in itself and must be prolonged. Art is the means to live through the making of a thing; what has been made does not matter in art.[3]

Potebnya's image has been replaced by a stone; thought is ousted by cold, hard substance. What are we to make of this substitution? How does it relate to modernism's new interest in the material bases of poetry? And what does this substitute for the image reveal about the apparent contradiction at the heart of Shklovsky's theory of art, which promises to "restore the sensation of life" even as it declares its exclusive interest in the "complication of form"?

In part due to his close personal ties with Futurism, Shklovsky's earliest articles have sometimes been cast as a retrospective effort to provide a theoretical framework for the movement and particularly its invented transrational "language," *zaum'*, with which several of these articles deal. This view has rightly been criticized as too simplistic; but it was an opinion voiced by Formalist scholars themselves. Boris Eikhenbaum, who regarded the Futurists irritably as "mechanics" rather than poets proper, blamed their influence for early Formalism's narrow focus on sound—to his mind, a significant weakness of the essays in the first issue of the *Poetika* series, since this led to the neglect of semantic meaning.[4] This point has been taken up in later scholarship. Early Formalism, typified by Shklovsky, was "mechanistic," as Peter Steiner's landmark study of the movement has it—too wedded to a conception of the work as "a mechanical aggregation of its parts" to account for the full complexity of poetic language as a system.[5]

Certainly, there is a large dose of the manifesto's crude iconoclasm in Shklovsky's early essays, the shortcomings of which, as Shklovsky himself conceded, can be traced to their determined "negation of what others are doing."[6] For example, the strict demarcation of art and *byt*—or of literature and non-literature—at the heart of the mechanistic model was a direct and polemical negation of the views of another influential nineteenth-century philologist, Alexander Veselovsky.[7] Specifically, Shklovsky resisted the notion that literary evolution is driven by "developments in social life and corresponding transformations in the human spirit."[8] Yet Shklovsky's alternative remained tied to the basic premises of this tradition: although *ostranenie* positions the evolution of art as that which revitalizes the automatized forms of life (rather than, as for Veselovsky, vice versa), it nonetheless assumes that there is—indeed, must be—some relationship between life and literature. Hence the ambiguity at the heart of this theory: does art refresh our perception of art, or of *byt*? Does it draw our attention to artistic form, or to the stoniness of stone?

This marriage of old and new was, Peter Steiner finds, "at least in part . . . responsible for the quick aging of the mechanistic model."[9] Others, too, have noted the limitations imposed by the determinedly interstitial quality of Shklovsky's approach. Caught between idealism and positivism, historicism and formalism, his role as a theoretician and his own practice as a writer of fiction, Shklovsky's work was, in Tihanov's terms, fundamentally informed by its origins in an era of transition from one regime of relevance to a new one.[10] Given that this is the case, I propose here to take *ostranenie* on its own terms: what does this concept tell us about the "interparadigmatic stage in the evolution of Slavic literary scholarship" that it epitomizes? After all, as Basil Lvoff contests, it is perhaps the fact that Shklovsky "does *not* speak to us in the language of established categories" that accounts for the enduring intellectual appeal of his most famous concept.[11]

In this view, to hew too closely to existing definitions in our interpretation of Shklovsky's central terms is to make the very same mistake we ascribe to Shklovsky. If we are to avoid turning Shklovsky's work—and with it, Russian Formalism—into an "endless sentimental journey," we must read it according to its own radically innovative terms.[12] When placed in the context of what Oushakine terms Russian modernism's "media project," *ostranenie* turns out to be a device aimed not so much at renewing perception as at revealing the work of mediation by which perception is structured: the "medium is the message," to borrow the famous adage of a more familiar media theorist, Marshall McLuhan.[13] This chapter will expand on this position. My contention will be that Shklovsky's early theoretical contributions demonstrate an interest less in some specific medium (voice *rather than* text, for example) than in the intermedial processes that poetic language sets in motion. This position is informed by debates around the image, the very device against which Shklovsky appears to inveigh.

ESTRANGING THE IMAGE

Clearly, the stone is intended in part to bring art back down to earth. It contributes to Shklovsky's polemic against Symbolists like Bely, who repeatedly turned to images of petrification (*okamenenie*) and ossification to describe what they saw as the decay of language in the modern world. This was a theory of language drawn from the work of Potebnya. In simplified terms, Potebnya's mythic view of language proposed that all words originally established a direct connection between objective reality and subjective inwardness thanks to the absolute harmony of their "outer form" (external sound qualities) and their "inner form," that is, the etymon whence the word is derived: one example that Potebnya gives is the word *stol* (table), which refers to an object with many attributes, but which is represented by the single attribute present in the Slavic root /STL/, "covering"). Together, these produce the word's "content." Potebnya saw an analogous tripartite structure in poetry, with the image functioning as the equivalent of the inner form of the word. It is on the basis of this set of relationships that he defines poetry as "thinking in images." By restoring the original unity of signifier and signified, poetry restores the immediacy and freshness of perception; this, in turn, eases cognition.

This last point is the aspect of Potebnya's theory to which Shklovsky objected most vociferously; on the contrary, he contends, "the language of poetry is difficult, laborious language, which puts the brakes on perception."[14] Part of what Shklovsky takes issue with here is Potebnya's terminology and his loaded distinction between poetic language, which is imagistic and "living," and prosaic language, defined by the absence of images and as "the oblivion of inner form."[15] The Formalists objected to these labels on the grounds that they were conceptually confusing. Prose, too, could "have an independent poetic purpose," as Brik put it.[16] The relevant distinction, they argue, is not between poetry and prose but between the differing functions of poetic and practical language: while prosaic language ("the language of thought") exists primarily as a means of communication, poetic language does not.[17] Images can be found in both poetic and practical language, Shklovsky contends; it is their role in each that differs. Whereas the purpose of images in practical language is indeed to ease cognition, their function in poetry is quite different. Poetic images disrupt the established relationship between word and referent, signifier and signified, and thereby contribute to the larger goal of art, which is to make unrecognizable and *strange*.

Shklovsky and the Formalists were in fact responding to a much-filtered version of Potebnya's theory, which, in the decades leading up to and after his death, took on multiple lives of its own—both in the work of Potebnya's avowed followers, the motley crew of "Potebnyaist" critics grouped around the journal *Questions of Theory and the Psychology of Creativity* (*Voprosy teorii i psikhologii tvorchestva*), and in that of Russian Symbolists. While the ideas promoted by these figures were not without basis in Potebnya's work, they tended to exaggerate its central claims. The idea that the poetic image "economized" effort by making content more immediately available to consciousness is a case in point. This idea had in fact been put forward by Boris A. Lezin, the editor of *Voprosy*, and distorts Potebnya's original argument significantly.[18] Such distortions were generally the result of the co-optation of his ideas about language for some other goal.

Potebnya himself was building on the work of the German philosopher and linguist Wilhelm von Humboldt (1767–1835), for whom "inner form" denotes that which guarantees the vital energy of language and its generative force; it is what protects language from becoming *ergon*, a dead and finished thing, and sustains it as *energeia*, the ceaseless activity through which "humans form concepts and express them to each other."[19] In his influential 1862 monograph *Thought and Language* (*Mysl' i iazyk*), Potebnya sought to make these claims more precise by identifying the empirical basis of inner form; doing so, he believed, would clarify the relation between thought and language. Potebnya found one concrete foundation for the vague notion of "inner form" in linguistics. The equation of inner form with the word's etymon rendered it newly quantifiable since, according to Potebnya, these etymons are always ethnic (*narodnye*) and hence have measurable limits. Potebnya also identified a psychological dimension to inner form, which he aligned with the "presentation" or "impression," the trace left by sense perception on the mind. Inner form—and, in poetry, the image—acts as something like a pair of brackets, Potebnya argued, demarcating a certain set of this preexisting mental data, in relation to which it positions the new impression; the constellation that results is what we apprehend as the "content" of the word.[20]

According to Potebnya's psycholinguistic theory of poetic imagery, then, the image eases the initial moment of perception. In this sense, Potebnya does claim that the image facilitates at least the first stage of cognition; this is the idea that Shklovsky disputes. However, Shklovsky fails to recognize the creative effort that Potebnya regards as a necessary feature of the subsequent stage of cognition, the discovery of the image's content. The image in Potebnya's conception is inherently polysemous; its meaning exceeds its own narrow bounds, and its value lies in the active process of cognition that it sets in motion. This is what differentiates poetic reference from mythic reference, on the one hand, where the image is identical with meaning, and from scientific reference, on the other, where the image falls away entirely.[21] Holding signifier and signified in dynamic relation, the image and the creative effort it necessitates are what define the work of art as *energeia*, activity—and hence, what sustain the vitality of the connection between thought, language, and the world.

Shklovsky and Potebnya thus in fact share an interest in the restorative potential contained in art and the creative effort demanded by its central device—whether we call this, alongside Potebnya, "image" or, echoing Shklovsky, *ostranenie*. Nonetheless, it would be quite wrong to conclude, as some have, that the only significant difference between them therefore lies in Shklovsky's preference for what Potebnya calls "outer form," the sound of the word. Such a formulation renders trivial the fundamental reorientation to which Shklovsky's interest in the word's sensory qualities alerts us. Shklovsky is interested not in refreshed perception itself so much as *how* art refreshes perception; when he turns his attention to the "outer form" of the word, he looks to the processes of mediation in which the word as a physical object participates. This is where the real difference between Shklovsky and Potebnya lies.

In the context of the passage of "Art as Device" quoted above, the strangest thing about the stone is that it appears to be such a bad example. There are few things, if any, for which "the making" is more hidden than for stone, which forms without human intervention over a period longer than most human lives. It is an excellent example, however, if we understand Shklovsky's central point to be that art should help us to perceive language and things for what they are, rather than for what they used to be in some mythic time past: a stone, after all, is a stone; it did not exist before it became petrified. More than this, the stone stands in the passage for the essential change of emphasis that Shklovsky is proposing. The stoniness of stone is primarily a tactile discovery, a "sensation" (*oshchushchenie*) that would not be possible without the active participation of the stone itself as an "external material [factor]."[22] As such, it points to Shklovsky's turn away from a subject-oriented, psychologizing theory such as that proposed by Potebnya and toward a more radical definition of poetic transformation based upon the specific materiality of poetic language.

ON POETRY AND TRANS-SENSE LANGUAGE: TRANSFORMING THE POETIC MEDIUM

Before expanding on this point, let us look more closely at how Shklovsky defines the physical, sensuous side of poetry, its materiality. The first issue of the Formalist collective volume *Poetics* (*Poetika: Sborniki po teorii poeticheskogo iazyka*)—devoted to the OPOIAZ rebuttal of Potebnya—is concerned almost exclusively with sound, which is the basis of the new definition of poetic language that the Formalists were proposing. In poetic language, sound "acquires an independent value," as Lev Jakubinsky writes.[23] It is largely on this basis that scholars have highlighted the links between Formalism's redefinition of poetic language and Russian Futurism. As I have already begun to suggest, the ostensible phonocentrism of this movement has sometimes distracted scholars from more careful consideration of how they and Shklovsky conceived of poetic materiality.

It will help here to consider in more detail Shklovsky's essay "On Poetry and Trans-Sense Language" ("O poezii i zaumnom iazyke," 1916), which also appears in this first issue of *Poetika*. This essay, concerned with the foundational role of "trans-sense" language in poetry, appears to be as phonocentric as the Futurist texts that inspired it: as its opening lines state clearly, "words in a poem are not chosen for their meaning nor for their rhythm, but for their sound."[24] A recurrent theme in the essay, moreover, is that of "sound images" (*zvukoobrazy*), a direct translation of the German term "Lautbilder," an idea enthusiastically promoted by Wundt, the associationist psychologist encountered briefly in chapter 2. It is precisely Shklovsky's engagement with this concept, however, that reveals the subtler understanding of the poetic materiality he is proposing.

In Wundt's definition, "Lautbilder" are a kind of punning, onomatopoeic-but-not phenomenon whereby words "express not an acoustic but rather an optical or other idea, but in such a way that a certain correspondence is felt between this idea and the choice of sounds in this sound image type of word."[25] Taking issue with this notion of imitation, Shklovsky turns his attention instead to "words without image or content." These words, as Ana Hedberg Olenina summarizes, "cannot be said to exhibit any imitative articulation, for there is nothing to imitate." Instead, they point to "a connection between sound-movement, empathetically reproduced as some mute spasms by the listener's organs of speech, and emotion."[26] The example that Shklovsky provides is *tilisnut'*, a nonexistent verb found in Dostoevsky's *Notes from the House of the Dead*. "Is there a similarity between the articulatory movement of the word *tilisnut'* and the movement of a knife sliding over and cutting into the human body?" Shklovsky asks. "No, but this articulatory motion describes as well as possible every instinctive state of the facial muscles during the specific feeling of pain in the nerves experienced by us when we imagine a knife sliding along the skin (but not stuck into the body)."[27]

Emphasizing the role of emotion in his discussion, Olenina argues that Shklovsky regards "the choice of phonemes in a poetic text as motivated by the workings of the poet's psychology."[28] As she concludes, Shklovsky's essay replaces Wundt's notion of iconic mimesis with mimesis taken quite literally: mime. Rather than some concrete meaning contained within the image itself, what is most important here is the meaning generated through the physical act of poetic utterance, which, according to ideas then gaining ground in psychology, gives rise to a specific emotional response.[29] As Shklovsky states directly later in the same article, "when we hear, we reproduce the mimicry of the speaker and therefore we experience his emotions."[30]

Leaving aside for now the disputed issue of whether and in what ways Formalist theory drew on contemporary psychology, it is important to note that the central position in all of this is occupied not by emotions but by the body, which repeatedly serves as the intermediary between the poem and its emotional effects. It might be objected that this is just the point: psychology was at that time interested precisely in the role of the body in producing certain emotions. Nonetheless, a psychologizing approach neglects the prominence given in Shklovsky's essay to the physicality of this intervening process. The focus here is not so much on emotional effects as it is on the bodily processes that precede and produce these emotions. The emphasis falls upon the process of mediation, rather than its end result—upon the *making* of the thing (or emotion), rather than what has been or will be made.

Shklovsky's argument is not with Wundt, or Potebnya, or any of the other figures he singles out so much as with the dominant "imagistic" view of artistic thought and the intellectual paradigm whence it emerged.[31] This helps to explain the muddled sense in which he uses the term "image": rather than referencing a specific literary device, the term becomes shorthand for the whole notion that there is some necessary connection between language and the world beyond it. In essays such as this one, the early Shklovsky pushes against the subject/object binary at the heart of this view of language, and seeks instead to introduce a new paradigm centered on the work of the medium itself.

This is the work with which "On Poetry and Trans-Sense Language" is concerned, and which its discussion of sound seeks to locate more precisely. This is less straightforward than at first appears, as the essay's opening series of statements suggests: the "sound" of poetry is not the same as the sound of music, Shklovsky writes, but neither is it synonymous with that of words or language—although they are *speech* sounds. As he writes toward the end of the article: "it already seems clear that we can't call poetry a phenomenon of language, nor language a phenomenon of poetry."[32] Not only is the language of poetry something distinct from language in its ordinary usage, it is actually a separate médium, with its own material qualities.[33] These qualities are defined quite specifically, despite the vague, even contradictory terms in which they appear to be described.

For all his preoccupation with poetic sound, Shklovsky does not ground his distinction between practical and poetic language in terms of the division between printed text, on the one hand, and sounding text, on the other. This lack of differentiation recalls Kruchenykh's careful emphasis on both the written and sonic element in *zaum'*, as illustrated by the introductory note printed alongside "Dyr bul shchyl" when it first appeared ("written in my own language"). Likewise, Shklovsky seems to find it quite unproblematic that poetry as "wordless sound language" might be written down. It might be objected that this is simply a concession to the necessity of communicating via the still-dominant medium of written language. In the context of the article as a whole, however, it serves as evidence of what I propose we term Shklovsky's "transmedial" understanding of poetic materiality.

Modernist poets understood the specific materiality of language in the intermedial terms of their age. This is demonstrated by the three devices that organize this book (rhythm, image, and voice), all of which were hotly contested during this period as poets and theorists sought to describe poetry via its overlap with music, visual art, and speech. When experiments in sound or concrete poetry or in *zaum'* texts exaggerated or omitted one or other of these qualities, this was also a means of drawing attention to the other potential material realizations of the text. The intermedial quality of the poetic medium is particularly evident when we compare poetry with painting: whereas abstract painters can spurn figurative representation entirely and instead explore the flat surface of the canvas and the texture of paint or its pigment, even the most "transrational" of poets must grapple with the verbal element inherent to language. To borrow a coinage from James Joyce (later adopted by McLuhan), language is always "*verbi*vocovisual" (my emphasis): it signifies by definition, and while each of these three elements may be more or less prominent in any given utterance or text (assuming a literate rather than an oral culture), they are all always nonetheless co-present.[34]

A central claim in Shklovsky's article, if not one made wholly consciously, is that poetic language is not only inherently intermedial but in some sense is always already "transmediated"—that is, "mediated for a second (or third, or fourth) time by another technical medium."[35] Elleström regards transmediation as a discrete process that necessarily comes after an initial process of mediation. When we read a poem on the page, however, we are arguably simultaneously aware of (and perhaps—silently or aloud—even realizing) its potential for transmediation by the voice because of the way the poem is arranged on the page. This is the case even in extreme examples: at least part of the interest of concrete poetry stems from imagining the vocal acrobatics that would be required to read it aloud. The same holds true in reverse. Some portion of the graphic scaffolding of a poem—line breaks, stanzas, and so on—is audible when the poem is read aloud, such that a poem that is performed always draws our attention to its potential transmediation by the page. All of these effects were exaggerated during the modernist period, when challenges to graphic convention made this aspect of the poetic medium particularly salient and a whole range of experimental poetry explored the *transfer* of media characteristics that poetic language sets in motion.[36]

The numerous examples of trans-sense language provided in Shklovsky's article seem designed to foreground this quality of poetic language, particularly in light of its extensive discussion of articulation: these snippets of text repeatedly tempt us to read the printed page aloud. Some portion of the article's original readers had no doubt heard examples of similar texts at the poetry evenings that were then ubiquitous, further amplifying this effect.

This transmedial view of poetic materiality comes into clearer view if we compare it with Osip Mandel'shtam's "Word and Culture" ("Slovo i kul'tura," 1921), an essay that engages with Potebnya and the phenomenon that Shklovsky here refers to as "inner sound-language."[37] As Mandel'shtam, whose poem "Silentium" (1910) Shklovsky cites as one of his examples, writes:

> The poem is alive through its inner image—that sounding mold of the form [*zvuchashchim slepkom formy*] which prefigures the written poem. There is not a single word yet, but the poem is sounding already. This is the sounding of the inner image, palpated by the poet's hearing.[38]

Like Shklovsky, Mandelshtam is trying to describe the element in poetry that is "[wordless] but in sounds . . . not in the sounds of music . . . but in the sounds of speech"—that which distinguishes poetic language from both practical language and music.[39] This part of poetic language is somehow both substantial (the poet's hearing *palpates* the "inner image," in Mandel'stam's formulation, which has a kind of physical shape) and insubstantial, prior to and distinct from the written or sounding poem.

Although there appears to be considerable overlap between the two theorists, what Shklovsky is proposing here is something quite distinct from Potebnya's tripartite model of the word, where the unity of "outer form" and "inner form" produces "content." The sound of the word ("outer form") is integral to Potebnya's model, but is in an important sense also secondary to it: what Potebnya is most interested in are the mental processes that outer form sets in motion, and in which inner form plays the decisive role. Shklovsky, by contrast, as though collapsing Potebnya's terms, defines the "inner image" first and foremost through its physical presence. The physicality of his model of the word is emphasized further through the distinction he draws at various points throughout the essay between the word's "image element" and its "sound element." Again, the similarities with Potebnya are only superficial. These separate parts of the word are just that: separate parts, physical pieces rather than abstract constructs. Instead of the unity of signifier and signified, what moves to the fore is the manner in which these distinct pieces fit together and interact—the *making* of the word, to paraphrase Shklovsky's own formulation once again.[40]

As others have noted, there is an intriguing parallel to be drawn here with McLuhan's definition of media as "extensions of man." This is a definition that Shklovsky himself approaches in *Zoo, or Letters Not About Love* (*Zoo, ili Pis'ma ne o liubvi*, 1923) when he writes: "The tool not only extends man's arm but is itself extended in him" (*Orudie ne tol'ko prodolzhaet ruku cheloveka, no i samo prodolzhaetsia v nem*).[41] When McLuhan states that "the medium is the message," he means that the invention of a new medium fundamentally reorganizes the way we perceive and interact with the world and the things around us. As Lvoff points out, Shklovsky's view of the artwork is similar. Art is not a "tool separated from the individual" but "a certain *system* of the individual's perceptual activity, which dynamically sustains the connection between the individual and the world."[42]

This is not the only place where touch appears in Shklovsky's early writings. The stoniness of the stone is primarily a tactile discovery, when soft flesh (or shoe, or wife) comes into contact with cold, hard surface. This moment of contact is also one of transfer or translation—that "felt hesitation" between different material strata which I am suggesting was for Russian modernists the basic definition of poetic materiality, and which Shklovsky seems to be trying to articulate in the passage just cited. "Our very word 'grasp' or 'apprehension' points," as McLuhan writes, "to the process of getting at one thing through another, of handling and sensing many facets at a time through more than one sense at a time . . . 'touch' is not skin but the interplay of the senses."[43] Touch is a fitting figure for the material specificity of poetic language because it implies continuous movement between one kind of sensory experience and another. It is, as Michael Serres writes, "at the origin, the medium."[44]

When Shklovsky defines the device as that which "transforms extra-aesthetic material into the work of art by providing it with form," therefore, he resolves the problem of what might be said to constitute the material medium of poetry by circumventing it: poetic language is defined by its work of transformation; it is language that continuously generates its own materiality.[45] In this sense, his theory offers a corrective to the notion, common since Lessing and reinforced by Potebnya's emphasis on thought, that poetic language is immaterial and that images are the domain of the imagination. The process that Shklovsky describes is physical, rather than an abstract or cognitive one. Its effect is to make its own invisible transactions, the work of mediation, perceptible. It is this sensation (*oshchushchenie*) to which art draws our attention: not its psychological effect, but the moment of contact between two unlike things that produces this effect.

We should therefore take quite seriously the moment toward the end of "On Poetry and Trans-Sense Language" when Shklovsky posits that this wordless sound language may one day become its own medium: having shed the burden of mimesis, poetry will instead be concerned only with its own materiality. Again, it is not so much our sensory experience of the poem that is at stake here as the work of the medium itself, work that Shklovsky's essay locates, to borrow a phrase from McLuhan, in poetry's continual "translat[ion of] one kind of experience of one sense into all the senses."[46] The "message" of the poetic medium is not the emotional response that it produces in the reader, but the processes of translation and transformation that precede and determine this response.

What Shklovsky shares with (borrows, steals from) Potebnya, then, is not a vague notion that the image or poetic language in general can revive perception of the word and the world, but rather the desire to pinpoint and describe the moment of transformation or transfer that the poetic image, as device, entails. Potebnya attempts to explain this via the mediating work of inner form, which acts as a kind of prism, drawing together new perceptions and the existing data of consciousness and refracting them to produce new understanding. (As he writes, "to name with a word is to create a new thought in the sense of a transformation, in the sense of a regrouping of the former store of thoughts under the pressure of a new impression.")[47] Shklovsky instead remains focused on the process and conditions of refraction. "The goal of all imagery," as he writes toward the end of "Art as Device," is "the *transference* [*perenesenie*] of an object from its usual sphere of experience to a new one" (my emphasis).[48] The content of the image has been put to the side; its formal function is what remains.

Neither statue nor urn, the stone appears to be a stowaway in this article about art, its resolute refusal to signify only highlighted further by its potential to do so. The stone is stony, an adjective that is simultaneously inadequate as a description (what are the qualities of this stoniness?) and the most adequate description that language has available (any other description would, after all, need to be extended: the stone is grey, *and* cold, *and* hard, *and* so on). Even more than the other "things" in Shklovsky's work, the stone and the (in)adequacy of its epithet highlight "the process of dissimilation [*raspodoblenie*] to which the material world was subject in the process of its textual representation, in the course of the translation [*perevod*] of the world of objects into the language of literature."[49]

In this sense, it is perhaps the very randomness of the stone that is most important here. For Potebnya, we recall, the image represents a shield against arbitrariness—the hidden logic that governs the names that we give objects and hence our knowledge of them. For Shklovsky, by contrast, the work of art guarantees arbitrariness: this is what *ostranenie* restores. Randomness is also the inevitable consequence of Shklovsky's emphasis on the moment of encounter, which holds art open to "the kind of violation that cannot be anticipated."[50] Art is teleological in the sense that it is created intentionally, with a goal in mind, yet that goal is necessarily obscure; indeed, the whole purpose of art is to restore the element of surprise. This is the mode of the riddle, a genre with which Shklovsky explicitly compares the image in a late text, *Bowstring: On the Dissimilarity of the Similar* (*Tetiva: O neskhodstve skhodnogo*, 1970). The riddle, Shklovsky writes, is a form in which the answer always sends us back to the question, in delight and surprise—a temporal structure much like that of *ostranenie*, where, as Tihanov notes, "the new is hailed as the savior of the old or ever extant."[51] In both cases, this back-and-forth motion becomes art's defining characteristic—the "felt hesitation" which ensures that art is never fully "inside" the system that, though it can never escape it fully, art works continuously to reveal.

This is not to say that Shklovsky conceives of the poetic medium as working along a linear trajectory between A (perceiving subject) and B (perceived object). Rather, the back-and-forth motion reveals the work of the medium as the infrastructure that enables "things and humans" to come together in "heterogeneous assemblages," to adapt Oushakine's apt formulation.[52] McLuhan also saw media as, first and foremost, infrastructures—the systems and processes, both large and small, which organize human society, from heavy and fixed infrastructures such as railways, roads, and cities to portable systems such as the written word, games, and law. What these diverse examples have in common is their mundanity; as another media scholar points out, "they *are* infrastructures only to the degree that they are normalized as taken-for-granteds."[53] It was against this general "somnambulism" that McLuhan directed his energies.[54] For Shklovsky, too, infrastructural awareness is an ethical imperative. *Ostranenie* and the theoretical approach for which it has become shorthand were never "just" about the surface of the text, the look or feel of stone, the sound of the poem. Rather, Formalism was a movement alive to the work of *mediation* at the center of all art—the invisible infrastructure that is the ground for our experience of this surface. The next chapter considers Boris Pasternak's fascination with this same issue.

Chapter Five

Boris Pasternak's Poetic Configurations

TRANSFER FEATURES prominently in discussions of Boris Pasternak's imagery. In "Marginal Notes on the Prose of the Poet Pasternak" ("Randbemerkungen zur Prosa des Dichters Pasternak," 1935), to take one influential example, Roman Jakobson identifies metonymy as Pasternak's most characteristic device, a figure that involves the transference of qualities between contiguous objects.[1] Jakobson's comments reflect the frequency with which the personified features of Pasternak's poetic landscape take on each other's qualities, whether of their own volition or when brought into contact by the profusion of storms, rain showers, or gusts of wind—themselves the meteorological embodiment of the emotional exuberance that is perhaps this poetry's defining characteristic.

Pasternak spoke frequently of realism, which, like reality itself, he defined as fundamentally dynamic and subjective. As he writes in *Safe Conduct* (*Okhrannaia gramota*, 1931), "art is realistic . . . in that it did not itself invent metaphor but found it in nature and faithfully reproduced it . . . There is nothing except the mobile language of images."[2] Pasternak's exuberant depiction of nature and human emotions has often led readers to focus on the first part of this statement, seeing Pasternak's "precision of detail" as testament to his desire to faithfully reproduce certain scenes and experiences.[3] As Yury Lotman argues, for instance, Pasternak disregards the convention that attaches specific words to particular things; instead of "the world of words and phrases," he strives simply to describe as precisely as possible what is "seen and felt."[4] Others draw analogies with photography. Attempting to "capture and immortalize" phenomenological experience without "wrench[ing]" that experience "from the flow of time," these readers argue, Pasternak's poetry resembles nothing so much as a snapshot of reality caught in motion.[5]

While such accounts are careful to emphasize the dynamism of these poem-photographs, they remain based upon a linear conception of the relationship between the poem and the experience (now past) that it records or reproduces. This neglects the second part of Pasternak's statement: "there is nothing but the mobile language of images." Art is realistic "as activity," he writes (*PSS* 3:187)—that is, not because it reproduces specific images from nature, but because it operates according to the metaphorical logic it finds there.[6] Art does not capture reality but engages in an ongoing dialogue with it; and this exchange is conducted in the transformative language of the image-as-activity.

Like much of Pasternak's theoretical writing, the passage in which these reflections appear is dense and allusive. What is clear, however, is his interest in something like what I am suggesting we call the "infrastructural" work of the image: its significance as the invisible ground that sustains both reality and art. My aim in this chapter is to explain more fully what this means. As I hope to show, the most important quality of Pasternak's images is not what they depict but what they do—not the precision with which they capture reality but, rather, the new "perspective for understanding" that they make available.[7]

Comparisons between Pasternak's poetry and visual art or photography acknowledge this fact when they note the perceptibility of medium in his work. This acknowledgment may be tacit, as when Marina Tsvetaeva speaks of Pasternak's "light writing" (*svetopis'*), as she terms it in the essay "A Downpour of Light" ("Svetovoi liven'," 1922); or it may be more explicit.[8] As Lotman describes, for example, Pasternak animates his landscapes via "a deliberate shift from a predictable set of referents to another, unexpected one and a parallel substitution of linguistic functions. Thus, instead of 'the candle gutters,' we find 'the print gutters,' 'the word gutters,' or a 'guttering book.'"[9] Whereas Lotman and others seek to reconstruct the visual scene that such linguistic fragmentation conceals, I think here instead about what Pasternak's images tell us about how he conceived of the work of poetry as medium. As I will argue in the first part of this chapter, the apparent immediacy of Pasternak's poetry belies its interest in the interface between the material medium of poetry and the reality it depicts. In the second part of the chapter, I reflect at more length on how poetic materiality is conceived in Pasternak's early, "painterly" poetry and how, consequently, we should understand its often obscure meaning. Turning at the end of the chapter to consider one of Pasternak's most famous poems from this period, "Marburg" (1916), I argue that Pasternak shares with Shklovsky not only the intermedial conception of poetic language common to his generation, but also an infrastructural interest in the image as the interface between poetry and the world.

A MOBILE LANGUAGE OF IMAGES: POETRY AND/AS REALITY

The early poem "February . . ." ("Fevral' . . . ," 1912) has become shorthand for Pasternak's "ecstatic" poetics, the exuberant forays into the landscape for which his poetry is known. As such, it provides a useful vantage point from which to survey the terrain. Where and how do this poem and reality meet?

Февраль. Достать чернил и плакать!
Писать о феврале навзрыд,
Пока грохочущая слякоть
Весною черною горит.

Достать пролетку. За шесть гривен
Чрез благовест, чрез клик колес
Перенестись туда, где ливень
Еще шумней чернил и слез.

Где, как обугленные груши,
С деревьев тысячи грачей
Сорвутся в лужи и обрушат
Сухую грусть на дно очей.

Под ней проталины чернеют,
И ветер криками изрыт,
И чем случайней, тем вернее
Слагаются стихи навзрыд.[10]

February. To get ink and weep!
To write about February, sobbing
While the rumbling snow melts
And burns with black spring.

To get a cab. For a coin
Through church bells, the chirp of tires
To be transported to a place where the downpour
Is louder still than ink or tears.

Where, like charred pears
From trees a thousand rooks
Fall into puddles and cast
Dry sorrow to depths of eyes.

Beneath it black patches of thaw,
And the wind is rent by cawing,
And the more randomly, the surer
Poems are sobbingly composed.

Working backwards from the poem's striking final assertion, many readers have regarded the poem as a metapoetic commentary on the origins and nature of poetry. "Verse comes about spontaneously, unplanned and unpremeditated," as Olga Hughes glosses the poem, "under the influence of direct, immediate emotion."[11] Spontaneity certainly appears to be the poem's governing mood: February has arrived, and with it an uncontrollable torrent of emotion that the speaker, his tears mingling with his ink, rushes to put into words. So intense are these feelings that he races out into and through the spring landscape for a direct encounter with nature that only redoubles his emotions and the "sobbing" flow of poetry in turn. The poem rushes to completion as though compelled, drawn as inevitably as pears from a tree.

This sense of the poem's spontaneity appears to be confirmed by the story of its origins. Pasternak, we are told, composed this poem on the fly—*eksprompt*, as Russian has it, while sitting in Moscow's bohemian Café Grecque with Konstantin Loks, the friend to whom the poem was dedicated when it was first published in the almanac *Lirika* in 1913.[12] Like many poems in Pasternak's oeuvre, however, "February . . ." was revised repeatedly over the course of his lifetime. As Lazar Fleishman has shown, such revisions often served only to make Pasternak's poetry more complex.[13]

And indeed, there is plenty in "February . . ." that is puzzling, not least the source of the compulsion by which it is propelled. Likewise, despite the apparent specificity of the poem's first word, its temporal backdrop is hard to make out: the first thaws of spring are typically still some months away in February. So, too, the precise direction of the speaker's movement "to a place" (*tuda*, lit. "thither") remains vague, a feeling that is only exacerbated by the emphatic precision of the twice-repeated "where" (*gde*) that follows. This spatial ambiguity is compounded by the confusing vectors of the third stanza, thrown into retrospective relief by the opening words of the fourth: beneath what, exactly?

The poem's ambiguous spatial and temporal axes frame what emerges as its central theme, that of the relationship between representation and reality. The various black features of the physical landscape seem to flow from the poem's own material components, the ink in which it is composed. Lending physical contours to the landscape that the poem's words describe, this black substance activates the second meaning of the Russian verb *pisat'*, a verb that means both "to write" and "to draw." This blurring of verbal and visual depiction reaches a peak in the third stanza, where ink becomes charcoal (*ugol'*, contained in the "charred pears" [*ob*ugl*ennye grushi*]). This is also the first stanza in which no reference is made to sound, and where eyes appear for the first and only time. It is this stanza in particular that has prompted some readers to compare the poem with Alexei Savrasov's painting "The Rooks Have Returned" ("Grachi prileteli,"1871).

Whatever the thematic similarities between Pasternak's poem and Savrasov's painting, however, "February . . ." is clearly not an ekphrastic poem. The opaque reference to spatial position with which the final stanza begins ("beneath it") serves as a reminder that, as visually striking as its description may be, the poem is written in language; this verbal dimension cannot be ignored.

In this regard, these two short words, "beneath it" (*pod nei*), are a crucial moment in the development of the poem's larger theme, a semantic stumbling block that turns attention to the work of the image and its interaction with the material of the poem and the world. The virtual space depicted *in* the poem collides against the space *of* the poem as our eyes travel upwards in search of the pronoun's referent. This appears to be "sadness" (*grust'*), the nearest feminine noun. Transformed by its collision with the spatial preposition "beneath" (*pod*), this abstract emotion becomes concrete, something that takes up space in the poem's virtual landscape. This effect is further amplified by the echo in *grust'* of the falling pears at the beginning of the stanza (*grusha*), an effect that draws our attention again to the spatial arrangement of the poem on the page.

Indeed, as this inevitably rather lumbering description of the poem is intended to show, one way to read this text is as a dramatization of the work of poetic figuration. As in many of Pasternak's poems, this is signaled by the scene of literal transport at its center. Physical movement through the landscape (*perenestis' tuda, gde . . .*) enacts the figurative motion of metaphor, a term that comes from the Greek word meaning "transfer" (in Russian, *perenos*). Alexander Zholkovsky identifies this as a common theme in what he terms "infinitive writing," a small but substantial corpus of Russian poetry united not only by the use of infinitive verbs, but also by their meditative mode and the moment of transition or transformation—between life and death, imagination and reality, this world and the other—toward which this contemplation is oriented.[14]

Although Zholkovsky includes "February . . ." in this tradition, the dynamic he describes is complicated in this poem by the ambiguity of the movement in question. This applies not only to the direction in which the cab itself travels, indicated only by the deictic "thither" (*tuda*, rendered "to a place" in the above translation), but also to that of the many other transformations that run through the poem. Although clear parallels are drawn between the ink, tears, rain, and thawing snow, the precise direction of these comparisons is never quite established: is the ink like the black earth that shows through the melting snow? Or is this earth itself like a line of poetry, written upon the landscape? Does the ink flow like the speaker's tears or like the rain? Or do the rain or the tears themselves flow like ink? In other words, is poetry like spring, or spring like poetry?[15] The appearance of an actual vehicle amplifies this restless motion, each element shifting in and out of focus, now literally itself, now figuratively standing for something else, now—seemingly literally—transformed into that other. This ambiguity is intensified further by the poem's return, in the final stanza, to the scene of writing with which it begins, as well as the involvement of the poem's own material (its echoing sounds and shape on the page) in the creation of this shifting scene.

The idea that "certain names belong properly to certain things" underpins one long-standing conception of figurative language, according to which "figurative words are substituted for proper words or to fill a lexical gap." Consequently, "to explain a trope is to find the absent proper word."[16] In this definition, the "proper" word is implicitly that which has the most direct connection to its referent. Yet the existence of this word is at the same time called into question by the moment of invention implied by the "lexical gap": whether used literally or figuratively, the connection between "names" and "things" is only ever a matter of convention.

This tension is brought to the surface in "February . . . ," where ink and rain mingle and merge: the "proper" word cannot be found. Holding tenor and vehicle in a state of emphatic flux, the poem challenges the basic premise that words refer *back* to reality conceived as something stable and fixed in relation to linguistic convention. Rather, the poem and reality exist as equal partners in an ongoing and transformative exchange. It is not linear transition but this back-and-forth motion and the infrastructure it makes visible with which this infinitive poem is concerned.

If Pasternak's poetry concerns itself with "the close-at-hand and the concrete," as Andrei Sinyavsky so aptly asserts, among the objects it calls the reader to examine is the poem itself.[17] As Pasternak writes in "Black Goblet," an essay published in 1916 but begun in 1913, the same year that "February . . ." was first composed, the essential question for poets is

> how life should be folded up [*kak dolzhna slozhit'sia zhizn'*] so that it can be transported by the heart of the lyric poet, that repository of transferred meaning with its sign of the black goblet and the inscription: "Fragile. This side up." (*PSS* 5:16)[18]

When critics of his earliest work complained of it being "overcomplicated, too "overloaded" (*peregruzhennyi*) with images to be comprehensible, this misses the point.[19] The "complexity" (*slozhnost'*) of Pasternak's earliest poetry stems in part from its interest in the physical dimensions of the poetic medium and the manner in which—the more randomly, the surer—the material of this medium folds together with the material of the world.[20] It is to more detailed consideration of these operations that I now turn.

OVER THE BARRIERS: INTERMEDIALITY AND THE IMAGE

So far, I have avoided talking at length about Pasternak's images in visual terms and have instead focused on what I am calling their infrastructural quality. In particular, I have tried to argue that we should think of Pasternak's images not as precise representations but as a continuous action or process. In this section, I look more closely at the connections between Pasternak's early poetry and the artistic milieu in which it was composed in an attempt to describe in more detail how he conceived of the material qualities of poetry as medium.

As the son of the visual artist Leonid Pasternak and with formal training in music composition, Pasternak was profoundly aware of the demands and possibilities of different artistic media.[21] In the early 1910s, he participated in seminars at the Symbolist Musaget publishing house, a center of modernist debate about artistic form. He was, moreover, closely acquainted with many of those avant-garde poets and artists who were experimenting most radically with the limits of visual representation and poetic speech. He was a founding member of the literary group Lirika, which became the Futurist group Tsentrifuga, and a good friend of figures such as Sergei Bobrov, the de facto leader of these groups and a visual artist by training; and Nikolai Aseev, who was later involved in the avant-garde "Left Front of the Arts" (LEF) alongside Vladimir Mayakovsky, whose "Cubo-Futurist" verse Pasternak greatly admired.

This kind of inter-artistic dialogue and exchange would appear to run counter to the notion of medium specificity. Pasternak himself later emphasized the influence of visual art on his poetry of the period 1914–16, identifying this as the peak of his interest in Cubism; during these years, as he describes it, his poetry was characterized above all by its "painterliness" (*zhivopisnost'*).[22] John E. Malmstad argues convincingly that some of Pasternak's early poems were directly inspired by particular avant-garde paintings, highlighting in particular the time Pasternak spent at the apartment-studio of Aristarkh Lentulov, a meeting place for a wide variety of avant-garde and establishment figures during these years.[23] In general, it is the strikingly visual quality of his poetry that has tended to mark it out; "Pasternak *sees* in verse, whereas I *hear*," as Tsvetaeva would observe.[24]

Nonetheless, Pasternak composed poetry during these years, not paintings. The presence of painterly techniques and visual motifs in his work tells us at least as much about how he conceived of the specificity of poetry as a medium as it does about his interest in visual art. As Rajewsky reminds us, inter-artistic experimentation blurs the boundaries between different media but, in so doing, it also calls attention to these borders and to the particular qualities of the media they separate; "it is only due to our constructing borders in the first place that we are able to . . . transcen[d] or subver[t] those very boundaries."[25] Refracting poetry and the poetic image through the intermedial lens of its time, Pasternak asks what it means to see *in verse.* Just as Cubist painters attached scraps of newspaper and other realia to the canvas to make their paintings visible as objects in the world as well as representations of that world, so Pasternak's "precision of detail" draws our attention to the poem's own substance.[26]

The poem I want to consider in this connection is "Dedication" ("Posviashchenie"), the first poem in the 1916 collection *Over the Barriers* (*Poverkh bar'erov*). This may seem an unlikely candidate: while the poem begins with a description of an urban courtyard, as a whole the poem can hardly be called visual or painterly. The landscape it depicts is often rather difficult to discern, as the poem moves precipitously through a series of only loosely connected, sometimes rather puzzling images. Precisely for this reason, however, the poem is a useful one for describing in more detail some of the ways that intermediality shaped modernist conceptions of poetic materiality beyond instances of explicit ekphrasis or graphic experimentation, and for beginning to think about the connection between the "painterliness" of Pasternak's poetry of these years and what has been identified as its often obscure meaning.

Посвященье

Мелко исписанный снежной крупой,
Двор—ты как приговор к ссылке,
На недоед, недосып, недопой,
На боль с барабанным боем в затылке!

Двор! Ты, покрытый усышкой листвы,
С солью из низко нависших градирен;
Шин и полозьев чернеются швы,
Мёрзлый нарыв октября расковырян

Старческим ногтем небес, октября
Старческим ногтем и старческим ногтем
Той, что, с утра подступив к фонарям,
Кашляет в шали и варит декокт им.

Двор, этот вихрь, что, как кучер в мороз,
Снегом порос и по брови нафабрен
Снегом закушенным—он перерос
Черные годы окраин и фабрик.

Вихрь, что, как кучер, облеплен; как он,
Снегом по горло набит и, как кучер,
Взят, перевязан, спален, ослеплён,
Задран и к тучам, как кучер, прикручен.

Двор, этот ветер тем родственен мне,
Что со всего околотка, с налёту,
Он объявленьем налипнет к стене:
Люди, там любят и ищут работы!

Люди! Там ярость сановней моей.
Люди! Там я преклоняю колени.
Люди, там, словно с полярных морей,
Дует всю ночь напролёт с Откровенья.

Крепкие тьме—полыханьем огней,
Крепкие стуже—стрельбою поленьев!
Стужа в их песнях студеней моей,
Их откровений темнее затменье!

С улиц взимает зима, как баскак,
Шубы и печи и комнат убранство,
Знайте же—зимнего ига очаг
Там, у поэтов, в их нищенском ханстве.

Огородитесь от вьюги в стихах
Шубой; от ночи в поэме—свечою.
Полным фужером—когда впопыхах
Опохмеляется дух с перепою.

И без задержек, и без полуслов,
Но от души заказной бандеролью
Вина, меха, освещенье и кров
Шлите туда, в департаменты голи.[27]

Dedication

Written all over with fine-grained snow,
Yard—you're like a sentence to exile,
To lack-of-food, lack-of-sleep, lack-of-water,
To pain that pounds like a drum in the back of the head!

Yard! You, covered with a dryness of leaves,
With salt from low-browed graduation towers;
The seams of tires and runners show black,
The frozen abscess of October is picked open

By the old man's nail of the skies, of October
The old man's nail and by the old man's nail
Of she, who, standing by the street lamps since morning,
Coughs in her shawl and prepares them a decoction.

Yard, this blizzard, which, like a coachman in the frost,
Is overgrown with snow, brows plastered
With champed-at snow—it has outgrown
The black years of the outskirts and factories.

The blizzard, which, like a coachman, is completely encrusted; like him,
Up to its neck in snow and, like the coachman,
Taken, bound, scorched, blinded,
Shredded and screwed, like the coachman, onto the clouds.

Yard, this wind is akin to me, in that,
From all over the neighborhood, at high speed,
It will attach itself as an announcement to the wall:
People, there they love and are seeking work!

People! There, rage is statelier than mine.
People! There I bow my knees.
People, there, as from the Polar seas,
All night a wind blows from the Book of Revelation.

Those who are bound to the darkness—by the blazing of fires,
Those bound to the bitter cold—by logs that crack like guns!
The cold in their songs is more bitter still than mine,
The darkness of their revelations is darker!

Winter, like a Mongol lord, exacts from the streets
Fur coats and stoves and fittings of rooms,
Know then—the hearth of the winter yoke
Is there, in the poets' place, their beggarly Khanate.

Protect yourself from the snowstorm in verse
With a fur coat; from the night in the poem—with a candle.

With a full glass—when your spirit
Hurries to take hair of the dog that bit it.

And without delays, and without half-words,
Whole-heartedly, by recorded delivery,
Send wine, furs, light and shelter
There, to the departments of the needy.

Like "February . . . ," "Dedication" hinges on the relationship between the poem and the landscape through which it rushes. As in "February . . . ," this relationship is depicted in emphatically material terms. Here, it is not rushing liquid but the precipitous motion of the wind that unsettles our efforts to interpret the poem, sweeping us forcefully out of the yard and—for reasons that remain obscure—into a distant place of exile. This motion is again driven by a mysterious sense of urgency, which only becomes more insistent as the poem proceeds. Before turning to consider all of this in the infrastructural terms I have proposed, let us first consider the structure of some individual images in the poem.

The first stanza opens with a seemingly straightforward metaphor that anchors us in the physical space of the yard and its visual appearance: winter is a poem, written in snow on the page of the yard. This metaphor is quickly extended through a simile, which likens this yard/piece of paper to a "sentence to exile." Already, complications arise. The yard resembles a written text, we understand from the first line, but the particular document it resembles complicates this initial visual comparison, implying a parallel acoustic one (the Russian for "sentence" [*prigovor*] contains the root of the verb "to speak"). At the same time, it introduces a performative dimension (in most legal systems, a sentence must be read aloud to take effect) as well as an emotional one (the simile appears to refer as much to the speaker's emotional response as to the physical qualities of the yard). The physical space of the yard is *like* the flat surface of the page—but this comparison adds dimensions to the page in return, revealing over the course of the stanza the multiple sonic, haptic, and emotional contours that poetry also comprises. Poetry has multiple potential material interfaces, in other words, of which the world itself is one.

This claim appears straightforward enough, but it has rather complex implications, as begins to become clear in this same stanza. What does it mean to fold the world into poetry, or vice versa? The stanza's language is inflected by the landscape and language commonly used to describe such scenes: "nedosyp" (lack of sleep) (l. 3) and "barabannyi" (drum-like) (l. 4) contain echoes of the verbs "sypat'" (to fall) and "barabanit'" (to pound), both of which may be used with "sneg" (snow) in Russian in some contexts.

At the same time, this language transforms these memories of sensorial experience—a specific visual memory of the yard and the more generalized haptic and sonic memories that are captured by common collocations—into the immediately perceived sensorial experiences generated by its own material qualities. Combined with the repeated prefix "nedo-" (lack-of-) and the predominantly regular dactylic tetrameter, the repeated plosives of the stanza's final line ("Na *b*ol' s *b*ara*b*annym *b*oem v zatylke!") lend the "sentence to exile" a physical reality of its own. I mean this both in the literal sense that these effects invite us to read these lines aloud (if only in our heads), making us freshly aware of the material qualities of the printed text as well as its acoustic counterpart, and in the figurative sense that this sonic over-satiety both conjures and counteracts the physical suffering associated with exile.

The effect, as I have already suggested, is something like Cubist collage: words both participate in the creation of the virtual space represented in the poem and assert their own physicality as words. This is complicated, however, by the verbal medium in which this scene is represented. The virtual space evoked in the final line of the first stanza is the vehicle of the extended comparison that begins in the second line of the poem ("Yard, you are like . . ."); it does not belong in the same virtual space as the yard itself, or at least not on the same plane of that space. This second virtual space is that conjured by the work of poetic comparison. Given physical weight in (or by) the poem's own material, however, its reality in the poem is equal to (or even greater than, at this early stage) that of the yard. This makes it hard to find our footing: where do we stand in relation to this scene? Where, indeed (if anywhere) are we to locate the figure implied by the final line's aching head? What is "really" there—and what does this even mean in this context?

This quality of the poem's imagery reaches its peak in the fifth stanza (ll. 17–20)—the climax of this first part of the poem. By this point, the wind has picked up, bringing with it a flurry of comparisons: the word "like" (*kak*) is repeated four times, each time attached to the coachman (*kucher*) and the moment of (figurative) transport that this figure implies. The rate of these comparisons might distract us from their strangeness, and particularly the incongruous material of the things they compare. The blizzard is, "like a coachman, plastered"—with snow, we infer; but the image is still curious, assigning solidity and dimension to what is essentially air. How can the wind be "plastered" with anything, let alone be "like [the coachman], / up to its neck in snow" (ll. 17–18)? And in what sense do any of the participles that follow ("Taken, bound, scorched, blinded // Shredded and screwed," ll. 19–20) apply to either blizzard or coachman? The violent physicality of the action these participles describe is echoed by the terseness of these mono- or disyllabic verb forms, which further amplify the staccato soundscape to which the cluster of repeated *-k-* and *-uch-* sounds give rise.

As in the first stanza, these images ultimately confound any attempt to distinguish between the memories of sensorial experience that they reactivate (say, of snow or a blizzard) and the sense-data generated by the poem's language. This causes a certain degree of interference, and seemingly even a sudden change of spatial location and historical setting—emphasized by the repeated "there" (*tam, gde . . .*) in the first lines of the wind's "announcement," as well as through the use of archaic vocabulary. The adjective "krepkii," for instance, which means "strong, firm" in modern Russian, is used in the now-obsolete sense, "bound" or "indebted to." The archaic sense in which "krepkii" is used is clarified by an explanatory footnote in later editions of the collection, but the reader of the 1917 edition is left to decode the phrase by parsing the unexpected dative of the noun that follows, "[to] darkness" (*t'me*). As others have noted, lexical choices like this reflect Pasternak's fascination with "the past of [Moscow]" and especially medieval Moscow.[28] In the context of this poem and the particular phrase in which the word appears here, however, this specific history is less important than its contribution to the material muddle I have been describing. The word "krepkii" emerges from the wintry conditions described in the poem and the common collocation "krepkii moroz," a "hard frost." This modern, concrete sense of the word is transformed by grammatical form into an abstract, archaic one, which itself stands in for the violent reality of the power relations it implies.

This play of substance and abstraction is key to what this poem suggests the material medium of poetry might be. Joining a web of motifs relating to winter, night, cold, and financial bondage, the adjective "krepkii" resonates on multiple levels simultaneously. Like the whole set of effects I have been describing, it helps to undermine the sense of the text as an "enduring, stable structure of meaning that corresponds directly with a set of verbal signs contained in a single material form to which we can gain direct sensory access."[29] Just as even the hardest of frosts will eventually melt, so the poem—unsettling not only the conventionally fixed relationship between words and the world but also the material fixity of the text itself—asserts the impossibility of establishing meaning with any kind of finality.[30] It is poetry's ability to move back and forth between verbal and visual, abstract and concrete, poem and world that is its most salient quality. Bringing unlike things into contact, the poetic image dramatizes the inherently mixed quality of the poetic medium, its journey between different material domains.

If the poem begins by attempting to capture the yard in words, it has, by its end, usurped the yard, taking on a material existence of its own against which the speaker warns us to protect ourselves:

Огородитесь от вьюги в стихах
Шубой; от ночи в поэме—свечою.

Protect yourself from the snowstorm in verse
With a fur coat; from the night in the poem—with a candle.

Why this warning? What, come to that, are we to make of the note of vague threat that runs through the whole poem? We might speculate that it has to do with the date of its composition, in the middle of a long war and with revolution in the air.[31] The poem itself, however, appears to identify this threat as something more permanent, an inherent feature of poetic language rather than a historical bug. It connects this threat directly with poetry's material presence, the snowstorm and the night against which we must protect ourselves. It is not only the meaning of this poem that is hard to make out, in other words: its very stuff, in Daniel Tiffany's memorable definition of "what passes for material substance in poetry," is "darkness visible," that riddling quality which—preventing poetry's complete assimilation to the world of rational logic—speaks to the fundamental uncertainty of matter itself.[32]

This conclusion seems to stand in stark contrast to Tsvetaeva's description of Pasternak's work as a "downpour of light" and her claim that he "sees in verse." In fact, it simply recasts this claim. What does it mean to "see" in verse, the poem asks. Highlighting the inevitable gap between world and text already implied by the dash in its first stanza ("Yard—you are like . . ."), the poem is not an attempt to capture a precise image of the world but to draw the reader's attention to the inevitable failure of this effort. In so doing, it highlights the new "perspective for understanding" which this failure, sending us back to examine the basic structures of reality and experience, makes available. As Tsvetaeva writes in a different essay about Pasternak, "what is obscure, lyric clarifies; what is clear, it obscures" (*Lirika temnoe uiasniaet, iavnoe zhe—zakryvaet*).[33] This riddling quality is at the center of "Marburg," the last poem in *Over the Barriers* and the final poem I will consider here.

MARBURG/MARBURG

Whereas "Dedication" is often cited as a typical example of Pasternak's work from this early period, "Marburg" tends to be regarded instead as a first step toward the more mature style of what Tynianov would later describe as Pasternak's "diary" in verse, *My Sister—Life*.[34] The poem was inspired by Pasternak's brief stint as a philosophy student in Marburg in 1912. It was during this stay that Pasternak finally abandoned philosophy in favor of poetry.[35]

The catalyst for this break, as Pasternak describes it, was the rejection his proposal of marriage received from Ida Vysotskaia, a childhood friend. This autobiographical event frames "Marburg," which describes the failed proposal and the speaker's subsequent rebirth as a poet. The poem thus stands at a "crossroads," as Sinyavsky remarks, in multiple senses of the word: the poem itself is concerned with Pasternak's turn from philosophy to poetry and is positioned by scholarship, which usually focuses on its 1929 redaction, on the threshold of Pasternak's mature writing.[36]

Turning to the 1916 redaction of the poem, however, what stands out most starkly is what I am calling the poem's riddling quality. The crossroads at which this version of the poem stands is not that at which poetry and (autobiographical) reality meet and merge, but the place where the work of the poem as medium becomes most visible:

Марбург

День был резкий, и тон был резкий,
Резки были день и тон—
Ну, так извиняюсь. Были занавески
Жёлты. Пеньюар был тонок, как хитон.

Ласка июля плескалась в тюле,
Тюль, подымаясь, бил в потолок,
Над головой были руки и стулья,
Под головой подушка для ног.

Вы поздно вставали. Носили лишь модное,
И к вам постучавшись, входил я в танцкласс,
Где страсть, словно балку, кидала мне под ноги
Линолеум в клетку, пустившийся в пляс.

Что сделали вы? Или это по-дружески,
Вы в кружеве вьюжитесь, мой друг в матинэ?
К чему же дивитесь Вы, если по-мужески—
мне больно, довольно, есть мера длине,
тяни, но не слишком, не рваться ж струне,
мне больно, довольно—
стенает во мне
Назревшее сердце, мой друг в матинэ?

Вчера я родился. Себя я не чту
Никем, и ещё непривычна мне поступь,

Сейчас, вспоминаю, стоял на мосту
И видел, что видят немногие с мосту.

Инстинкт сохраненья, старик подхалим,
Шёл рядом, шёл следом, бок о бок, особо,
И думал: «Он стоит того, чтоб за ним
Во дни эти злые присматривать в оба».

Шагни, и ещё раз—твердил мне инстинкт
И вёл меня мудро, как старый схоластик,
Чрез путаный, древний, сырой лабиринт
Нагретых деревьев, сирени и страсти.

Плитняк раскалялся. И улицы лоб
Был смугл. И на небо глядел исподлобья
Булыжник. И ветер, как лодочник, грёб
По липам. И сыпало пылью и дробью.

Лиловою медью блистала плита,
А в зарослях парковых очи хоть выколи,
И лишь насекомые к солнцу с куста
Слетают, как часики спящего тикая.

О, в день тот, как демон, глядела земля,
Грозу пожирая, из трав и кустарника,
И небо, как кровь, затворялось, спалясь
О взгляд тот, тяжёлый и жёлтый, как арника.

В тот день всю тебя от гребёнок до ног,
Как трагик в провинции драму Шекспирову,
Носил я с собою и знал назубок,
Шатался по городу и репетировал.

Достаточно тягостно солнце мне днём,
Что стынет, как сало в тарелке из олова,
Но ночь занимает весь дом соловьём
И дом превращается в арфу Эолову.

По стенам испуганно мечется бой
Часов и несётся осёдланный маятник,
В саду—ты глядишь с побелевшей губой—
С земли отделяется каменный памятник.

Тот памятник—тополь. И каменный гость
Тот тополь: луна повсеместна и целостна.
И в комнате будут и белая кость
Берёзы, и прочие окаменелости.

Повсюду портпледы разложит туман,
И в каждую комнату всунут по месяцу.
Приезжие мне предоставят чулан,
Версту коридора да чёрную лестницу.

По лестнице чёрной легко босиком
Свершить замечательнейшую экскурсию.
Лишь ужасом белым оплавится дом
Да ужасом черным—трава и настурции.

В экскурсию эту с свечою идут,
Чтоб видели очи фиалок и крокусов,
Как сомкнуты веки бредущего. Тут
Вся соль—в освещеньи безокого фокуса.

Чего мне бояться? Я твёрже грамматики
Бессонницу знаю. И мне не брести
По голой плите босоногим лунатиком
Средь лип и берёз из слоновой кости.

Ведь ночи играть садятся в шахматы
Со мной на лунном паркетном полу.
Акацией пахнет, и окна распахнуты,
И страсть, как свидетель, седеет в углу.

И тополь—король. Королева—бессонница.
И ферзь—соловей. Я тянусь к соловью.
И ночь побеждает, фигуры сторонятся,
Я белое утро в лицо узнаю.[37]

Marburg

Day was harsh and tone was harsh,
Harsh were day and tone—
Well, I'm sorry then. Curtains
Were yellow. The peignoir was delicate, like a *chiton*.

July's caress splashed in the curtain lace,
The curtain lace, rising, struck at the ceiling,
Above my head were hands and chairs,
Beneath my head a pillow for feet.

You rose late. You wore only fashionable things,
And knocking at your door, I entered a dance class
Where passion, like a crossbeam, threw beneath my feet
The checkered linoleum, which had broken into dance.

What did you do? Or is it as a friend
That you whirl in lace, my friend in a morning gown?
What is it that surprises you, if, like a man–
        I am hurt, enough, everything has its limit,
        you can pull, but not too hard, the string must not break,
        I am hurt, enough–
                                        If my overripe heart wails in me
My friend in a morning gown?

Yesterday I was born. I don't consider myself
Anyone, and I'm still not used to my gait,
Just now, I remember, I was standing on the bridge
And saw what few see from the bridge.

Survival instinct, old man toady,
Walked at my side, at my heels, cheek by jowl, apart,
And thought: "It's worth, in these evil days,
Keeping both eyes on him."

Take a step, and again—instinct repeated to me
And led me wisely, like an old scholastic,
Through the winding, ancient, damp labyrinth
Of heated trees, lilac, and passion.

The flagstones grew hot. And the street's forehead
Was swarthy. And from beneath its brow cobblestones peered
At the sky. And the wind, like a boatman, rowed
Through the lindens. And dust and drumming poured forth.

The paving stone shone like lilac copper,
But in the thickets of the park it's dark as pitch

And only insects take flight from the bush
To the sun, ticking like a sleeping man's timepiece.

Oh, on that day, like a demon, the earth peered,
Devouring the storm, out of the grass and bushes,
And the sky, like blood, clotted, burning itself
On that gaze, heavy and yellow, like arnica.

On that day all of you, from combs to feet,
Like a provincial actor a drama of Shakespeare
I carried with me and knew by heart,
Roamed the city and rehearsed.

The sun is hard enough for me in the day,
Which grows cold, like *salo* in a tin dish,
But night occupies the whole house as a nightingale
And the house turns into the Aeolian harp.

Along the walls in alarm tears the striking
Of clocks and the saddled pendulum rushes,
In the garden—you look with whitened lip–
A stone monument detaches itself from the earth.

That monument—a poplar. And a stone guest
That poplar: the moon is everywhere and whole.
And in the room will be both the white bone
Of a birch, and other petrified things.

The fog will place garment bags all around,
And a moon will be thrust into each room.
The visitors will provide me with a box room,
A *verst* of corridor and a black staircase.

Up the black staircase it is easy barefoot
To complete a most excellent excursion.
Only the house will melt with white horror
And with black horror—the grass and nasturtiums.

They go on this excursion with a candle,
So that the eyes of violets and crocuses might see,
How the lids of the wanderer are closed. This
Is the whole point—the illumination of an eyeless trick.

What do I have to fear? I know insomnia more thoroughly
Than grammar. And I don't have to wander
Along the bare tile like a barefoot lunatic
Among lindens and birches of ivory.

For the nights are sitting down to play chess
With me on the lunar parquet floor.
It smells of acacia, and windows agape,
And passion, like a witness, turns grey in the corner.

And the poplar is the king. The queen is insomnia.
And the queen is the nightingale. I am drawn to the nightingale.
And night wins, the figures move off,
I recognize white morning by its face.

As is clear, the autobiographical events by which the poem was inspired are present here only in oblique form. While the poem is clearly divided into three parts—the speaker's rejection at the hands of a female figure (ll. 1–20); the emotional turmoil that ensues (ll. 21–72); and the mysterious chess game with which the poem ends (ll. 73–84)—the details of this narrative as it is presented in the poem remain ambiguous. Even the titular Marburg features only dimly, as the "muddled, ancient, damp labyrinth / Of heated trees, lilac, and passion" through which "instinct" leads the lovelorn speaker. Instead, the abiding impression is of the indistinctness of the space through which this speaker moves and the strange logic of the many actions, comparisons, and progressions that animate this space.

I will focus for now on the second part of the poem (ll. 21–72), which, as in the poems considered above, again sees the speaker moving through the city (this time on foot). This part of the poem divides into two distinct halves. In the first (ll. 21–48), the personified features of the city reach out to one another. These objects form a network that is conjoined yet discrete, as emphasized by the alternation of dominant vowels in each ("plitn*ia*k *raskalialsia*. I *u*litsy lob / byl sm*u*gl"); their actions gain an accretive momentum through the repeated "and" which bursts forth in the storm of the tenth stanza. By contrast, the second half (ll. 49–72) is defined by all-pervasive transformation. Whereas the cumulative logic of the first half results in a labyrinth of connected but separate objects, here objects emerge from and merge into one another, detaching themselves from larger wholes ("A stone monument detaches itself from the earth," l. 54) and fracturing in order to enter new ones ("And a moon will be placed into each room," l. 62). This sense of everything being part of the same whole is reinforced by the rhymes and other sound patterns that echo across and between stanzas, as well as the repetition of individual words, which appear and reappear in different line-positions, grammatical functions, and combinations across the stanzas in this section of the poem.

The two halves of this central part of the poem thus enact the opposing directions contained in metonymic description, in which whole represents part or vice versa. Metonymic contiguity functions differently in each half, too, in the first half primarily on the level of language, as sound repetition connects adjacent words, and in the second on a metaphorical, or ontological level, as adjacent things bleed into and transform those in their vicinity. This would seem to align these two halves with Jakobson's distinction between metonymy, which he connects with prose, and metaphor, connected with poetry. This distinction is further emphasized by what we have identified as the cumulative (i.e., narrative) motion of the first half of this central part of the poem and the recurrence (i.e., poetry) typical of its second half. Nonetheless, to read the poem in an autobiographical key as a depiction of the speaker's progress from philosophy through disappointed love to poetry neglects an important part of its meaning.

The transformations and reversals of the second part of the poem offer a vivid illustration of what I would term the "multistability" of Pasternak's images. "Multistable" is the term used to describe optical illusions such as the well-known "duck-rabbit," which represents either a duck or a rabbit, depending on how one looks at it. Challenging the notion of a natural connection between visual representation and the object it depicts, such images "illustrate the co-existence of contrary or simply different readings."[38] They are multistable in the sense that our awareness of each stable possibility is always accompanied by our consciousness of the multiple other options that the image contains. This is the effect we have already observed more than once—the reversible quality of Pasternak's images and the multiple possibilities this encodes. A vivid instance in this poem occurs in stanza fourteen:

> Тот памятник—тополь. И каменный гость
> Тот тополь: луна повсеместна и целостна.
> И в комнате будут и белая кость
> Берёзы, и прочие окаменелости.
>
> That monument is a poplar. And the stone guest—
> That poplar: the moon is everywhere and whole.
> And in the room will be both the white bone
> Of a birch, and other petrified things.

The stanza begins by identifying the "stone monument" that first appears in the previous stanza as a poplar tree. It then immediately reverses this motion, transforming the tree back into a "stone guest." While the basic metaphor remains the same (TREE is STATUE), any sense of ontological hierarchy between the two things is erased by the alternation between them (monument—poplar—stone guest—poplar) and the light of the moon, "everywhere and whole." These transformations continue through the stanza. The moonlight penetrates into the room of the house, now conjuring a tree ("white bone / of birch") that appears to be metaphorical (a shadow-dappled shaft of moonlight, perhaps) but which retains the weight of the "real" (poplar) tree just described (indeed, given the often metonymic mode of Pasternak's metaphors, it may suggest a nearby birch). At the same time, the solidity of the monument is also reaffirmed, its qualities endowed upon the other objects in the room (turned by the moonlight into "petrified things"). The stanza is, in other words, a multistable "tree-statue" image in which tree and statue coexist, two parts of the same whole.

Multistability is not restricted to this section of the poem, but extends to the mirrored structure of the poem as a whole. I have already suggested that the second half of the poem's central part seems to mirror the first, reversing the initial movement from part to whole. This general tendency is realized on the level of the individual stanza, each of which is as though "reflected" by its counterpart in the other part of the poem. The first clue to this pattern is provided by the chess game in the final section of the poem, a transformed version of the "checkered linoleum" in the opening stanzas. Other echoes include the echo of the beloved's "peignoir" and "morning gown" in the "nights" and "white morning" of the final section; and the speaker's belated response to his own command, the imperative verb "*tian*i" (pull) (l. 17) reappearing in reflexive, first person form in the poem's final stanza: "Ia *tian*us' k solov'iu" (I am drawn to the nightingale) (l. 82).

Similar patterns are seen throughout the poem. To list just a few of these correspondences: the imagery associated with injury and treatment in the tenth stanza ("the sky, like blood, clotted shut," "arnica") and the twelfth (melted *salo* was commonly used as a poultice); the "clock" and "garden" in the thirteenth stanza and the "watch" and "park" in the ninth; the communing parts of the city in the eighth stanza and the labyrinth of images created by the fourteenth (discussed above); the appearance of figures external to the speaker in the fifteenth stanza ("priezzhie" [visitors]), presumably referring to the things the moonlight has brought into the room, and the personified "instinct" in the seventh; the twice-repeated "walked" of the sixth stanza and the "excursion" of the sixteenth, in which "white horror" and "black horror" also echo the "evil days" feared by "instinct"; and finally, the use of the verb "videt'" (to see) in the seventeenth stanza, for the first time since the fifth.

This symmetry enacts on a large scale the reversible metonymic motion from part to whole and whole to part that we observed in each section, with each stanza now seen on its own terms, now drawn into the larger structure of which it is part. This is not to speak of the many further patterns that these motifs, moving like chess pieces through the poem, establish and develop within this structure, nor of the shifting significance which these additional patterns bestow on these motifs. If we accept the view that the first half of the poem represents the world of reality, while the second depicts "the play of imagination,"[39] then the poem as a whole describes not a linear trajectory from one space to the other but the multidirectional movement of a chessboard—a space where the world ("And the poplar is the king"), subjective reality ("The queen is insomnia"), and art ("And the queen is the nightingale") exist in constantly shifting and productive relation to one another, like so many folds in the fabric of reality and the text.[40]

This helps us to understand better the current of fear that we encounter here again, and which the speaker shakes off only in its final stanzas. Again, it suggests that the origin of this fear may be the material of poetry itself—the "darkness visible," in Tiffany's terms, of its riddling speech. While "Marburg" lacks the brevity of a riddle, its many intricate patterns hint tantalizingly at the key ("vsia sol'"?) that might solve the strange logic of its progress. The riddling quality of the poem is further highlighted by the allegorical landscape through which the speaker moves, full of enigmatic signs. The second part of the poem, in particular, resembles an allegorical journey into the underworld—whether that of Orpheus, in search of his beloved; or, more hopefully, Persephone, whose annual return to earth brings the spring suggested by the flowers and grass of the sixteenth stanza. Most telling, however, is the poem's invocation of another legend, that of the Sphinx. Like this poser of ancient riddles, the speaker roams the streets of the city reciting verse; drawing attention to his gait, he calls to mind her famous question (What goes on four feet in the morning, two feet at noon, and three feet in the evening?); as though acting out the *answer* to her famous riddle, he appears now as baby ("Yesterday I was born"), now as a young lover, now as an old man ("Survival instinct, old man toady / Walked at my side").

But the riddle is not solved. If the speaker ceases to feel afraid at the end of the poem, this is due rather to his acceptance of the fundamentally enigmatic quality of poetic meaning ("I know insomnia more firmly than grammar"). Although much has been made of night's victory at the end of the poem, the present tense of this final section indicates that this victory is not final. The riddle of poetry is not that of the progress from infancy to old age but the insistent interstitiality of its position, on the brink between day and night, life and the underworld, reality and its reflection. Progressing from one image to the next via a contiguous motion that takes place on both the level of reality and on the level of language, "Marburg" and the metonymic ground along which it moves open up an avenue of exchange between world and text in which both occupy the position of both whole and part, cause and effect—in which "the noise of the dictionary" (*PSS* 5:23–26), as Pasternak describes his poetic material elsewhere, gives birth to life, just as "my sister, life" is the source of poetry. As Pasternak wrote to his father in 1916, the same year the poem was first composed, his turn to poetry occurred "instinctively, suddenly, and laconically [*bezotchetno, skoropostizhno i lakonichno*], like health and illness, like birth and death" (*PSS* 7:243). The turn from philosophy to poetry was, in other words, not a turn *from* death to life, from illness to health, but rather the entry into a domain where such incommensurable spheres exist simultaneously.

Over the Barriers, the collection in which "Marburg" appears, was thoroughly revised in 1928–29 before its republication in 1929. These revisions were initially composed on the back of the original manuscript, a book-palimpsest that epitomizes the type of ephemeral materiality proposed by Pasternak's poetry. The snow will melt; the wind will let the announcement drop; poems can be rewritten, and the story of his time in Marburg told and retold. These are poems in which, as Olga Peters Hasty insightfully observes, figuration cedes its place to *con*figuration—where images do not so much reproduce reality as emerge from the dynamically shifting constellations of its parts.[41]

By the same token, Hasty argues that Pasternak is opposed to photography and its drive to capture and fix, an argument that I have also made here. Nonetheless, Pasternak's poetry does share certain things in common with photography, an inscriptive medium that does not simply mimic reality but *shares* in it, produced by the collision between its own surface and the light that strikes it.[42] The contingency of this moment of collision between artistic material and the world is also at the center of Pasternak's poetry, where words and things, moving freely among one another, periodically collide and become, as Tynianov puts it, "fraternally entangle[d]."[43] Like photography, Pasternak's poetry is before anything else a record of this contingency, the unforeseeable event of its own birth. It is precisely in this sense, however, that poetry as Pasternak conceives it is less an inscriptive medium than an infrastructural one: shuttling between multiple material dimensions, bringing words and things into transformative contact.

PART III

Voice

"Every soul has its fundamental tone," an essay by the poet Maximilian Voloshin begins, "and every voice its own fundamental intonation."[1] The essay that follows does not concern the "voices of poets" in any literal sense, however, despite the promise of its title. Instead, Voloshin uses this term metaphorically as a synonym for all that is most unique about a poet's work. Still, it is precisely this metaphorical usage of the term that marks the essay as a product of its performance-centric time. In the decade after 1905, poetry readings and other such events became a fixture of literary life in the two capitals. Modernist poets cultivated highly individual vocal styles as part of the broader project of "life-creation" (*zhiznetvorchestvo*), a set of aesthetic practices that "blurred the boundary between art and life, actor and spectator, in effect transforming human existence into performance."[2] Blurring the boundary between poet and persona, it was the ambiguity of voice as both source and sign of individual genius that made it a source of such popular and poetic fascination.

In stark contrast, the Formalist Boris Eikhenbaum approached voice in impersonal terms as an element of the literary text conceived as a verbal composition or sound system. His conception of voice was also informed by the poetry evenings that were such a staple part of cultural life. This context was a crucial one for the arguments advanced in essays such as "Illusion of Skaz" ("Illiuziia skaza," 1918) and "How Gogol's Overcoat Was Made" ("Kak sdelana *Shinel'* Gogolia," 1919), which position writing as "a living, dynamic activity, formed by voice, articulation, and intonation and accompanied by gestures and mimicry."[3] However, the ubiquitous poetry readings of the era only confirmed Eikhenbaum's conviction that the object of Formalist scholarship was not the unique sound of the author's voice (physical or metaphorical), but, rather, the voice of the text itself.

The opposition between theatrical life-creation and the work-centered approach advocated by Formalists such as Eikhenbaum recalls the animating tension of lyric discourse more generally—defined, as Roland Greene has argued, "by the dialectical play of ritual and fictional phenomena."[4] "Ritual" in this definition refers to all those features of poetic utterance that make it "uniquely disposed to be re-uttered," or what Jonathan Culler describes as "writing for readers to enunciate"—that is, to those formal aspects of the poem that make us want to read it aloud, commit it to memory, and recite it.[5] In this sense, poetry, as "potentially immediate . . . speech," represents a "real world utterance," in Kate Hambürger's terms (I may not *really* be addressing a nightingale, but I am literally articulating a series of poetically patterned lines).[6] At the same time, lyric poetry often relies upon "images of voice," where "the fiction of a speaker and explicit address" tethers its speech to one (fictional) voice or situation in particular.[7] As scholars have argued, it is the interaction of these two poles—the ritual and the fictional; the iterative and the singular—that renders the highly personal expression typical of the lyric available for repetition by others.[8]

It is no surprise, then, that these features of poetic speech moved to the fore in the early decades of the twentieth century, a period when the growing pressures of the mass literary marketplace, the invention of recording technologies, and political circumstances sharpened questions around originality, reproducibility, and literary personality more broadly. The following chapters consider the consequences of these circumstances for conceptions of poetry during this period. What happened to poetry and ways of thinking about poetry when poets and audiences regularly met face-to-face and the difference between poetic and real-world utterances became blurred? And how did poets and their audiences respond to the increasingly commercialized, mediatized domain in which these encounters took place?

As we observed in the chapters on the poetic image, modernism in Russia and throughout Europe witnessed a resurgence of interest in the material qualities of poetic language. Focusing now on voice, I turn from sound's significance for conceptions of poetry as an artistic medium to consider the intersections between poetry and medium in one of the more modern senses of the term—as (mass) communication medium. By contrast with the numerous recent studies devoted to the phenomenon of the modernist poetry reading and the sound of individual poets' voices, I aim to describe how changing practices of performance and oral recitation of verse formed part of a broader set of reflections on the nature and status of poetry in a mediatized age.[9]

As a term in poetics, "voice" has its origins in ancient Greece, when poetry was sung to a lyre. Although oral performance ceased to be intrinsic to the practice of lyric with the invention of writing, it endured in the lyric's first-person mode and a thematic interest in song, and poetry remained a form intended primarily for oral performance well into the medieval period.[10] Perhaps counterintuitively from a modern vantage point, this proximity to physical voice correlated by and large with a lack of interest in individualized lyric speakers. Even as poetry gradually became the domain of private meditation and poetic voice lost its literal basis in sounding speech, poems continued to offer definite but unspecified subject positions for readers to occupy as they "performed" these lyrics in private.[11] If lyric came increasingly to be regarded as a form for the expression of personal feeling, its iterative qualities remained at the fore.

As expressive theories of literature became dominant in the Romantic period, poetic voice became more firmly attached to an individualized subject, and devices such as rhythm or rhyme that had previously invited readers to inhabit a poem's voice now became the mark of its individuality.[12] This equation of poet and speaker also led to the emergence of the dramatic monologue as a separate genre in which the speaker was explicitly fictionalized and identified as separate from the poet. Whether "casting off . . . complete masks of the self in each poem" or testing the physical voice with elaborate sonic arrangements, modernists reacted to these earlier models by adopting "egregiously artificial voice[s]" that undermined not only the notion of poetic speech's origins in a unique individual but, often, the existence of a stable and coherent self at all.[13]

Such radical mutability was, in some sense, the logical end point of the rise of print and its detachment of poetic voice from literally sounding speech. Yet the context for such experimentation was, in fact, a resurgence of interest in oral performance, from Gustave Kahn's *samedis popularies* to the Italian Futurist *serate*, from Zurich's Cabaret Voltaire to St. Petersburg's Stray Dog.[14] Researchers across Europe, Russia, and the United States paid new attention to the sound of poetry and particularly poetry recitation, and the relative status of the printed and the recited poem was hotly debated. This was, in other words, an era when "voice" ceased to be a merely metaphorical term and became once again a literal feature of poetic texts. As a consequence, it was also one during which the full complexity of lyric discourse and its interstitial position moved to the fore.

This was particularly the case in Russia, where the relationship between *I*-author and *I*-speaker within the poem had long been "productively ambiguous."[15] This ambiguity was amplified by modernist poets, who challenged the dominance of professional theatrical declaimers by taking to the stage to read their own verse. Modernist poets came increasingly to be identified with their voices, so that "familiarity with how a poet read his poems became one key for interpretation of his poetry."[16] At the same time, these poets were guided by the formal qualities of the poem rather than its semantic content, as in the case of the dramatic style preferred by professional declaimers; their idiosyncratic style of reciting their verse thus highlighted those aspects of poetic speech that make it easily memorable and amenable to repeated readings. Not coincidentally, the rise of authorial readings during this period was matched by new enthusiasm for poetry recitation among the general population. One of the bestselling books of the first decades of the century, for example, was *Reader-Declaimer* (*Chtets-deklamator*), a selection of poems for reading aloud that came out in multiple volumes and editions.[17] The picture was further complicated by the invention and proliferation of new technologies for sound recording, reproduction, and communication, as well as the demands of the commercial literary marketplace.[18]

Blurring the boundaries between established categories, the ubiquity of poetry recitation raised a number of questions about the nature of poetic language and the identity of its speaker. The new focus on topics such as verse "melodics" and intonation also forced researchers to grapple with more fundamental methodological issues. In chapter 6, I will look closely at some of the debates with which studies on these topics were engaged, focusing particularly on Eikhenbaum's work in this area and that of his colleague, Sergei Bernshtein. Both were involved in research on sound and poetry performance then underway at the Institute of the Living Word (Institut zhivogo slova), established in Petrograd in 1918. Disagreements centered on the relationship between the formal composition of a given poetic text and the declamation of that text: was there a particular, authoritative way to recite the poem, or were multiple different interpretations possible (and permissible)? And what was the correct way to study this aspect of poetry: through new methods of sound-based analysis or with reference to the printed text? As I argue, these seemingly rather dry methodological debates got to the heart of the deeper issues tied up with theoretical approaches to poetry during these years. While Eikhenbaum's efforts to account for the voice of the poetic text rather than the poet were (and continue to be) criticized for failing to acknowledge its life beyond the page, his dogged defense of the work-centered approach was in itself an effort to identify and describe what he saw as literature's most vital qualities.

The opposition between singularity and repetition is also a crucial one for chapter 7, in which I consider the work of Vladimir Mayakovsky, whose near-total erasure of the boundary between *I*-author and *I*-speaker has earned him a reputation as, at best, one of modernism's foremost romantics and a self-promoting egomaniac, at worst. Returning to the early period of his work and public performances here, I argue that this attitude speaks to a concern not so much with the unique individuality of the speaker so much as the multiplicity of the text. Mayakovsky's work from this period tests the boundaries between printed text and oral recitation as part of a broader exploration of the role of poetry and the place of the poet in a new media landscape. Mayakovsky responded to rapid urbanization and the growth of the urban entertainment industry not by lamenting the poet's loss of cultural authority or by attempting to shore it up, but by devising an alternative model of poetic speech that embraced the multiplicity of roles this context made available.

Chapter Six

Boris Eikhenbaum, Sergei Bernshtein, and the Melodics of Verse

THE EXTENT OF INTEREST in the "living," "live," or "spoken" (all translations of the Russian adjective *zhivoe*) word and the "sounding" (*zvuchashchee*) word in Russia in the first decades of the twentieth century cannot be overstated. This interest reached a peak with the creation in 1918 of Petrograd's Institute of the Living Word, where, as Eikhenbaum writes in "On Poetry Reading" ("O chtenii stikhov," 1919), "this topic is debated late into the night."[1]

The institute revived a plan first outlined in 1914, when Iurii Ozarovskii (1869–1924), the director of St. Petersburg's Aleksandrinskii Theater, sought to bring together in person the diverse contributors to *Voice and Speech* (*Golos i rech'*), a journal that had flourished briefly in 1913–14 in conjunction with a series of declamation workshops headed by Ozarovskii beginning in 1910. Ozarovskii's plans were prevented by financial and political difficulties caused by the outbreak of the war. The institute was eventually founded on the initiative of Vsevolod Vsevolodskii-Gerngross (1882–1962), who raised the idea at a meeting of the Theater section of Narkompros, the newly established People's Commissariat for Education, in 1918.[2] When the Institute of the Living Word finally became a reality, it sought to gather a range of well-known scholars and artists in a multidisciplinary space where specialists with a broad range of expertise—from literary scholars and specialists in theater and performance to linguists, physiologists, and psychologists—would study and teach the "living word" in all its forms.

The phrase "living word" (*zhivoe slovo*) had grown in popularity in the latter half of the nineteenth century, when it was invoked in relation to pedagogical discussions around language teaching. Here, the phrase was used to mean something like "colloquial speech," as academics and pedagogues argued for the inclusion of language "as it is spoken" in textbooks, rather than phrases contrived for the purpose of teaching grammatical examples.[3] It is frequently used in a sense close to the English "spoken word" to refer to the live performance of literary texts—also commonly referred to as "declamation" (*deklamatsiia*) or "reading" (*chtenie*).[4] The phrase originates in the Bible (the "living word" of God), and frequently appears in descriptions of religious oration, where it gained the additional expressive sense "divinely ordained." During the modernist period, all three senses of the phrase were combined as writers sought, through poetry and poetry declamation, to reverse what they regarded as the decay of language, often adopting the role, already well established for Russian writers, of secular prophet as they did so. (I discuss this trend at more length in the next chapter.) It was in this hybrid sense that the phrase arrived in the name of the institute itself; as Vsevolodskii-Gerngross rather loftily opined during its opening ceremony, citing the famous final line of Pushkin's poem "The Prophet," "The words 'And with your word ignite men's hearts' were once just a beautiful image; now they are . . . a beautiful reality."[5]

There were immediate causes for the spike of interest in the living word as a research topic in the wake of the October Revolution. Contending with shortages of paper and other materials, literary writers and academics had to disseminate their work orally; this led to heightened interest in orality in a wide variety of forms.[6] The revolution also opened up new venues and opportunities for ordinary citizens to engage in public speech. This shift was considered "crucial for a social democracy," and made rhetoric and the spoken word important topics for practical education as well as research.[7]

Interest in the spoken word was not unique to Russia, but followed western European developments in philology and linguistics. Particularly important was the rise of "Ohrenphilologie," the method of sound-based analysis championed by the German philologist Eduard Sievers (1852–1932) and discussed briefly in the chapters on rhythm. This was one symptom of the more general turn to empirical research methods fueled in no small part by the new availability of sound recording and other technical devices. This enthusiasm was shared by Vsevolodskii-Gerngross, who in 1919 set up a working group on "Speech Melody" (*Melodiia rechi*) at the institute for the express purpose of recording the voices of actors and other professional speakers in order to analyze the melodic structure of their speech; in April of the same year, this became the "Committee on Speech Melody" (Komissiia po melodike rechi).[8] The first part of this chapter considers several of the theoretical texts to emerge from these initiatives, chiefly Boris Eikhenbaum's book-length study of the "melodics" of Russian lyric poetry and Sergei Bernshtein's essays on poetry and declamation. The two theorists worked together under the aegis of the committee to compile a bibliography on the topic of melody in speech and poetry that was included as an appendix in Eikhenbaum's book.[9] However, they disagreed on a number of issues, including the definition and correct usage of key concepts such as "melodics" and "intonation." These disagreements speak to the urgent methodological questions raised by the turn to sound-based analysis and "melodics": where was the line to be drawn between poetics and linguistics? To what extent could or should the text be treated independently of context? And how was the object of literary analysis to be properly defined?

THE SOUNDING WORD: POETRY FOR THE EYE OR EAR?

A key point of debate during this period was the nature of the relationship between the written poetic text and its "sounding" counterpart: which had priority? The prevailing consensus among linguists was that the spoken word provided a more proper foundation for linguistic analysis than its written counterpart—since, as Lev Shcherba wrote in 1923, "one can normally only call 'language' that which is pronounced [*to, shto proiznositsia*], even if this is only in one's head."[10] These ideas carried over into the study of literature, reinforcing the intuitive sense among many researchers working on poetry that poetic language, defined as it was by prosodic features such as rhythm, sound patterning, and intonation, could only be properly understood if read aloud. As Eduard Sievers wrote in 1912, "in order for it to have its full effect, a poetic work that has been fixed in writing must be brought back to life through oral interpretation, through performance."[11]

This was the sentiment behind Sievers's turn to "Ohrenphilologie" and the study of the sounding text, discussed briefly in chapter 2. Sievers's basic assumption was that there is one correct way to recite any given poem, and that this is inscribed by the formal structure of the poem itself. This is what he called the "objective sound shape" of the poem.[12] This "sound shape" is expressed via a poem's rhythmic and melodic features and could, he argued, be "brought back to life" if the poem were read aloud in the correct way.[13] Only by reciting the poem could readers and researchers identify and reproduce the "suggestive idea of melody" that had originally inspired it. Even a writer working in silence, Sievers held, "continually produces imagined melodies, even if he is not conscious of this aspect of his production."[14]

Despite its apparent basis in objective analysis of sonic form (including pitch, interval size, modulation, and tone-steps), Sievers's notion of what he called "melodics" reproduced long-standing biases regarding the proximity of oral speech to authenticity or truth.[15] The "objective sound shape" provides a tangible trace of the poet's intentions to which reading the poem aloud gives direct access.[16] These assumptions led Sievers to adopt the method known as "mass reaction." This involved asking large numbers of people to recite the same set of poems aloud. If two readers "melodized" the poem in the same way, this could be taken to be a true reflection of the "sound shape" of the poem.[17] On the basis of these studies, Sievers concluded that poems did indeed inscribe certain "rules" for correct recitation that reflected the intentions of the author, and that verse melodics are inherent to a poem's composition.

Eikhenbaum vigorously disputed this and other similar assertions. His opposition to the growing dominance of sound-based analysis stemmed largely from his desire to draw a clear line between poetics ("a humanist science" [*nauka o dukhe*]) and linguistics ("a natural science").[18] The study of the acoustic and phonetic features of a poem as realized in the physical qualities of one particular voice (analyzing timbre, pitch, and so on) was the realm of linguistics, he insisted. While Eikhenbaum conceded that linguistics could be a source of useful tools for the literary scholar, he was quite firm that it should not distract from the main task of poetics, namely, to understand the immanent laws whereby the text is constructed. As he cautioned, the "drawing together of neighboring disciplines can only be fruitful so long as it does not develop into some new subordination."[19] Sound-based analysis led many researchers to forget that "the printed text is not a fact, but a problem"; it is thus from this text that any attempt at analysis must begin.[20]

This was the task that Eikhenbaum set himself in *Melodics of Russian Lyric Verse* (*Melodika russkogo liricheskogo stikha*, 1922). Eikhenbaum began work on this study in the spring of 1918. He had come to the topic through his work on the nineteenth-century poet Vasily Zhukovsky, and saw it as a possible solution to the problem of accounting for that elusive element which makes the work of individual poets recognizable as their own. This cannot be the product of metrical organization or rhyme alone, Eikhenbaum argues, since these formal elements recur across poems and poetic traditions; nor can this quality be explained solely with reference to lexicon, since this neglects the role played by form.[21] Rather, we must look to the place where rhythm intersects with semantics, namely syntax and the intonational system to which it gives rise.

The choice of "melodics" to label this element of poetic speech is evidently an effort to avoid using the term "voice," with its ambiguous proximity to the spoken word and the figure of the individual poet. As Eikhenbaum states in the book's introduction, part of his intention is also to dispel vague talk of poetry's "melodiousness." Still, his use of the term "melodics" indicates that he recognizes the reality that such language seeks to describe. The similarities between poetry and music must be acknowledged and accounted for if we are to understand the differences between them and articulate the specific nature of *verse* melodics.

At the same time, Eikhenbaum is clear that he does not regard sound-based analysis as suited to this task. Instead, he focuses solely on identifying and analyzing "melodic-syntactical figures" in the work of several Romantic and post-Romantic poets in what he terms the "song-like" or "melodious" (*napevnyi*) category of Russian verse. Even when discussing Zhukovsky's use of elegiac questions or anaphora in the work of Afanasy Fet, the study studiously avoids any mention of physical voice or the analysis of musical qualities such as pitch or dynamics. Clearly, there are limits to such an approach, as Eikhenbaum's own frequent use of musicological terminology implies; I will come back to these in a moment. But Eikhenbaum's insistence on analyzing the written text should not be dismissed out of hand. The text-based analysis he undertakes represents a serious attempt to clarify the claim implicit in Sievers's sound-based analysis: how *does* the text inscribe "melodics" and "intonation," by what compositional means?

At the other end of the spectrum, or so it would appear, we find Sergei Bernshtein, the most ardent adopter of Ohrenphilologie and its methods in Russia. Bernshtein's enthusiasm for the sounding text was such that, in 1920, he set up and led a new project under the aegis of the Committee on Speech Melody dedicated to the study of poetry recitation.[22] To this end, he set about recording poets reading their poetry aloud. This work progressed at a remarkable pace; by 1922, he had already recorded more than 6,000 poems, performed by 30 different poets and actors.[23] It is thanks to Bernshtein that we can hear the voices of poets such as Akhmatova, Bely, Blok, Briusov, Mayakovsky, and others today.[24] These recordings formed the basis of his analysis.

One of Bernshtein's stated aims in studying these recordings was to test Eikhenbaum's theories regarding the melodics of verse: how did his findings stand up to those derived through sound-based analysis? Bernshtein also sought to refine the method proposed by Sievers, whose approach he critiques at length in the essay "Poetry and Declamation" ("Stikh i deklamatsiia," 1924). The method outlined in this 1924 essay is thus offered as a corrective to the work of both Sievers and Eikhenbaum. Whereas Sievers insists on the absolute priority of oral recitation and Eikhenbaum analyzes only the written text, Bernshtein tries to get to grips with the full complexity of the relationship between the two.

Bernshtein took particular issue with Sievers's method of "mass reaction," which he argued could not be the basis for conclusions about the structure of the poetic text.[25] The manner in which any given reader recites a poem is influenced by a number of factors external to the poetic text itself, he argued (regional accent, for example); hence, the study of non-authorial readings can tell us only about how individual readers interpret the text, not the author's intentions in writing it. What the method of "mass reaction" makes most apparent is the fallacy of viewing the poetic text as a set of authorial instructions for the reader. These issues are reflected in the problematic categories that the method of "mass reaction" led Sievers to devise. On the basis of his experiments, he sorts readers into two groups: "Autorenleser," or those who stuck closely to these authorial instructions, and a smaller group of "Selbstleser," who took a freer, more individualized approach to recitation of the text. According to these categories, Bernshtein points out, contemporary Russian poets would have to be filed under "Selbstleser," since the quirks of their vocal delivery were rarely directly motivated by the poetic text.[26] While attaching importance to insignificant extra-textual features and failing to account for common trends in contemporary declamation practices, Bernshtein concludes, Sievers's method not only does little to illuminate the relationship between the poetic text and the manner in which it is declaimed, but also demonstrates clearly that there is no necessary connection between the two.[27]

Where Sievers seeks to classify modes of declamation, Bernshtein instead identifies two different types of poetry, "declamatory" (*deklamativnyi*) and "non-declamatory" (*nedeklamativnyi*). The former type tends to emphasize those aspects of a text that contribute to its "material sounding" (*material'noe zvuchanie*); the latter does not.[28] Neither type "needs" to be read aloud; nor is it the case that "declamatory" poems necessarily lend themselves better to recitation. Blok's poetry, for instance, belongs to what Bernshtein terms the "non-declamatory" category—despite Blok's deserved reputation as a reader of his own verse. This is not a contradiction; as Bernshtein argues, both declamatory and non-declamatory poetry are suited to recitation to a greater or lesser degree, depending on the formal structure of the poem in question.[29] All of this leads Bernshtein to conclude, contrary to Sievers, that verse melodics and intonation are not part of the basic composition of a poem. Declamation is a secondary phenomenon, and is interesting and useful only because (or when) it helps us to perceive more clearly the prosodic features of the poem itself—or, conversely, when it is studied as a linguistic phenomenon in its own right.[30]

This appears to be much the same conclusion as that reached by Eikhenbaum. Yet Bernshtein faults Eikhenbaum's study precisely for its failure to consider the materially sounding text. Why does Bernshtein criticize Eikhenbaum in these terms? As we have just seen, Bernshtein himself regards this sound text as separate from the basic composition of the poem. I would argue that it stems from his concern with the methodological problem posed by the relative status of the written and the spoken texts. In refusing to engage with the issue of recitation without a full understanding of the melodics of the printed text, Eikhenbaum comes close to reproducing Sievers's rather dubious claim that a written text provides precise instructions for recitation and the "sound shape" of its author's intentions. For Bernshtein, the task at hand is to better understand the nature of each as independent phenomena.

Eikhenbaum's study has also been criticized for its apparently sketchy grasp of its core terms. Despite his professed interest in melodics, Eikhenbaum makes no mention of musical qualities such as pitch at all. Moreover, he undermines his own efforts to separate poetics from linguistics by relying on the now-disproved notion that certain fixed intonational structures correspond to different syntactical constructions.[31] Eikhenbaum would likely object that the aim of his study is to describe *poetic* intonation, rather than music or speech patterns; his intention is precisely to avoid analogies with these two spheres.

Nonetheless, Bernshtein and others are right to caution that this narrow focus limits his study. Eikhenbaum discounts the materially sounding text because he wants to resist the "subordination" of poetics to linguistics; as Bernshtein's critique implies, however, it may be Eikhenbaum who is letting linguistics in by the back door. Focusing exclusively on the role of syntax in determining melodics, Eikhenbaum ends up making the same mistake as Sievers—precisely for the reason that he *does not* analyze declamation. Both of them work from the mistaken assumption that melodics "is part of the poetic composition," i.e., that each poem has a particular, "correct" intonation, which is inscribed by its formal structure.[32] The only difference is that, for Sievers, this is demonstrated by reading the poem aloud; whereas, for Eikhenbaum, it is encoded by syntax in the written text.

Bernshtein, by contrast, believes that there is more than one way of reciting a text. The formal composition of the poem cannot on its own account for these multiple possibilities. Bernshtein's objection to Eikhenbaum's neglect of the materially sounding text therefore has nothing to do with his desire, as a linguist in literary scholar's clothing, to bypass the text and instead "study the voice on the basis of poetic material," as Eikhenbaum claimed of sound-based analysis more generally.[33] On the contrary, he wants to demonstrate the independence of the poetic text proper from its declamation (and hence also of poetics from linguistics). He does so by demonstrating why discussion of melodics and the sounding text must be bracketed off from consideration of the written text and its composition. Despite their apparent disagreement, in other words, Bernshtein achieves what Eikhenbaum sets out to do: to carve out a space for a scientific poetics that is distinct to linguistics.

In some sense, the main issue here is a terminological one. Bernshtein and Eikhenbaum are working with slightly different definitions of their two key terms, "melodics" and "intonation." Intonation is a notoriously difficult phenomenon to describe, even from a purely linguistic point of view; the sheer variety of methods employed by linguists in their efforts to transcribe it, as Eric Griffiths observes, indicates that the trouble is a "permanent conceptual intractability in the material rather than . . . a mere cussedness of the equipment."[34] The matter becomes even more complex when the talk turns to poetic intonation, since here we are dealing not only with the question of *how* to decipher spoken intonation from written notation, but also *whether* to do so and how much room for *interpretation* is left for us when we do. Eikhenbaum states at the beginning of his study that his intention is to move away from vague, metaphorical terms such as "musicality" (*muzykal'nost'*), but "intonation," for all its ring of scientific rigor and objectivity, is no less metaphorical when applied to a written poetic text. What does it refer to in this context—the metrical, rhythmic, and syntactical structure of the poem (Eikhenbaum)? The literal intonations of the voice that recites it (Bernshtein)? Or the (emotional) implicatures of the poem-as-utterance, as Viktor Zhirmunsky, in another critical review of Eikhenbaum's study, seems to have in mind?[35] If there is such a thing as poetic intonation, how does it compare to ordinary speech intonation? And does intonation, whether poetic or "ordinary," sound the same when we "mentally 'hear' a text" as when we were to hear the same words spoken in conversation?[36]

The failure to reach scholarly consensus on these seemingly rather basic points speaks to the larger question mark that the rise of Ohrenphilologie and sound-based analysis had placed over the nature of poetic speech and the appropriate parameters for the study of it. Despite his skepticism regarding the relevance of oral renditions of the text for our understanding of melodics, Eikhenbaum nonetheless classifies poetry into three types—declamatory (*deklamativnyi*), spoken (*govornoi*), and song-like (*napevnyi*)—all of which are defined in relation to the sounding voice.[37] Bernshtein does not question this basic classification, whatever his other objections to Eikhenbaum's methods and conclusions. He follows his own concluding remarks about the need to distinguish clearly between declamation and poetry with a discussion of the "speech elements" (*rechevye elementy*) in poetry that listening to recordings can help us to describe. Both scholars agree, in other words, that poetry contains *some* trace of the voice (if not one voice in particular)—even as each struggles to locate and describe the specific nature of that trace.

In the end, therefore, it is not the relative status of spoken and written texts that is at stake so much as the challenge that their coexistence presented for scholars seeking to define their object of study. Eikhenbaum's mistake is that he fails to fully acknowledge the basic fact that a poem can be both written down and read aloud; whatever the relationship between these two versions of the poem, they are proof enough already that a poem cannot have one single, correct intonation; its "voice" is inherently multiple.

As we will see in the next section, Eikhenbaum was to some degree aware of this dynamic. Turning to consider in more detail his engagement with the common practice of reading poetry aloud in public, this section considers how this tension between singularity and multiplicity factored into his understanding of how poetry communicates emotion.

VOICE AND EMOTION

If Bernshtein is critical of Eikhenbaum's claim to distinguish between linguistics and poetics, Viktor Zhirmunsky takes most issue with the neglect in *Melodics* of the "psychological element." It is this psychological element, Zhirmunsky holds, and not some abstract "system of intonation," that "turn[s] the sounds of our speech into an artistically meaningful and aesthetically valuable fact."[38] In his view, Eikhenbaum fails to move beyond formal analysis of the text and account for the important role played by our response to the semantic content of the words and their "emotional coloring."[39] Of course, this is precisely Eikhenbaum's methodological gambit, and part of his determined effort to move away from the kind of semantic or psychological interpretation of the verse phonotext epitomized for him by Andrei Bely's reading of Pushkin's champagne-popping prosody ("Is poetry, then, simply a rebus?"), which was so prevalent in Russian criticism of the time. Sounds in verse "are self-sufficient and self-signifying," he writes; "they do not 'accompany' and do not simply 'correspond.'"[40]

The divide between Zhirmunsky and Eikhenbaum mirrors quite neatly the division in modes of poetry declamation described by Eikhenbaum in *Melodics* and other work of this period. Zhirmunsky, who emphasizes the importance of semantic meaning and "logical" intonation, takes a position broadly in line with that of the "expressive" style preferred by professional declaimers.[41] Eikhenbaum's own preference, as he writes in "On Chamber Declamation" ("O kamernoi deklamatsii," 1923), was for the almost monotonous, inexpressive style adopted by modernist poets: "thanks to this, I perceived the text of the poem and experienced it as I wanted. I felt that the poem was being presented to me [*podaetsia*], rather than acted out [*razygryvaetsia*]."[42] The physical and audible presence of the poet has the paradoxical effect of making the *poem* more available to the audience. This is because poets, unlike professional declaimers, emphasize not content or emotional expressivity but formal organization; they are guided by rhythmic and strophic structure, rather than semantic or syntactic logic. "There is no 'staging' involved" (*nikakoi instsenirovki net*), as Eikhenbaum writes approvingly. The poet becomes a "third party" (*tret'e litso*) at the reading, no more than a mouthpiece for the voice of the poem itself. Nonetheless, this article represents an attempt to rectify some of the excesses of *Melodics* and to use Zhirmunsky's criticisms of the earlier study to strengthen the work-centered approach. In particular, Eikhenbaum seeks in his article to describe more precisely the role of emotion in poetry and art more generally.

What is wrong with the "expressive" mode of poetry recitation, in Eikhenbaum's view? First, that it is expressive at all. According to Eikhenbaum, a declaimer should strive for "the neutralization of personal emotions" in order to interfere as little as possible with the transmission of the poem.[43] This is because obtrusive interpretation (in the form of "play acting" [*razygryvanie*] or "mimicry" [*mimika*]) "deceives" the audience into responding viscerally rather than neutralizing *their* personal emotions and reacting to the piece as a work of art. It is not only the poem to which "expressive" reading "does violence," therefore; by seeking to blur the line between personal, emotive speech and the impersonal voice of the poem, it does violence to the audience, too.[44]

Eikhenbaum was not the first to notice the divergence between these two modes of declamation—"like actors" (*po-akterski*) and "like poets" (*po-poetski*)—in the years leading up to the revolution.[45] As he recalls in the essay, Eikhenbaum first became aware of the latter style at the evening in memory of the actress Vera Komissarzhevskaia in 1910. However, the inexpressive, "amateurish" (*neumelaia*) style of declamation he heard at this occasion had already been common practice among Symbolist poets for a number of years by that date. The relationship between theatrical declamation (*ispolnitel'skaia deklamatsiia*) and declamation by poets (*avtorskaia deklamatsiia*, henceforth "authorial reading") was, moreover, more complex than Eikhenbaum's description allows. While modernist poets certainly adopted a style consciously opposed to that of professional theatrical declaimers during the first decades of the twentieth century, authorial reading by no means developed in complete isolation from theatrical declamation. The "Saturday" gatherings held at Komissarzhevskaia's theater before her death, for instance, had featured a mixture of theatrical declamation and authorial reading, with each inevitably influencing the other; these gatherings set the stage for the 1910 event in her memory attended by Eikhenbaum.[46] This was a model that would be reproduced in the 1910s at cabarets such as the Stray Dog and the Comedians' Haven (Prival komediantov), and provides one explanation for the "theatrical" elements of readings by poets such as Mayakovsky during this period.

Part of Eikhenbaum's objection to the proliferation of courses and handbooks on expressive reading was that they paid so little attention to the specific qualities of poetry. Actors were advised to rewrite poems as lines of prose; to identify, based on the poem's semantic content, where the "logical" stresses should fall; and to use this as a guide for the delivery of the poem. Eikhenbaum is particularly outraged by the advice offered in these guides regarding the rhythm of the poem, which the declaimer is told as far as possible to "observe" (*sobliudat'*)—"just as, in polite company, one must 'observe decorum' [*sobliudat' prilichie*]."[47] Favoring semantic meaning over formal structure inevitably meant that such readings neglected rhythm and other formal organizational devices, and emphasized instead "emotion, emotional experience [*perezhivanie*], mood."[48]

Where all this goes wrong, Eikhenbaum argues, is in assuming that the most important element in the performance is the emotional experience of the declaimer. This was the approach favored in theater, and particularly by Stanislavsky, whose "emotion memory" method (*iskusstvo perezhivaniia*) may be what Eikhenbaum has in mind when he criticizes the emphasis that professional declaimers placed on "emotional experience" (*perezhivanie*). Stanislavsky, of course, had been among those pushing for theatrical delivery to move closer to ordinary, conversational speech, a shift directly opposed to the contemporaneous move among modernist poets toward monotonous chanting. This led, increasingly, to neglect of issues relating to voice and speech at the Moscow Art Theatre, a blind spot that did not go unnoticed by critics of the method but which was a conscious decision on Stanislavsky's part. As he wrote to Meyerhold, "I have completely lost faith in everything that serves the eye and ear on stage. I believe only in feeling [*chuvstvo*], emotional experience [*perezhivanie*], and, most importantly, in nature itself."[49]

Whereas Stanislavsky's focus is on the actor and his process, Eikhenbaum prioritizes instead the experience of the audience.[50] If art inevitably induces *some* kind of emotional response, Eikhenbaum has definite views about what kind of emotional response it *should* produce, and for whom. He makes frequent reference throughout "On Chamber Declamation" to his own strongly negative responses to theatrical declamation, which induces in him feelings of "awkwardness, embarrassment, and shame," and even "rage" (*gnev*).[51] He contrasts such feelings to his neutral response to authorial reading proper, when he "perceived the text and experienced [*perezhival*] it as [he] wanted."

These contrasting responses form the basis of the essay's discussion of two types of emotion: on the one hand, the personal or "soulful" (*dushevnyi*), an epithet probably meant to evoke Stanislavsky's notion of "soulful naturalism" (*dushevnyi naturalizm*); and on the other, the "formal" (*formal'nyi*), "intellectual" (*intellektual'nyi*), or "spiritual" (*dukhovnyi*), terms Eikhenbaum uses interchangeably. Emotions in the former category, which includes such feelings as joy, anger, and passion, belong to our private lives. Those in the latter category, by firm contrast, "are not connected with the intimate content of personal life and are not born immediately and instinctively of this content, but relate to personal life as form does to material."[52]

Though labeled "intellectual," these "spiritual" emotions are repeatedly tied in Eikhenbaum's account to physical experience. This is evident already in an earlier piece, "On Tragedy and the Tragic" (1919), one of the first in which the scholar addresses the issue of emotion in art directly, writing that the emotions it produces are "held in the hands along with one's opera glasses."[53] The account in "On Chamber Declamation" is more subtle, implicitly contrasting the physicality of the "violent force" (*nasilie*) exercised by actors upon poems (and, subsequently, audiences) with the "special emphases [*nazhimy*] (sometimes even with the help of gestures . . .)" used by poets to communicate the poem's rhythmic structure.[54] Still, a kind of solidity is imputed to the emotional experience that results: rhythm is an emotion, Eikhenbaum writes, and as such must be *constructed*.[55] As Olenina points out, this view of rhythm chimes with Formalism's interest in architectonics, according to which the artwork is an assemblage of distinct elements. The audience must actively engage with these elements in order to understand the relationship between them. Formal emotions emerge from the awareness of the text's structure that results.[56] In other words, poetry "moves" us most when we are least carried away by its content and the emotional experiences and events it depicts—when we are most aware of it as conventionalized performance, and of the iterable quality of the emotions it conveys.

"Verse declamation is currently becoming an issue every bit as vital as obtaining firewood, matches, boots, etc.," Eikhenbaum wrote in the winter of 1919.[57] Reading "On Chamber Declamation," we begin to get a sense of why, during this harsh and hungry time, this might be so. While Zhirmunsky may lament Eikhenbaum's failure to account for the "psychological element," it is precisely by circumventing this kind of personal response to poetry that Eikhenbaum's work-centered approach seeks to explain its more essential emotional role. The monotonous, inexpressive style adopted by poets enables the mechanism by which poetry communicates intellectual emotion to stand out more clearly and hence to work more effectively. Rather than catharsis, it is this emotion, constructed through interaction with the formal structures of the poem, that Eikhenbaum identifies as the proper sphere of art and the source of its value as spiritual support.

The Formalists and their work-centered approach came under increasing attack as the 1920s continued. Seen from the perspective of his detractors, the difficulties that Eikhenbaum encountered in studies such as *Melodics* demonstrate the limitations of an approach that sought to explain the literary text in complete isolation from adjacent or even overlapping spheres such as speech, performance, and music. More sympathetically, we might say that Eikhenbaum's efforts to describe the specific way that poetry speaks to audiences were aimed precisely at understanding the particular role that literature plays in emotional and spiritual life. The difficulties that Eikhenbaum encountered as he strove to explain poetic voice (or melodics, or emotion) without falling back on empirical analysis of the individual vocal performance were not, in any case, entirely of his own making. The challenge that all these theorists encountered was how to articulate the animating tension of lyric discourse, that between singularity and repetition. This was a problem with which poets also grappled during this period, as the next chapter will describe.

Chapter Seven

The Many Voices of Vladimir Mayakovsky

VLADIMIR MAYAKOVSKY: A Tragedy, first published in March 1914 in a run of 500 copies, was not originally intended for circulation in print. The copy of the play that Mayakovsky submitted to the censors for approval in November 1913 did not include typographical effects or any other indication that Mayakovsky conceived the play with publication in mind.[1] Indeed, so minimally formatted was this manuscript that the censors—so the story goes—mistook the author's name for the title of the play. Nor did Mayakovsky contribute substantially to the preparation of the edition, which was published a few months after the play's premier at St. Petersburg's Luna Park on December 2, 1913: the design, typeface, and illustrations of this volume were left almost entirely to his friends and fellow Futurists, David and Vladimir Burliuk. In short, Mayakovsky composed his tragedy first and foremost for performance on the stage.

Precisely for this reason, the play and its first print edition raise interesting questions about the relationship between text and performance, voice and print. As we saw in the previous chapter, this relationship has often been conceived of in hierarchical terms, with either the spoken or the written text given priority or viewed as the more authoritative source. Where did Mayakovsky's loyalties lie? Numerous contemporaries attest to Mayakovsky's habit of composing his poetry out loud.[2] Reading this work in front of audiences in his trademark baritone was a constant feature of his literary activities. Yet Mayakovsky did not neglect the written text entirely; perhaps his most enduring legacy is the stepladder or *lesenka* line, an innovation that arose precisely at the interface between voice and graphic layout. As this chapter will argue, Mayakovsky's interest in the interplay between print and oral performance formed part of a broader investigation into the nature of the poetic text and the status of the poet in the mediatized age.

As in many Futurist publications at the time, the first edition of *Vladimir Mayakovsky: A Tragedy* makes playful use of typographic effects, italicizing certain letters, blowing others up to disproportionate size, setting certain words in bold, and so on.[3] These effects are visually arresting but pro-

Милостивые Государи

Заштопайте мне душу

Пустота сочиться не могла бы

Я не знаю **плевок** обида или
Нет

Figure 7. "Ladies and Gentlemen / patch up my soul / so that the emptiness can't leak out / I don't know whether a gob of spit is an insult or / Not." Extract from original edition of *Vladimir Mayakovsky: A Tragedy* (March 1914), designed by David and Vladimir Burliuk. From Al'fonsov and Krasitskii, *Poeziia russkogo futurizma*, 141.

Я овенчаюсь моим безуміеМ

Figure 8. "I will crown myself with my madness." Extract from original edition of *Vladimir Mayakovsky: A Tragedy* (March 1914), designed by David and Vladimir Burliuk. From Al'fonsov and Krasitskii, *Poeziia russkogo futurizma*, 145.

vide little information as to how the text was or should be performed aloud, as extracts from this edition make clear (see figures 7 and 8).[4]

The apparently random use of capitalization, emphasis, italics, and font size in these lines bears little obvious relation to intonation. In the absence of any explicit or consistent indication as to volume, timbre, or tone, a degree of subjective interpretation is required in order to read these lines aloud. In this sense, this edition of the play is functionally no different from a written text produced without oral performance in mind. Those minimal instructions for performance that written texts do usually possess—chiefly, punctuation marks—are frequently omitted, as in the case of the missing commas in the final line of figure 7. As with other graphic effects used in these lines, this omission appears to lack any particular "expressive purpose or . . . practical goal," and indeed serves primarily to further obscure the intended intonation of the line.[5]

If the random typographical effects that characterize the print edition of *Vladimir Mayakovsky* do not offer precise guidance as to how its lines should sound when read aloud, might the relationship between the printed text and performance work in the opposite direction? The play's premier was a scandalous success—even if, by most accounts, it was also a somewhat shambolic affair. This was not entirely intentional While the cast was from the start made up almost entirely of students with little acting experience, the unexpected resignation of many of these cast members two days before the show meant, as Ol'ga Matiushina recalls, that a number of roles were played by last minute recruits from among Mayakovsky's acquaintances. (The original cast, Matiushina says, had heard rumours that some audience members were planning to throw rotten meat and fish at them and beat them up.).[6] The vocal delivery of these amateurs left something to be desired, as one attendee at the show's premiere recalls. "They acted badly, and read their words badly and unintelligibly . . . The audience, meanwhile, was not listening carefully enough to make out any of what was coming from the stage."[7] Despite these problems, the play prompted intense reactions, from the emotional to the outraged. The chaotic typography of the first printed edition might thus be understood as an attempt to capture the disruptive spirit of the original performance of the play. As one scholar has argued, Mayakovsky's addition of stage directions to the printed edition represented an attempt "to convey to the reader the images and impressions that the viewer took from the show," rendering the printed edition less a set of instructions for future performances than a record of the Luna Park show as a singular event.[8]

The idea that the printed edition of the play seeks primarily to preserve or capture some aspect of the original performance positions the written text as secondary to that performance. Conversely, to consider the accuracy with which the printed text communicates instructions for its performance prioritizes the written word. The latter is the more common assumption when it comes to poetry performance. Terms such as "declamation" (*deklamatsiia*) and "reading" (*chtenie*) "imply a secondary voicing of a pre-existing text," where the text exists separately from (and prior to) its vocal presentation.[9]

Clearly, this binary view of the matter fails to account for the complex relationship between the written word and its spoken counterpart. The complexity of this relationship was particularly perceptible during the first decades of the twentieth century, when poets such as Mayakovsky regularly performed their work in public, as well as publishing in magazines and putting out books. If the typographic effects in the first edition of *Vladimir Mayakovsky* tell us anything, it is arguably that the ubiquity of performance during this period produced an alternative view of the text as such. This new orientation is similar to that described by Charles Bernstein in his theoretical account of poetry in performance, inspired in part by his own experience as an avant-garde poet: rather than weighing up the originality of the performance or the written document against its copy, he argues, we should attend to the "plural event" of the work in all its forms. As Bernstein writes, "the work is not identical to any one graphical or performative realization of it, nor can it be equated with a totalized unity of these versions or manifestations."[10]

The difference here is between a view of the text as something fixed and prior to performance and a conception of the text as essentially plural.[11] It is this distinction to which the typographic effects in the first edition of *Vladimir Mayakovsky* ultimately draw our attention. Highlighting nothing so much as the distance between the printed text and its first as well as all subsequent performances, the printed edition of the play—by dint of its very fixity—undermines the status of the text as a stable object. Viewed from this angle, Mayakovsky's addition of stage directions to the printed edition only emphasizes the multiple future lives that the play might lead: the singularity of the poem's original performance becomes the basis for its repetition in future. The printed text and the spoken word exist not in hierarchical relation to one another but simply as variant possibilities. This is much the same conclusion as that reached by Sergei Bernshtein, as we saw in the previous chapter. In Mayakovsky's poetic practice, it becomes the basis for a wide-ranging exploration of the nature of poetic speech and the authority of the poet.

I, MYSELF? POETRY AND/AS MEDIATIZED PERFORMANCE

What I have just identified as the multiplicity of *Vladimir Mayakovsky: A Tragedy* stands in tension with the play's apparent obsession with the singularity of its author, main character, director, and starring actor, whose name supplies its title: Vladimir Mayakovsky. Arrogant and ostentatiously lacking in regard for the limits of good taste, this character seems the epitome of avant-garde *épatage*, determined to shock his public out of the comfortable conventions to which they are accustomed. Luxuriating in the "velvet of [his] own voice" even as he uses this voice to describe lurid and grotesque scenes, the larger-than-life speaker of *Vladimir Mayakovsky* and the author's early poems sets himself against his audience; seeking to goad them into response, he mingles statements with mocking exposure of their inability to resist this boor's charms: "ladies love my meat," as the speaker of "A Fop's Blouse" ("Kofta fata," 1914) has it.

The apparently self-obsessed quality of Mayakovsky's earlier work conceals a larger set of questions regarding originality and authenticity that emerge from the strange multiplicity at the heart of performance. As performance scholars note, the tension between singularity and repetition that is inherent to drama as a genre, where each individual production is both unique and but one more iteration of the play. In taking a poet as its main character, *Vladimir Mayakovsky* amplifies this tension and uses it to dramatize the familiar problem of the relationship between *I*-author and *I*-speaker.

When poetry is read aloud, the ambiguity of this relationship is intensified by the (poet-)performer, whose presence blurs the boundary between fictive persona and autobiographical person still further and adds yet a third voice to the text. In *Vladimir Mayakovsky*, these ambiguities occupy center stage. Are the words of this "poet" fictional, a dramatic monologue of sorts in which the *I*-speaker takes center stage? Or should they be understood as the direct utterance of the *I*-author? If the latter, is this author a character that the real-life Mayakovsky is representing (as is conventional in theatre), or is Mayakovsky presenting himself? Where is the line between this performed self and his "true self"? How singular is the author himself?[12]

If Mayakovsky's regular cameos in his own work imply a certain degree of arrogance, these multiple personae also represent so many "versions" of the author, who willingly makes copies of himself for distribution among his audience. In this sense, the important distinction is not between the play or poem as performed and as written down, but rather that between live and mediatized performance. The Futurists were among the first artists in Russia to energetically engage in self-advertisement, as well as to actively court the attention of the press. This attests to the wide net these renegade artists knew they had to cast were they to succeed commercially despite their position on the fringes of the main art market; lacking social standing as well as funds, the artists were conscious of the insecurity of their patronage and became canny self-promoters. Unable to print their writing in large runs due to limited financial means, they undertook instead to tour the country in person—a sort of living radio *avant la machine*, designed to broadcast their artistic program to as wide an audience as possible. (This tour began immediately after the premier of *Vladimir Mayakovsky* in December 1913.) The Futurists also planned to release a collective "phonobook" of poetry; though this idea never came to fruition, they created and released their first film, *Drama in Cabaret No. 13*, as early as 1914.[13]

In other words, Mayakovsky and other Futurists were well aware that their work would not only be experienced live but also through a variety of media, and indeed they counted on this fact. *Vladimir Mayakovsky* again provides a useful case in point. As memoir accounts of this first performance make clear, many in the audience were deeply moved by the show, despite its imperfections; and this was thanks largely to Mayakovsky's compelling delivery and presence on stage. Yet many who were not at the first performance were equally moved: to judge by the innumerable reviews of the play to appear in provincial newspapers, this audience-at-a-distance was, for the most part, outraged. Both of these reactions fulfilled important functions for Mayakovsky, and help to explain the apparently conflicting tendencies in his work of these years, which veers between the scandalous and the sensitive. As Mayakovsky puts it in *A Cloud in Trousers* (*Oblako v shtanakh*, 1915),

Хотите—
буду от мяса бешеный
—и, как небо, меняя тона—
хотите—
буду безукоризненно нежный,
не мужчина, а—облако в штанах!

If you want,
I'll be red-blooded and raging,
and, changing tone, like the sky,
If you want,
I'll be absolutely tender,
Not a man, but a cloud in trousers![14]

These lines recall Shklovsky's memorable commentary on *Vladimir Mayakovsky*: "The poet has spread himself out on the stage, holding himself in hand as a card player holds his cards. Here's Mayakovsky the deuce, the three, the jack, the king."[15] Such moments are typically considered in terms of what they tell us about Mayakovsky himself. Yet these multiple personae speak just as eloquently of Mayakovsky's awareness of the multiple audiences to which his mediatized person spoke and through which he would be refracted.

A similar dynamic can be seen in Futurism at large. Resisting the homogeneity of the mass-produced object, Futurist typography and handmade books evince a desire to preserve a trace of the individual poet, on the one hand, and to reinvigorate the individual reader's relationship with the text, on the other. At the same time, these artists goaded the press, putting on countless debates and exhibitions designed to lure in and outrage as large an audience as possible. These apparently conflicting practices were in fact evidence of artists looking to adapt to a new media landscape: despite their proclivity for the rude and the shocking, the Futurists thought carefully about how to communicate with their audience. The well-known poem "But Could You?" ("A vy mogli by," 1912) illustrates this point. As we might expect for this period, this is a poem about artistic media (paint and musical instruments); but it is also one that makes clear how mediatized performance changed the way that Mayakovsky thought about audience and poetic communication.

Much like *Vladimir Mayakovsky*, and in keeping with the rest of Mayakovsky's work of this period, the poem appears straightforwardly to assert the authority of the poet as a uniquely talented individual. The strident speaker displays his own prowess before throwing a challenge to the bourgeois crowd that, we infer, is hardly likely to be met:

А вы могли бы?

Я сразу смазал карту будня,
плеснувши краску из стакана;
я показал на блюде студня
косые скулы океана.
На чешуе жестяной рыбы
прочёл я зовы новых губ.
А вы
ноктюрн сыграть
могли бы
на флейте водосточных труб?[16]

But Could You?

I suddenly smeared the weekday map
splashing paint from a glass;
I pointed out on a plate of aspic
the ocean's slanted cheeks.
On the scales of a tin fish
I read the summons of new lips.
And you
perform a nocturne
could you
on a drainpipe flute?

The poem is emphatic about its own singularity: paint is splashed randomly across the canvas in a gestural motion that connects the resulting marks with the body of the individual who produced them. But what is perhaps most striking here is the tension between the speaker's claim to absolute originality and the democratic gesture that the poem's final challenge conceals: even as the speaker proclaims his own genius, he undermines his claim to special talent. Poetry can be heard wherever there is a drainpipe and some rain.

The ambiguities of this stance stem in part from the poet's repeated encounters with audiences during these years. These performances were an opportunity to display the unique qualities of his individual voice; at the same time, they made the contradictions inherent in the role of the modern poet—performing his singularity each night in front of paying crowds or selling it on film—more tangible. The significance of Mayakovsky's performance practice for the final form taken by the poem becomes clearer when we compare it to an earlier version of the poem, published in *Trebnik troikh* in 1913:

На чешуе жестяной рыбы
Прочел я зовы вещих губ
А вы, ноктюрн сыграть могли бы
На флейтах водосточных труб?
Я стер границы в карте будня
Плеснувши краску из стакана
И показал на блюде студня
Косые скулы океана.[17]

On the scales of a tin fish
I read the summons of prophetic lips
And you, could you perform a nocturne
on drainpipe flutes?
I erased the borders on the weekday map
having splashed paint from a glass
And pointed out on a plate of aspic
the ocean's slanted cheeks.

Here, the challenge upon which the later version of the poem turns is much less prominent. Not only does the poem lack the provocative title of later versions, but its address to the reader—embedded near the beginning of the poem and in lines of the same length as the rest—loses much of its stridency. The presence of the "I" in this earlier version is also much attenuated; it is not yet the first word of the poem, nor repeated so frequently. The later version of the poem—which first gained staggered lines in the 1916 collection, *Simple as Mooing*—gives more prominence to its speaker, as we might expect for a version of the poem finalized after the initial period of performance. Yet the increased prominence of the speaker also shifts further attention onto the reader-addressee. Broken up and isolated on separate lines, the phrases "but you" and "could [you]" in the later version render the poles of the poem's I-you axis more starkly opposed. Precisely in so doing, the lines stage an encounter between them. In this sense, the staggered lines of the later version capture on the page a version of what Mayakovsky did on stage when he turned, as memoirists recall, to address the audience directly.[18]

Mayakovsky would explain his later adoption of the *lesenka* or stepladder form via reference to the audience: rather than providing instructions for recitation, this graphic form is designed to make his poetry more *comprehensible*—"to make things so that they could reach the greatest quantity of listeners."[19] Yet though Mayakovsky criticizes his earlier work for being "incomprehensible," he was far from neglectful of these issues in that work.[20] To the contrary, a great deal of his early output, including *Vladimir Mayakovsky*, concerns at least on some level the question of communication:

what does it mean to communicate in verse? How and why does the poet communicate—and with whom? These questions took on new urgency in the mediatized age in which Mayakovsky found himself, and form the basis of a broader exploration of the changing status of the poet in the modern era, to which I now turn.

THE POET PROFITS: VOICE AND THE LITERARY MARKETPLACE

Russia has a history of oral poetry and verse recitation that predated the period examined here, from folk traditions to the ceremonial odes that were such an important feature of eighteenth-century literary production and the lively salon culture of the Romantic era and beyond. Literary readings and lectures first became a regular feature of public cultural life in the late nineteenth century, however. This resurrected a trend that had flourished briefly thanks to a short-lived relaxation of censorship (the first period of glasnost') during the era of the Great Reforms.[21] Such evenings became so ubiquitous in the post-1905 period as to move Alexander Blok to complain in 1908 of St. Petersburg's "raging literary-musical-vocal epidemic" (*PSS* 8:55).

Blok makes quite clear his perturbation at the nakedly commercial spirit of such evenings—which, he observes in the same essay, were often little more than an opportunity for the "public herd" to gawk at practitioners of the newly fashionable "new art." As such, Blok insists, these events were an inappropriate venue for the recitation of modernist verse, which should be reserved for audiences who would understand and appreciate its value.[22] This kind of division of labor was common among Russian modernists, many of whom sought to protect their artistic independence and the charismatic authority traditionally endowed on the "poet-prophet" in Russian culture in the face of the sordid imperatives of the cultural marketplace, while at the same time profiting from their growing popularity. Blok's essay illustrates well the contortions this required. "I myself have read at evenings of 'new' and not-so-new art many times," he admits midway through his piece, before hastening to add, "I have always been left feeling as though I have done something wrong [*kak budto ia sdelal chto-to durnoe*]" (*PSS* 8:57). And indeed, despite the essay's firm conclusion—such evenings are "unworthy" of any poet as "an artist and a citizen" and should be avoided at all costs—Blok continued regularly to read at such events until he died in 1921.

The trope of the "poet-prophet" was "a by-product of secularization transferring to writers the authority of theologians and monastic scribes as carriers of the divine Word" that cast writers as "moral and spiritual teachers, socio-political prophets, as well as martyrs speaking truth to power and aspiring to Christlike self-sacrifice in the service of greater good."[23] The special authority of the writer in Russian culture was undermined in the early twentieth century by the rapid development of a cultural marketplace made newly competitive by the commercialization of the entertainment industry and the growing popularity of new technologies such as the cinema and the gramophone.[24] Whereas Symbolists scorned commercial culture and struggled to protect the traditional status of the Russian poet and Russian literature more broadly as "a charismatic institution," Mayakovsky instead embraced this crisis and the need to reimagine the relationship between poets and their audiences that it brought with it. [25]

The Futurists were quite open about their desire to turn a profit. Four main categories of Russian Futurist performance can be identified during the early period of their activities, from roughly 1910 to 1914: spontaneous (or purportedly so) street "happenings"; advertised lectures and debates in university and museum lecture halls; advertised and impromptu performances in cabarets, restaurants, and other middle- and upper-class venues; and, finally, more formal performances in traditional theater settings, such as the 1913 performance of *Vladimir Mayakovsky: A Tragedy* in St. Petersburg's Luna Park.[26] This newly commercialized venue had previously been home to V. F. Komissarzhevskaia's drama theater, directed by Vsevolod Meyerhold; for at least one contemporary, the invasion of its stage by the rowdy young Futurists was yet another symptom of cultural decline.[27]

The scandalous atmosphere cultivated at such events was geared toward generating publicity—and with it, cash. "When Mayakovsky needs money, he creates yet another sensation," as Marina Tsvetaeva writes; "the public rushes to watch the scandal and brings its money along."[28] This was an unashamedly exploitative relationship. As Leonid Livak notes, entrance to the Stray Dog cabaret for outsiders cost as much as a private box at the Bolshoi theater—the difference, of course, being that performances at the latter did not tend to revolve primarily around insulting those in attendance.[29] Taking money from their audiences with one hand while throwing slurs at them with the other, the Futurists in this account are canny operators interested primarily in how to have their cake and eat it, too.[30]

But was their mockery of the audience merely a more open, Futurist variety of the aversion expressed by Blok—"yet another mechanism for negotiating artistic involvement in the free market" and for making a show of their disdain for the commercial hordes?[31] This description is accurate in certain important senses, but it does not do justice to the fundamental change in orientation that the Futurists, and particularly Mayakovsky, were proposing—a shift that sought not to protect authorial charisma from the dangers of the marketplace, but to renovate it for the modern age and a modern audience.

Despite their pointedly provocative and disdainful stance, the Futurists, particularly when compared with the coterie-centric mode of the Symbolists, were very much turned outward. Where Blok used the audience's incomprehension to draw a clear line between initiates and outsiders—the "integral" audience and the "accidental," in the terms used by the performance scholar Richard Schechner—the Futurists were interested precisely in the challenge of communicating with an audience increasingly likely to be largely outsiders or accidental. Schechner defines these terms in part with reference to the audience itself: an integral audience has been invited, is known and "in-the-know," whereas accidental audiences are more likely to have paid to attend and are also more likely to pay attention once there, given their lack of familiarity with what is about to happen.[32] But the distinction between integral and accidental audiences has also to do with the role this audience plays in determining the status of the performance. "In short, an accidental audience comes 'to see the show' while the integral audience is 'necessary to accomplish the work of the show.'"[33]

The shift from integral to accidental audiences—from an audience of initiates to one made up of paying members of the public—was one symptom of what some have termed the modernization of poetry performance. In the absence of alternative forms of domestic entertainment technologies such as gramophones or the radio, poetry readings and musical recitals had traditionally played an important role in the life of many households; most frequently, such recitals took place in front of an audience of intimate acquaintances and involved the recitation of the work of others. Authorial readings became increasingly common early in the twentieth century as readings moved into a public domain where poets had to compete for an audience.

Faced with largely accidental audiences and in an increasingly crowded cultural marketplace, the Futurists put on an entertaining show. Much to their chagrin, even establishment figures found it hard to deny Mayakovsky's ability to liven the atmosphere. As one account of an evening of talks about Futurist aesthetics at Moscow's Polytechnical Museum writes, "Although the auditorium was again full, the public was obviously bored during the talks." When time came for discussion, Mayakovsky—calling for the museum to be blown up—"was the first to clamber onto the stage, despite being scheduled to appear seventh. In fact, he saved a rather dull evening. . . . he turned to the auditorium and shouted at the top of his voice, 'Gentlemen! I ask for your protection from the arbitrariness of this bunch, smearing drool on the aspic of art!' The auditorium was completely delighted and demanded he continue."[34]

The Futurists did not use insults and shocking tactics simply to titillate audiences, however. These moments also served to convert accidental audiences into integral audiences—to demand active participation and draw them into "the work of the show." Their attacks on the institutions of art were meaningless unless they provoked a reaction, after all. Although insults were the more memorable part of Futurist performances, the audience's lack of familiarity with modern art fed into these events in more constructive ways, too; the majority of such evenings were explicitly pitched as educational occasions, with recitation of Futurist verse usually taking place only after lectures on modern art or Futurist aesthetics. It is hard to see the motivation for this as purely cynical, although clearly there was some profit to be made by educating audiences to appreciate modern art.[35] On a deeper level, the Futurists' preference for the debate and the dispute demonstrates their desire to engage the audience and critics in a public exchange that did not rely simply upon the privileged authority of the poet's voice. Instead, the Futurists embraced the ephemeral temporality of participatory performance and the inherent challenge to fixed cultural hierarchies that this posed.[36]

How did this spirit inform the kind of poetry that Mayakovsky wrote during these years? The poem "Me Again" ("Eshche ia") begins to give us some idea. Here is the poem as it appeared in the *First Journal of Russian Futurists* in 1914:

Ещё я

Улица проваливалась как нос сифилитика
Река сладострастье растёкшееся в слюни
Отбросив белье до последнего листика
Сады похабно развалились в июне.
Я вышел на площадь выжженный квартал
Одев на голову как рыжий парик
А людям страшно что у меня изо рта
шевелит ногами непрожеванный крик
Как трактир мне страшен ваш страшный суд
Ведь меня одного сквозь горящие здания
проститутки как святыню на руках понесут
и покажут богу в свое оправдание
И бог заплачет над моею книжкой
Не слова а судороги смешивая комом
и побежит по небу с моими стихами под мышкой
и будет задыхаясь читать их своим знакомым.[37]

Me Again

The street caved in like the nose of a syphilitic
The river lust oozing outward into strings of spit

Having stripped off their bed sheets down to the last leaf
Gardens lasciviously collapsed in June.
I came out into the square the scorched block
Placed on my head like a red wig
And people are frightened that out of my mouth
with swarming feet a half-chewed shout
Your last judgment is as frightening to me as a tavern
After all, I am the only one who through burning buildings
prostitutes will bear in their arms like a saint
and show to God in their defense
And God will burst into tears over my book
Not words a sticky lump of clotted spasms
And run across the sky with my poems under his arm
and read them breathlessly to his acquaintances.

The project of *épatage* might seem to dictate that the avant-gardist adopts a stance diametrically opposed to his audience, a position seemingly exemplified in the unabashedly self-centered title of "Me Again." The poet is capitalizing on his notoriety as a public personality, appearing here again as the impudent Futurist hooligan who shouts frightening and incomprehensible words at the gathered crowd: that same Mayakovsky the public all so enjoy abusing, in the press and on the stage. Closer examination, however, reveals the encounter between speaker and addressee here to be rather ambiguous. The oozingly repulsive landscape of the first stanza, for example, is clearly calculated to provoke the reader's disgust; precisely for this reason, however, it also forces us to examine our own aesthetic tastes and value judgments. The reader who is outraged by the inclusion of such distasteful material in art moves to blame the speaker, yet is stopped short by the speaker's own clear revulsion before the landscape he describes and the diseased society it implies. Do we condemn the speaker or the society he himself condemns, in other words—are we to trust our aesthetic instincts, or our moral ones?

This ambiguity is heightened in the fifth line as the speaker acquires body and strides out into this horrifying landscape, not least given the thin line this figure walks between arrogant joker and tragic cannibal. Again, our emotional and aesthetic responses flounder as we attempt to identify our position in relation to the scene: do we count ourselves among the insensitive crowd, an extension of the repulsive street, or as one of the few who understand the unintelligible mouthings of this debased prophet? Do we side with the cliquish literary culture of the Symbolists (seemingly evoked here via the poet Konstantin Bal'mont's 1900 collection, *Burning Buildings*) or with this loutish poet's retinue of down-and-outs? And if we are to understand the poem as an essentially sincere call for sympathy and understanding, what are we to make of the rather comical depiction of God with which the poem ends? For even as the speaker declares the affective power of his own poetry—it touches even God—he undermines its value by parodying in this portrait its own claim to divinity.

The scene imagined in these final lines draws to a conclusion the numerous challenges to authority that run through the poem. These echo the challenges that Mayakovsky himself was continually mounting against his literary opponents during his early period of intensive performance. My suggestion that the burning buildings in this poem are meant to evoke Bal'mont may appear farfetched until we recall the numerous occasions on which Mayakovsky directly confronted Bal'mont in the years 1913–15. Bal'mont had become famous following the publication of his collection *Burning Buildings* (*Goriashchie zdaniia*) by the Symbolist publishing house Scorpio (Skorpion) in 1900, and he remained a prominent figure on the literary scene throughout the pre-revolutionary period. Whether polemicizing with Bal'mont in debates, showing up at the train station upon Balmont's return to Moscow to congratulate him "in the name of his enemies," or interrupting an evening of poetry readings put on in his honor to "[declare] the backwardness of Bal'mont's work," Mayakovsky repeatedly attacked the older poet during this period.[38] Bal'mont's enduring popularity as a poet may have made him a particularly tempting target, but to a large extent he served simply as a totemic representative of the whole generation of writers that Mayakovsky and his fellow Futurists had determined to rout: he may be the first contemporary poet named in their manifesto, "A Slap in the Face of Public Taste," but he is by no means the only one mentioned.

Mayakovsky's attacks on Bal'mont were not simply an effort to undermine cultural authorities past, however, just as "Me Again" as an avant-garde speech act cannot be said to have a straightforwardly negative effect on the audience, but functions as a perlocutionary gesture through the very incongruity of the conflicting emotions it evokes. Both this poem and Mayakovsky's confrontations were designed to prompt reflection on the notion of cultural authority as such and to highlight its basis in social consensus. In this sense, the most important image in the poem is the reference to the Russian folk carnival contained in the square-worn-as-wig, which evokes the mummery common during such events. The carnival provided a space outside of everyday life in which ordinary hierarchies of power and authority could be temporarily reversed.[39] The speaker of Mayakovsky's poem is arrogant, but any authority he possesses, this image suggests, is provisional at best. Challenging fixed (opposed) positions, the poem instead models a particular kind of "flexible" communicative event—not "shackled" but "in essence dynamic," as Mayakovsky put it in one 1913 article (*PSS* 1:275–77)—in which the audience must find their own footing.

Two years after its publication in the *First Journal of Russian Futurists,* "Me Again" was republished in Mayakovsky's collection *Simple as Mooing* (October 1916). In this printing, the poem is fully punctuated, divided into quatrains, and gains a stanza, the third of the new version:

> Но меня не осудят, но меня не облают,
> как пророку, цветами устелят мне след.
> Все эти, провалившиеся носами, знают:
> я—ваш поэт.
>
> But they will not judge me or howl me down,
> as for a prophet, they'll strew my path with flowers.
> All of those with caved-in noses know:
> I—am your poet

The striking truncated line with which the stanza ends sounds a commanding and suddenly serious, even lyrical note—an abrupt change of tone that is simultaneously the poem's first real moment of direct address. This moment might be regarded as another instance of self-fictionalization, an act of self-aggrandizement that hijacks the authority of a centuries-long tradition to position this speaker, maligned though he may be, as the divine emissary of the mob. Viewed from another angle, however, the line underlines the provisional nature of the speaker's status, which depends on the will of the crowd. This crowd is addressed via a statement that simultaneously endows them with the power of speech. It is they who have named the speaker prophet—just as it is their "last judgment," as the next line implies, who can take it away. "I" and "you" exist only in relation to one another, as the line's striking dash makes graphically clear.

Mayakovsky's invocation of the poet-prophet in this poem is not unique. Anxiety about the status of the poet during this period was often articulated in these terms, particularly via reference to Pushkin's well-known poem "The Prophet." The poem had become closely associated with both poetry performance and an elevated notion of the Russian writer's mission following Dostoevsky's legendary recitation of the text at the Pushkin celebrations in 1880.[40] When Blok complains about the uninspiring quality of poetry readings at charity events in 1908, he compares these unfavorably with Pushkin's poem.[41] Mayakovsky himself frequently references this tradition, as in *Vladimir Mayakovsky* and even "But Could You?" whose original version includes the line "I read the summons of prophetic lips" (*Prochel ia zovy veshchikh gub*).[42] This trope appears in parodied form in "Me Again," with the speaker's "half-chewed shout" perhaps intended to approximate the best sound that Pushkin's original prophet—whose tongue is ripped out and who has a burning hot coal placed in his chest—might, in fact, have hoped to make. If we can also read this "half-chewed shout" as a reference to the *zaum'* language that was the Futurists' most notorious trademark (though not employed by Mayakovsky himself), this sly comment is further extended, positioning the Futurists—who, we recall, many felt were threatening to "turn poetry into nothing"—as the rightful and inevitable heirs of the very Pushkin they had thrown off the steamship of modernity.[43]

More provocatively, at least from the point of view of modernist attitudes, the speaker's alignment with prostitutes in this poem positions the poet-prophet within the context of the commercial theater and the *café chantant*—both of which modernists viewed with distaste as "a form of prostitution." This accusation, borrowed from Nietzsche and Wagner, combined with other fears around sexual pollution to create a potent symbol of the dangers inherent in the commercialization of art.[44] Identifying himself as the voice of the prostitutes, the speaker in Mayakovsky's poem points to the hypocrisy of this position, which obscured modernists' active participation in the commercial market they affected to despise. More than this, it showcases the new model of authority that Mayakovsky's poetry of this period proposes. The poet-prophet is now the intermediary between the prostitutes and God; he must negotiate the commercial world into which he has fallen. Accepting this position, the speaker acknowledges his own ordinariness: if the word is made flesh, then all flesh might be the word. By the same token, any member of the audience—or all of them—has an equal claim to the position of poet.

The disorienting series of shifts in "Me Again" and the stratification of emotional response they induce reflect the newly fluid relationship between poets and their audiences. This provides one key to understanding the new title under which the second redaction appeared, "But Still" ("A vse-taki"). Hovering somewhere between discourse connective and contrastive conjunction, this title points to the poem's underlying concern with the interstices between utterance, speaker, and hearer, and models the constant modifications of response that the poem demands and implicitly identifies as central to poetry as communicative—as well as commercial—exchange.

LISTEN!! DISSEMINATING VOICE

Modernist anxiety about commercialization and its challenge to poetic authority was in some sense merely an extension of concerns that had existed since at least the Romantic era, when the shift from the patronage system made writers increasingly dependent upon success in the literary marketplace, and the wider availability of print meant that writers "spoke" to ever more distant audiences. Mayakovsky responded to rapid urbanization and the growth of the urban entertainment industry not by lamenting the poet's loss of cultural authority or by attempting to shore it up. Rather, as we have seen, his poetry of the early 1910s celebrated the multiplicity and flexibility of roles that were the result of the cultural marketplace, its anonymous masses, and an increasingly mediatized entertainment sphere. This final section of the chapter turns back to consider the implications of this new attitude for Mayakovsky's understanding of poetic voice and communication in verse.

Many of Mayakovsky's poems of these years stage moments of failed or miscommunication. This often involves a confrontation between the speaker and an uncomprehending crowd—whether in the poem or implied as its addressee. "To You!" ("Vam!" 1915), a poem so offensive that it led to the closure of the Stray Dog by the authorities, is a prime example. This poetic stance overturned earlier models of poetic communication as an intimate dialogue between the speaker and his chosen addressee. In Mayakovsky's poetry, we find instead a communicative model that has more in common with *dissemination.*

The clash between dialogue and dissemination encapsulates the contests around authority and control over communication that are the inevitable corollary of shifts in the media landscape. While dialogue is "specifically addressed and reciprocal in form," the media scholar John Durham Peters points out, dissemination is "indifferent to the receiver's person and one-way in form." [45] Whereas dialogue usually implies a communicative situation based upon some kind of (physical) presence and relies upon mutual understanding and exchange, dissemination is not predicated upon a response. Like the printed word, it is indiscriminate, unconcernedly addressing myriad potential listeners rather than one specially selected interlocutor.[46] Mayakovsky's enthusiasm about technologies such as the radio "as medi[a] through which the poet can converse with listeners" is emblematic of the change in orientation his poetry proposed.[47]

The conflict between dialogue and dissemination is dramatized in "Listen!" a poem written in 1914 and published in the *First Journal of Russian Futurists*:

Послушайте!

Ведь если звезды зажигают
Значит это кому нибудь нужно?
Значит кто то хочет чтобы они были?
Значит кто то называет эти плевочки жемчужиной
И надрываясь в мятелях полуденной пыли
Торопится на небо боится что опоздал

Плачет и целует жилистую руку
И просит чтоб обязательно была звезда
Клянется что не перенесет эту беззвездную муку
А после ходит тревожный и
Спокойный наружно
И говорит кому то ведь теперь тебе ничего не страшно

Да?
Послушайте?!

Ведь если звезды зажигают
Значит это кому нибудь нужно
Значит это необходимо чтобы каждый вечер над
крышами
загоралась хоть одна звезда![48]

Listen!

I mean if stars are lit
Does that mean somebody needs it to be that way?
Does that mean someone wants them there?
That means someone calls those spitballs pearls
And sobbing in storms of midday dust
Rushes to the sky fears he's late
Cries and kisses the veiny hand
And asks that there definitely be a star
Swears that he won't survive this starless torture
And afterwards goes agitated and
Superficially calm
And says to someone I mean you're ok now not afraid

Right?
Will you listen?!

I mean if stars are lit
that means somebody needs it to be that way
That means it's absolutely necessary that every evening over
the rooftops
at least one star lights up!

The poem's imperative title is followed by a series of questions ("If stars are lit / does that mean somebody needs it to be that way? / Does that mean someone wants them there?). Critical accounts of the poem demonstrate a surprising readiness to take these questions at face value, both thematically (it is a reflection on "[the poet's] experience with the thought of a starless night" that expresses his "sense of worried wonder about the origin of the world") and tonally (with reference to its fabric of "alarmed questions and agitated, half-spoken thoughts").[49] Yet, as the poem's title already implies, what is at stake here is not so much the presence or absence of stars as the status of poetic communication and the receptiveness of the audience upon which it relies.

Like "Me Again," "Listen!" appears to explicitly invoke Symbolist culture. Stars featured prominently in numerous Symbolist publications, including Viacheslav Ivanov's 1903 collection of verse *Pilot Stars: A Book of Lyric Poetry* (*Kormchie zvezdy: Kniga liriki*) and his 1909 essay collection *By the Stars* (*Po zvezdam*), as well as in the names of Symbolist institutions: the constellations that gave names to the Symbolist journal *Libra* (*Vesy*) and the publishing house Scorpio (Skorpion), for instance. Symbolists made frequent reference in their critical and philosophical writings to Pythagorean teachings about world harmony and the "night-time music of the stars."[50] This original "concert," Leo Spitzer writes, "was no performance on a narrow stage, to be witnessed by an audience of neutral observers. It was a song in praise of God, uttered by nightly-ordered nature, and by the human community serving as an echo."[51] For Blok, it was the job of the poet to communicate this harmony on earth—a daunting task, as the anxiety of Mayakovsky's speaker as he rushes between God and the earth suggests. Another common trope during this period was fear of stars (or "starry terror" [*zvezdnyi uzhas*], to borrow Bely's phrase), which reflected "widespread fears of cosmic catastrophes and a new wave of apocalyptic expectations."[52] "Astraphobia"—originally a term denoting fear of storms but turned by the popular imaginary into a term meaning fear of stars—was even added to lists of neurological disorders; associated with endlessness and eternity, stars were regarded as a cause of agoraphobia and neurasthenia more generally.[53]

The speaker in Mayakovsky's poem fears not the stars themselves but their absence. Nonetheless, his extreme agitation suggests that Mayakovsky may have "starry terror" and its popular association with neurological disturbance in mind. It is not just the starry content of Symbolist poetry that he targets, however. The agitation of the speaker in Mayakovsky's poem draws our attention to the basic assumption upon which poetic communication had hitherto been founded. Oriented toward an insular moment of poetic communion between poetic speaker and mute listener, poetry traditionally operates according to the non-interactive mode of what Jonathan Culler identifies as one typical mode of poetic address, apostrophe.[54] Apparently directed toward an absent or inanimate addressee (an urn, say, or the west wind), Culler argues, apostrophic address is in fact always a performance for the benefit of a third party who is very much *present* as reader or listener. Obsessively—even excessively—interactive in mode, Mayakovsky's poem and its hypersensitive speaker draw attention to this truth: the poem is not a private dialogue but an ostentatious display.

In this sense, Mayakovsky's larger-than-life persona simply represents an exaggerated version of the stance adopted by all poets. In amplifying this aspect of poetic communication, however, Mayakovsky also subverts it: openly acknowledging the third party that is the poem's true addressee, he dispenses with any notion of poetry as intimate dialogue. The new orientation his poetry instead proposes is indicated already by the volume of Mayakovsky's physical voice, which, in stark contrast with the almost inaudible tones of a poet such as Blok, drew comparisons from contemporaries with anything from a "loudspeaker" to "the din of factory machinery."[55] This was poetry written for performance in public and recited for the benefit of whoever was willing to pay the entrance fee or even just happened to wander by—poetry for dissemination.

As John Durham Peters has argued, the ultimate "disseminator" is Jesus, who, like other prophets before him, scatters his parables over the ground in full knowledge of the fact that some of these seeds will not germinate.[56] In this sense, the turn to dissemination shifts attention from the authority of the speaker to the attentiveness of the audience. In "Listen!" despite the emphasis placed on speaking, it is hard to tell who is actually the source of its various statements. Does the "listen!" of the title, for example, come from the same mouth as the "listen?!" repeated later in the text? Possibly so. This reading is by no means the definitive one, however. Much depends on how we understand its tone: are we to take the poem's questions seriously, as the earnest speech of the poem's author? Or does the poem make fun of its speaker, adopting a verbal mask in the manner of *skaz* narration? In the latter case, the title might equally be read as a playful reference to the live performance situation, an exhortation to the audience to listen to the poem that follows; or as a mocking echo of the desperate plea embedded in the text.

Leaving all these possibilities open, the poem and its resolutely protean tone dramatize the lack of control that the disseminator has over the reception of his poetry. Just like his biblical counterpart, this poet-prophet speaks to an audience that may or may not listen—an audience that might interpret his words one way, or the other. In much the same way, Mayakovsky's *lesenka* layout and other aspects of the printed text can suggest how the poem should be read aloud but not control it entirely.[57] Indeed, the *lesenka* encapsulates the attitude toward voice I have been trying to describe here: rather than resisting mechanical reproduction and defending the unique authority of the author, Mayakovsky embraces the multiple singular lives that the poetic text leads, both on the page and off. If his egotistical poetic persona and his distinctive speaking voice have led to an emphasis on the self-aggrandizing aspects of his poetic practice, these qualities in fact form part of a wide-ranging exploration of what it means to be the author of a poem in a mediatized age.

Conclusion

THIS BOOK HAS BEEN concerned with modernist efforts to identify and describe the strange matter of poetry. For this reason, I have avoided lengthy discussion of particular print editions, graphic or visual designs, and of specific recordings of poetry being recited, preferring instead to highlight how modernist culture framed poetry as a material phenomenon in its own right. The medium of poetry was not ordinary, practical language but "poetic" language, the Formalists famously argued; but what remained to be determined was the material medium of that language, the specific qualities of poetry itself as medium.

To focus on poetry as a distinct medium clearly runs the risk of rehashing the essentialism of outdated theories of modernism such as that proposed by Greenberg. As I hope to have shown, however, interest in the specific qualities of the individual medium need not be synonymous with monomediality or media purity. In the case of Russian modernism, such discussions emerged from a culture of intermedial experimentation and exchange and articulated the specific qualities of poetry in terms of the indeterminacy of its material limits; poetry was understood to be an inherently mixed medium, one that inhabits multiple material strata, from spoken word to printed text and recorded sound.

Medium is itself an inherently indeterminate concept. Although typically used in contexts that imply some concrete set of material constraints, the term ultimately refers only to a theoretical construct, what Sybille Krämer calls a "theoretical abstraction" (*Abstraktionsleistung*).[1] As Rajewsky writes, "in dealing with medial configurations, we never encounter 'the medium' as such . . . but only specific individual films, individual texts, and so on."[2] Highlighting the importance of creative and theoretical engagement with concrete examples for the work of the modernists considered here, I have sought to push back against the charge of excessive abstraction so often leveled against Russian Formalism and to show that any universal laws that these theorists did derive were conceived on the basis of encounters with specific texts. These laws were, moreover, fundamentally informed by the heightened sensitivity to the constructed character of poetry as medium that was so characteristic of this era, to which the explicitly media-historical terms in which they were so often framed attest.

My larger goal in asking how these figures thought about poetry as medium has been to provide an answer to the perennial question of how to define and understand modernism itself. A conclusive account of this movement remains elusive, undermined in no small part by the slipperiness of its central term: does "modernism" name a particular period of time, a specific mode of representation, a particular collection of connected cultural artifacts, or a certain attitude—a way of being and perceiving, or, as T. J. Clark has suggested, a particular kind of hope?[3] If this book has not offered a definitive account, it is in part because the new understanding of poetry as medium I have been describing demonstrates once again the complex interaction of all of these factors in modernism conceived as a dynamic cultural milieu. The particular understanding of poetry and its material qualities that emerged in late imperial and early Soviet Russia was fundamentally shaped by this historical and cultural context, the processes of technological change then in motion, and poetry's position in the media landscape of the time. It also flowed from modernist hopes and aspirations regarding poetry's potential as a transformative tool for social change. The most significant shift in conceptions of poetry during the period I have considered here was not the turn to statistical analysis but the notion that the formal analysis of verse should take place, to borrow one media theorist's analogy, "in the ablative case"—that it should examine poetry as a set of formal, technical qualities "*by means of which*" concrete things could be achieved.[4]

I end my discussion with some brief thoughts on how this account of modernism changes when we view it in the terms proposed by more recent attempts to define it as a "planetary" phenomenon. As Susan Stanford Friedman and others have argued convincingly, inherited notions of modernism that identify the movement with a narrow set of artists and the work they produced in western Europe and North America in the late nineteenth and early twentieth centuries are based on a flawed binary of center and periphery. According to this model, modernism was pioneered in the West before being copied by the "rest."[5] Friedman rejects this diffusionist ideology in favour of a planetary approach to a phenomenon that she argues should be defined simply as "the *expressive dimension of modernity*" (Friedman's emphasis), whenever and wherever it is experienced.[6] Viewed from this perspective, modernism is inherently multiple—a polycentric phenomenon that takes different forms in dialogue with the distinct modernities it inhabits.

The scale of Friedman's argument is very different from my own. I have followed scholars such as Livak, who proposes that Russian modernism is best thought of as a community, a minority culture created by a network of people and practices active in a particular time and place (albeit one that came to span multiple countries following the 1917 revolution and ensuing mass emigration).[7] To put this in Friedman's terms, "Russian modernism" names the distinctive set of responses to modernity as experienced by a small set of the cultural elite in the capital cities of late imperial and early Soviet Russia. Acknowledging the limitations of the present study—which restricts its view not just to the already narrow sphere of Russian modernist culture, but to a select group of poets and theorists working within that culture—I would nonetheless like to suggest that it also offers a planetary answer to the question at its heart. What was "modernist" about Russian modernist poetry and theory was a factor not only of its response to the particular conditions in which it developed but also the way these figures conceived of form, a term that I have intentionally been avoiding but to which I now return.

Form occupies a prominent position in debates about world literature and interactions between the local and the global. Caroline Levine, for instance, argues that "precisely because they are abstract organizing principles, shapes and patterns are iterable . . . They can be picked up and moved to new contexts."[8] So, too, Franco Moretti finds that "form is . . . the repeatable element of literature."[9] One effect of framing world literature in these terms is that poetry tends to be neglected: since world literature is so often read in translation, and since poetic form is more closely tied up with linguistic specificity (the count of syllables, and so forth), prose literature has appeared more suited to analysis of the multiple linguistic contexts in which the original text comes to circulate. It is on this basis that Tihanov positions Shklovsky as a precursor to modern discourses of world literature. Unlike Jakobson, who tended to work with poetry in its original language, Shklovsky more often than not worked with translations of prose texts. This reflects their opposed interpretations of the key Formalist concept, "literariness," which for Jakobson was located at the linguistic level but which Shklovsky understood as primarily a matter of structure and composition. Only in this latter sense, Tihanov argues, does literariness become portable like form, a quality that can be transposed largely unchanged from one linguistic context to another.[10]

Another corollary of this framing of world literature, Jahan Ramazani points out, is that "one of the most pervasive models for 'world' and 'global' literature has been the formula *foreign form and local content*."[11] According to this model, the "abstractive formal dimensions of a text are almost entirely associated with the Western metropole," while the "peripheries" provide "raw materials."[12] This view perpetuates the imbalance that Friedman's work seeks to correct. As she writes, "the West, for Moretti, is the site of discursive creation, while the non-West is 'local materials,' a center/periphery binary that ignores the often-long histories of aesthetic production among the colonized."[13] Or, in Ramazani's pithy phrase, "doesn't the rest of the world have any 'patterns' of its own?"[14]

In this view, poetry may actually be the best way into a global literary tradition, since it exists in a world understood as "a profoundly uneven totality" made up of "multiply differentiated space-times" that coexist.[15] And indeed, as Ramazani has so brilliantly shown, the notion that poetry is "the most provincial of the arts," in W. H. Auden's phrase—uniquely local in its attachment to the poet's homeland and mother tongue, particularly when compared with the mobility of modern digital media—obscures the many intersecting currents that have shaped modern poetic traditions around the world.[16]

Russian modernist poetry illustrates this dynamic well. Modernists of all stripes relied heavily on translation from French and other European languages, particularly in the earliest days.[17] Creative adaptation of these models played a crucial role in shaping its aesthetic. As we saw in the chapters on rhythm, however, these adaptations were informed by local conditions. The particular direction in which Russian modernist versification developed was influenced not only by forms imported from the West, but also by a number of local factors, including the relative youth of syllabotonic verse in Russia; the growing interest in folk forms; and the norms established by nineteenth-century predecessors. Experiments in this area were also shaped by the changing material conditions of modern life in the city and technological advances, as well as by cultural factors such as ongoing efforts to excavate and reclaim (or, occasionally, invent) a "native antiquity," as Irina Shevelenko and others have described.[18] These factors also impacted the study of versification, which was shaped by philological interest in the oral genres of folklore and the mechanisms through which the elements of such genres come to form a local tradition (*predanie*), to borrow Veselovsky's term.[19]

At the same time, Russian modernists wanted to make claims about the universal qualities of poetic language, and turned to a markedly international set of concepts in order to do so. Free from the restrictions of syllable count or rhyme, the concepts discussed in this book proved much more portable than specific formal structures such as the alexandrine or fixed poetic forms such as the sonnet, the ghazal, or the tanka. Debates about rhythm, image, and voice turned on broadly similar issues in Russian, western European, and Anglo-American contexts, despite considerable local divergence as far as developments in the formal organization of poetry are concerned. If these debates took on particular local inflections and led to conclusions that differed in certain crucial respects, they nonetheless shared an awareness of the inherent contingency of these conclusions—a sense of mutability and change that, as we saw in the Russian context, often became part of the definition of these terms. The widespread interest in these concepts and others like them during this period registers, moreover, a broader shift in thinking about poetic form, which was increasingly viewed not as a set of restrictive shapes or patterns but in the relational terms suggested by rhythm, image, and voice—as impulse, mode, or attitude.

Whether Russian modernist poetry combined foreign form with local content or vice versa is thus an open question. What is clear is that a binary model is not particularly useful here, since it fails to account for the multiple and multiplying transformations that occur when foreign and local forms or themes collide, interact, and coincide. These competing tendencies recall the tension between transnational aesthetics and nationalism that has been identified as a feature of modernist artistic production more broadly, so often characterized by a "particular mixture of radicalism and patriotism, of a worldly international outlook and a violently nationalist faith."[20] As Harsha Ram comments in this connection, understanding global modernism may be a case not of resolving these contradictions but simply of learning to recognize and identify the interplay of multiple scales that they express, from the imperial to the national, regional, and local.[21]

Applied to the narrower question of form, a similar logic suggests one solution to the ongoing dispute between formalist and historicist approaches regarding the relationship between literary form and historical or sociopolitical concerns. Pushing back against the perception that formalist studies neglect these broader issues, scholars such as Levine have been keen to emphasize the relevance of the study of literary form for grappling with them, a relationship that she and others locate on the level of analogy: by attending carefully to literary form, we learn to recognize the formal structures that organize the social and political world at large.[22] What Friedman, Ramazani, and others highlight is that we need not reach for parallels of this sort to demonstrate the profound interconnections between form and sociopolitical life. Literary form is itself always embedded in its historical moment and shaped by the "geography of mobility and interculturality" to which the conditions of modernity give rise.[23] Close reading has an inherently planetary dimension, in this sense.

None of this was lost on the modernists themselves. Awareness of these clashing forces and scales crucially informed the view of poetry as medium that I have tried to describe. Investigating rhythm, Bely, Tynianov, and Blok sought to move beyond static, foot-based conceptions of metrics and scansion and instead viewed rhythm in relation to a mobile set of contexts, one not limited to the individual line or poem, the poetic cycle, book, or canon, but also including the printed page and the spoken or recorded word and the overlapping temporalities brought into dialogue by these multiple frames. Debates about the image, similarly, explored the interface between material of the text and material of the world, asking not how poetry captures or mimics the world but how it brings distinct spheres into transformative contact. Finally, poetic voice became one focus for thinking through the tensions that were amplified by new technologies for the reproduction of sound and the mediatization of culture more broadly, in particular poetry's ability to straddle singularity and multiplicity, the intimate encounter and the public stage. Returning repeatedly to the multiple borders across which poetry asks or enables us to move, modernists sought to describe the specific qualities of poetry as medium because it was only through such description that its relationship with a wider context could be understood. The theoretical positions that emerged were also importantly shaped by this (global, mediatized) context and its conflicting demands. Viewed from this angle, the seemingly opposed interpretations of literariness identified by Tihanov demonstrate simply the multiple scales across which modernism operated, from the "territorial logic of the nation-state" (Jakobson's linguistically specific model) to the "deterritorializing logic of market exchange" (Shklovsky's translational mode), from cultural specificity to universalizing frameworks.[24]

The difficulty in defining modernism lies not in the variety of aesthetics or styles associated with the movement both across and within geographical contexts so much as in its own refusal of fixed positions. Rather than novelty or shock, the work of the poets and theorists considered in this book is characterized by its heightened sensitivity to the dynamic nature of tradition and the porousness of poetry, conceived in terms of its interaction as medium with multiple spheres. This way of thinking about poetry is open and nodal, relational in much the same way as Friedman suggests modernism itself is best understood.

Notes

INTRODUCTION

1. Following this initial publication, the poem was reprinted in numerous places, including Kruchenykh and Khlebnikov's manifesto, "The Word as Such" ("Slovo kak takovoe"). For facsimiles of the poem and discussion, see Gerald Janecek, *Zaum: The Transrational Language of Russian Futurism* (San Diego, CA: San Diego State University Press, 1996); Gerald Janecek, "Kruchenykh contra Gutenberg," in *The Russian Avant-Garde Book: 1910–1934*, ed. Margit Rowell and Deborah Wye (New York: Museum of Modern Art, 2002), 41–49; and Marjorie Perloff, *The Futurist Moment: Avant-Garde, Avant Guerre, and the Language of Rupture* (Chicago: University of Chicago Press, 1986), 121–26.

2. Valerii Briusov, "Novye techeniia v russkoi poezii: Futuristy," *Russkaia mysl'* 3 (1913): 129.

3. Vadim Shershenevich, *Futurizm bez maski* (Moscow: Tipografiia "Moskovskoe Izdatel'stvo," 1913), 74.

4. M. Rossiianskii (L. Zak) [1913], "Perchatka kubofuturistam," in *Russian Futurism: A History*, by Vladimir Markov (Berkeley: University of California Press, 1968), 90.

5. Perloff, *The Futurist Moment*, 124.

6. The most exhaustive accounts are found in Janecek, *Zaum*, 49–70; and N. Å. Nilsson, "Kručenych's Poem 'Dyr bul ščyl,'" *Scando-Slavica* 24 (1978): 139–48.

7. Nilsson, "Kručenych's Poem 'Dyr bul ščyl,'" 143–45.

8. Janecek, *Zaum*, 62.

9. Iurii Tynianov, "Valerii Briusov," in *Problema stikhotvornogo iazyka*, by Iurii Tynianov (Moscow: Sovetskii pisatel', 1965), 265.

10. For discussion of these and related issues, see Thomas H. Ford, "Poetry's Media," *New Literary History* 44, no. 3 (2013): 449–69.

11. Clement Greenberg, "Avant-Garde and Kitsch," *Partisan Review* 6, no. 5 (Fall 1939): 34–49; and Clement Greenberg, "Towards a Newer Laocoön," *Partisan Review* 7, no. 4 (July–August 1940): 296–310.

12. For useful overviews of this tendency and associated critiques, see Douglas Mao and Rebecca L. Walkowitz, "The New Modernist Studies," *PMLA* 123, no. 3 (2008): 737–48; Eric Hayot and Rebecca L. Walkowitz, eds., *A New Vocabulary for Global Modernism* (New York: Columbia University Press, 2016); and Cara L. Lewis, *Dynamic Form: How Intermediality Made Modernism* (Ithaca, NY: Cornell University Press, 2020), 3–11. A cogent account of new modernist studies in relation to paths forward for scholars of Russian modernism can be found in Leonid Livak, *In Search of Russian Modernism* (Baltimore, MD: Johns Hopkins University Press, 2018).

13. Ilya Kliger and Boris Maslov, "Introducing Historical Poetics," in *Persistent Forms: Explorations in Historical Poetics*, ed. Ilya Kliger and Boris Maslov (New York: Fordham University Press, 2015), 13. See also Jessica Merrill, *The Origins of Russian Literary Theory: Folklore, Philology, Form* (Evanston, IL: Northwestern University Press, 2021); Ilona Svetlikova, *Istoki russkogo formalizma: Traditsiia psikhologizma i formal'naia shkola* (Moscow: Novoe literaturnoe obozrenie, 2005); and Galin Tihanov, *The Birth and Death of Literary Theory: Regimes of Relevance in Russia and Beyond* (Stanford, CA: Stanford University Press, 2019).

14. Serguei Oushakine, "'Ne vzletevshie samolety mechty': O pokolenii formal'nogo metoda," in *Formal'nyi metod: Antologiia russkogo modernizma*, ed. Serguei Oushakine, 3 vols. (Moscow: Kabinetnyi uchenyi, 2016), 1:35. The poets at the center of this study have occasionally been discussed as contrasting pairs. See, for example, Boris Eikhenbaum's comments regarding Vladimir Mayakovsky's influence on Alexander Blok in "Trubnyi glas," *Knizhnyi ugol* 1 (1918): 3–5; Marina Tsvetaeva's essay comparing Mayakovsky and Boris Pasternak, "Epos i lirika sovremennoi Rossii (Vladimir Maiakovskii i Boris Pasternak)," *Novyi grad* 6 (1933): 28–41; or Roman Jakobson's comments on Mayakovsky in "Randbemerkungen zur Proza des Dichters Pasternak," *Slavische Rundschau* 7 (1935): 357–74.

15. For a thorough commentary on these and other, similar terms, see Livak, *In Search of Russian Modernism*, 38–56. The term "modernism" was first applied in a positive sense to literature in Central America, where a "new spirit . . . the spirit of modernism [*el modernismo*]" was hailed as early as 1890. Harsha Ram, "The Scale of Global Modernisms: Imperial, National, Regional, Local," *PMLA* 131, no. 5 (October 2016): 1375.

16. On earlier iterations of this stance and the "quarrel of the Ancients and the Moderns," see Matei Calinescu, *Five Faces of Modernity: Modernism, Avant-Garde, Decadence, Kitsch, Postmodernism* (Durham, NC: Duke University Press, 1987).

17. Ewa M. Thompson, *Russian Formalism and Anglo-American New Criticism: A Comparative Study* (The Hague: Mouton, 1971), 73.

18. Harsha Ram, "The Sonnet and the Mukhambazi: Genre Wars on the

Edges of the Russian Empire," *PMLA* 122, no. 5 (October 2007): 1557. On the latter, see Irina Shevelenko, *Modernizm kak arkhaizm: Natsionalizm i poiski modernistskoi estetiki v Rossii* (Moscow: Novoe literaturnoe obozrenie, 2017).

19. Susan Stanford Friedman, *Planetary Modernisms: Provocations on Modernity across Time* (New York: Columbia University Press, 2015), 33, my emphasis.

20. Marshall McLuhan, *Understanding Media: The Extensions of Man* (New York: McGraw-Hill, 1964), 19.

21. Jay David Bolter and Richard Grusin, *Remediation: Understanding New Media* (Cambridge, MA: MIT Press, 2000), 65.

22. Bolter and Grusin, *Remediation*, 15.

23. As they summarize elsewhere in the same volume, "hypermedia and transparent media are opposite manifestations of the same desire: the desire to get past the limits of representation and to achieve the real." Bolter and Grusin, *Remediation*, 53.

24. Bolter and Grusin, *Remediation*, 19.

25. John Guillory, "Genesis of the Media Concept," *Critical Inquiry* 36, no. 2 (Winter 2010): 324.

26. Clement Greenberg, "On Abstract Painting," in *Clement Greenberg: The Collected Essays and Criticism*, ed. John O'Brian, 4 vols. (Chicago: University of Chicago Press, 1986), 1:203.

27. Clement Greenberg, "Modernist Painting" (1965), in *Modern Art and Modernism: A Critical Anthology*, ed. Francis Frascina and Charles Harrison (New York: Westview, 1982), 5.

28. Bolter and Grusin, *Remediation*, 38.

29. Michael Fried, "How Modernism Works: A Response to T. J. Clark," in *The Politics of Interpretation*, ed. W. J. T. Mitchell (Chicago: University of Chicago Press, 1983), 227.

30. Bolter and Grusin, *Remediation*, 65.

31. Craig Dworkin, *No Medium* (Cambridge, MA: MIT Press, 2013), 32.

32. Bely's studies were not the first of their kind, nor even the most popular; I focus on them here because of their importance for later theorists. See E. I. Orlova, "'Mezh konturom i zapakhom tsvetka' (Iz istorii metodologicheskikh iskanii 1910-kh godov)," *Voprosy literatury* 4 (2002): 136–69.

33. Exceptions to this rule tend to focus on the relationship between poetry and contemporary media discourses. See, for example, Marjorie Perloff, *Radical Artifice: Writing Poetry in the Age of Media* (Chicago: University of Chicago Press, 1991).

34. Johann Joachim Winckelmann, "On the Imitation of the Painting and Sculpture of the Greeks" (1755), in Johann Joachim Winckelmann, *Writings on Art*, ed. David Irwin (London: Phaidon, 1972), 61–85.

35. See, for example, Lars Elleström, "The Modalities of Media: A Model

for Understanding Intermedial Relations," in *Media Borders, Multimodality and Intermediality*, ed. Lars Elleström (Basingstoke, UK: Palgrave Macmillan, 2010), 11–50; W. J. T. Mitchell, "There Are No Visual Media," *Journal of Visual Culture* 4, no. 2 (August 2005): 257–66; and W. J. T. Mitchell and Mark B. N. Hansen, "Time and Space," in *Critical Terms for Media Studies*, ed. W. J. T. Mitchell and Mark B. N. Hansen (Chicago: University of Chicago Press, 2010), 101–16.

36. Cecilia Sjöholm, "Lessing's Laocoon: Aesthetics, Affects and Embodiment," *Nordic Journal of Aesthetics*, no. 46 (2013): 18–34.

37. Greenberg, "Avant Garde and Kitsch," 37.

38. For an overview of these trends, see I. V. Koretskaia, "Literatura v krugu iskusstv," in *Russkaia literatura rubezha vekov (1890-e—nachalo 1920-x godov)*, ed. V. A. Keldysh, 2 vols. (Moscow: IMLI RAN, 2001), 1:131–90. See also the essays collected in Catriona Kelly and Stephen Lovell, eds., *Russian Literature, Modernism and the Visual Arts* (Cambridge: Cambridge University Press, 2000).

39. McLuhan, *Understanding Media*, 60.

40. Ford, "Poetry's Media," 457.

41. Mark Goble, *Beautiful Circuits: Modernism and the Mediated Life* (New York: Columbia University Press, 2010), 10. See also the discussion in Lewis, *Dynamic Form*, 1–17.

42. Cleanth Brooks, *The Well-Wrought Urn* (New York: Harcourt Brace, 1947), 198.

43. Anna Kornbluh, *The Order of Forms: Realism, Formalism, and Social Space* (Chicago: University of Chicago Press, 2019), 3.

44. For one example, see the essays collected in Susan J. Wolfson and Marshall Brown, eds., *Reading for Form* (Seattle: University of Washington Press, 2006).

45. Caroline Levine, *Forms: Whole, Rhythm, Hierarchy, Network* (Princeton, NJ: Princeton University Press, 2015).

46. Levine, *Forms*, 47, 150.

47. Kornbluh, *The Order of Forms*, 6.

48. Austin Warren and René Wellek, *Theory of Literature* (New York: Harcourt, Brace, 1949).

49. Merrill, *Origins of Russian Literary Theory*, 219; Levine, *Forms*, 18.

50. For a detailed discussion of differences, see Thompson, *Russian Formalism and Anglo-American New Criticism*.

51. The classic accounts of Russian Formalism and its origins are provided in Victor Erlich, *Russian Formalism: History—Doctrine* (The Hague: Mouton, 1955); Aage Hansen-Löve, *Russkii formalizm: Metodologicheskaia rekonstruktsiia razvitiia na osnove printsipa ostraneniia*, trans. S. A. Romashko (Moscow: Iazyki russkoi kul'tury, 2001); and Peter Steiner, *Russian Formalism: A Metapoetics* (Ithaca, NY: Cornell University Press, 1984). Examples of more recent accounts include Merrill, *Origins of Russian Literary Theory*; Svetlikova, *Istoki russkogo formalizma*; and Tihanov, *Birth and Death of Literary Theory*.

52. Merrill, *Origins of Russian Literary Theory*, 33.

53. Roman Jakobson, "Noveishaia russkaia poeziia," in Roman Jakobson, *Selected Writings, Volume 5: On Verse, Its Masters and Explorers*, ed. Stephen Rudy and Martha Taylor (Amsterdam: De Gruyter, Mouton, 1979), 305.

54. Merrill, *Origins of Russian Literary Theory*, 221.

55. Merrill, *Origins of Russian Literary Theory*, 223.

56. Oushakine, "Ne vzletevshie samolety mechty," 12–13.

57. Galin Tihanov, "Why Did Modern Literary Theory Originate in Central and Eastern Europe? (And Why Is It Now Dead?)," *Common Knowledge* 10, no. 1 (2004): 61–81; Jakobson, "Noveishaia russkaia poeziia," 305.

58. Merrill, *Origins of Russian Literary Theory*; Svetlikova, *Istoki russkogo formalizma*; Ian Levchenko and Igor' Pil'shchikov, eds., *Epokha "ostraneniia": Russkii formalizm i sovremennoe gumanitarnoe znanie: Kollektivnaia monografia* (Moscow: Novoe literaturnoe obozrenie, 2017).

59. Merrill, *Origins of Russian Literary Theory*, 6.

60. In-depth studies tend to restrict their focus to intersections with individual poets or periods. See, for example, V. V. Ivanov, "Pasternak i OPOIAZ (K postanovke voprosa)," *Tynianovskii sbornik* 3 (1988): 70–83; R. D. Timenchik, "Tynianov i 'literaturnaia kul'tura' 1910-kh godov," *Tynianovskii sbornik* 3 (1988): 159–73; and E. A. Toddes, "Mandel'shtam i opoiazovskaia filologiia," *Tynianovskii sbornik* 2 (1986): 78–102.

61. Tihanov, *Birth and Death of Literary Theory*, 19. This argument is advanced at most length in Krystyna Pomorska, Russian Formalist Theory and Its Poetic Ambiance (The Hague: Mouton, 1968). Links with Futurism are also discussed in Erlich, *Russian Formalism*; Hansen-Löve, *Russkii formalizm*; and Steiner, *Russian Formalism.*

62. Tihanov, *Birth and Death of Literary Theory*, 19.

63. Viktor Shklovsky, *Literature and Cinematography* (1923), trans. Irina Masinovsky (Champaign, IL: Dalkey Archive, 2008), 27.

64. Tihanov, *Birth and Death of Literary Theory*, 31–32.

65. Osip Brik, "The So-Called Formal Method," trans. Ann Shukman, in *Formalist Theory*, ed. L. O'Toole and A. Shukman (Colchester, UK: Holdman Books, 1977), 90–91.

66. When Viktor Shklovsky opposed "counting," he was, in this sense, in fact on Bely's side: his objection was to the "algebraic way of thinking" that he blamed for automatized perception—as a result of which, he argued, "we do not see [things] but recognize them by their initial features . . . Perceived in this way, the thing dries up." Viktor Shklovskii, "Iskusstvo kak priem," in *O teorii prozy*, by Viktor Shklovskii (Moscow: Federatsiia, 1929), 12. Translation cited from Alexandra Berlina, *Viktor Shklovsky: A Reader* (London: Bloomsbury, 2016), 79.

67. V. V. Polonskii, *Mezhdu traditsiei i modernizmom: Russkaia literatura*

rubezha XIX–XX vekov: Istoriia, poetika, kontekst (Moscow: IMLI RAN, 2011), 46; Steiner, *Russian Formalism*, 10.

CHAPTER ONE

1. See, for example, Jakobson, *Selected Writings*, 5:570; Boris Eikhenbaum, "Teoriia 'formal'nogo metoda,'" in *O literature*, by Boris Eikhenbaum (Moscow: Sovetskii pisatel', 1987), 378; and John Elsworth, *Andrei Bely: A Critical Study of the Novels* (Cambridge: Cambridge University Press, 1983).

2. I will use the Russian spelling of this title (*Simvolizm*) throughout the text to avoid confusion with Symbolism as a movement. For contemporary reviews, see A. V. Lavrov, ed., *Andrei Bely: Pro et contra* (St. Petersburg: Izdatel'stvo Russkogo Khristianskogo gumanitarnogo instituta, 2004).

3. See, for example, B. Griftsov, "Rets. na kn.: Andrei Belyi: *Simvolizm*," reprinted in Lavrov, *Andrei Bely: Pro et contra*, 319–22.

4. "Thus, the one destroying the other, two forces battle in A. Bely: the intuitive and the analytical . . . This battle explains the majority of the contradictions in [*Simvolizm*]." Griftsov, "*Simvolizm*," 321–22.

5. Steven Cassedy, "Bely the Thinker," in *Andrei Bely: Spirit of Symbolism*, ed. John E. Malmstad (Ithaca, NY: Cornell University Press, 1987), 320.

6. I omit discussion of Bely's later work on rhythm, given its inflection by Bely's turn to anthroposophy in 1912. See John Elsworth, "The Concept of Rhythm in Bely's Aesthetic Thought," in *Andrey Bely: Centenary Papers*, ed. Boris Christa (Amsterdam: Adolf M. Hakkert, 1980), 68–80.

7. Andrei Belyi, *Sobranie sochinenii*, 14 vols. (Moscow: Respublika, 1994–2014), 5:176–315. Unless indicated otherwise, subsequent references are to this edition of Bely's works, with the abbreviation *SS* and with volume and page numbers provided in parentheses in text.

8. W. J. T. Mitchell and Mark B. Hansen, "Introduction," in Mitchell and Hansen, *Critical Terms*, xxi.

9. For an account of the widespread sense of uncertainty that characterized this period in urban Russia, see Mark D. Steinberg, *Petersburg Fin de Siècle* (New Haven, CT: Yale University Press, 2011).

10. Shevelenko, *Modernizm kak arkhaizm*.

11. For more on Bely's dispute with the mystical anarchists, see A. V. Lavrov, *Andrei Belyi v 1900-e gody: Zhizn' i literaturnaia deiatel'nost'* (Moscow: Novoe literaturnoe obozrenie, 1995); and Bernice Glatzer Rosenthal, "The Transmutation of the Symbolist Ethos: Mystical Anarchism and the Revolution of 1905," *Slavic Review* 36, no. 4 (1977): 608–27.

12. A. Belyi, *Mezhdu dvukh revoliutsii*, ed. A. Lavrov (Moscow: Khudozhestvennaia literatura, 1990), 353.

13. V. F. Khodasevich, *Nekropol'*, in *Sobranie sochinenii*, by V. F. Khodasevich, 4 vols. (Moscow: Soglasie, 1996–97), 4:53.

14. Ilona Svetlikova, *The Moscow Pythagoreans: Mathematics, Mysticism, and Anti-Semitism in Russian Symbolism* (Basingstoke, UK: Palgrave Macmillan, 2013), 168.

15. Friedrich Nietzsche, *Sämtliche Werke: Kritische Studienausgabe*, ed. Giorgio Colli and Mazzino Montinari, 15 vols. (Berlin: Walter de Gruyter and Deutscher Taschenbuch, 1980), 7:38.

16. Valerii Briusov, "Otvet g. Andreevskomu," *Mir iskusstva* 1–6 (1901): 247.

17. Andrei Belyi, "Lirika i eksperiment," in Belyi, *Sobranie sochinenii*, 5:192. A translation of the essay can be found in Steven Cassedy, *Selected Essays of Andrei Bely* (Berkeley: University of California Press, 1985). Subsequent references to these editions of the essay will be provided in parentheses in text (Russian/English page numbers).

18. Zhirmunsky's view of the matter may be colored by Bely's work on rhythm in the period 1918–20. See Elsworth, "The Concept of Rhythm."

19. Lavrov, *Bely v 1900-e gody*, 265.

20. Andrei Bely, "K budushchemu uchebniku ritma," published as an appendix in S. S. Grechishkin and A. V. Lavrov, "O stikhovedcheskom nasledii Andreia Belogo," in *Struktura i semiotika khudozhestvennogo teksta: Trudy po znakovym sistemam XII* (Tartu, 1981), 119–29.

21. For a recent corrective to the idea that modernists rejected metrical convention in Anglophone literatures, see Ben Glaser, *Modernism's Metronome: Meter and Twentieth-Century Poetics* (Baltimore, MD: Johns Hopkins University Press, 2020).

22. Despite their later differences, the young Bely was much impressed and significantly influenced by Briusov's approach to versification. Both had been pupils of Lev Polivanov, who pioneered the application of elements of statistical analysis to modern Russian verse (the practice had been common for many years amongst classicists). See the discussion in T. Iu. Khmel'nitskaya, "Poeziia Andreia Belogo," in A. Belyi, *Stikhotvoreniia i poemy* (Moscow-Leningrad: Sovetskii pisatel', 1966), 5–66.

23. See Manfred Shruba, *Literaturnye ob"edineniia Moskvy i Peterburga 1890–1917 godov. Slovar'* (Moscow: Novoe literaturnoe obozrenie, 2004).

24. For further discussion, see Mikhail Gasparov, "Belyi-stikhoved i Belyi-stikhotvorets," in *Izbrannye stat'i: O stikhe. O stikhakh. O poetakh*, by Mikhail Gasparov (Moscow: Novoe literaturnoe obozrenie, 1995), 123–36.

25. I refer here to the totals listed in figure 3. I have counted only the first three rows for each poet, as it is not made clear whether subsequent rows, which list the frequency of omission of stress on multiple feet in one line, include feet already accounted for in the individual tallies.

26. See Avril Pyman, *A History of Russian Symbolism* (Cambridge: Cambridge University Press, 1994), 323–24.

27. Lessing is referenced in the footnotes to "Lyric and Experiment" in relation to the discussion of "means of artistic representation" (*sredstva khudozhestvennoi izobrazitel'nosti*) (Belyi, *SS* 5:428).

28. For a historical overview of the hierarchy between spatial and temporal arts, see Mitchell and Hansen, "Time and Space," 101–16.

29. Bernice G. Rosenthal, "The Spirit of Music in Russian Symbolism," *Russian History* 10, no. 1 (1983): 66–76.

30. See Steven Cassedy's observations regarding the "typographical dimension of the *Symphonies*": "One might say that the visual impression of the layout is in some way suggestive of a musical score . . . apart from the visual impression, the organization of these works into short segments is suggestive of musical phrases." Cassedy, "*Petersburg* and Music in Theory and Literature," in *A Reader's Guide to Andrei Bely's "Petersburg,"* ed. Leonid Livak (Madison: University of Wisconsin Press, 2018), 165. See also Robert Hughes, "Bely's Musical Aesthetics," in *Andrey Bely: A Critical Review*, ed. Gerald Janecek (Lexington: University Press of Kentucky, 1978), 137–45.

31. Gerald Janecek, "Intonation and Layout in Bely's Poetry," in Christa, *Andrey Bely*, 87. See also Khmel'nitskaya, who notes his interest in gesture and his "search for a syncretic form of expression in which the word, intonation, rhythm, and gesture form an indivisible whole." Khmel'nitskaya, "Poeziia Andreia Belogo," 8.

32. V. M. Zhirmunskii, *Vvedenie v metriku: Teoriia stikha* (Leningrad: Academia, 1925), 40. The English translation incorrectly translates "naimenee udachnaia chast'" (*least* successful part) as "most successful." V. M. Zhirmunsky, *Introduction to Metrics: The Theory of Verse*, trans. C. F. Brown (The Hague: Mouton, 1966), 44.

33. Zhirmunsky, *Introduction to Metrics*, 44.

34. The English translation expresses this more naturally as "the actual perception of rhythm" (Zhirmunsky, *Introduction to Metrics*, 45), but in so doing it loses the awkwardness of the original Russian and the caveats it implies, which relate to the debate around accentuation. Zhirmunsky argued for the introduction of two intermediate categories between "stressed" and "unstressed"—"a weaker stress ('half-accent') and a strong unstressed syllable (various degrees of making it heavier [*otiagchenie*])." Zhirmunskii, *Vvedenie v metriku*, 127.

35. Cassedy, *Selected Essays*, 69–89.

36. Cassedy, *Selected Essays*, 68.

37. Lisa Gitelman, *Always Already New: Media, History, and the Data of Culture* (Cambridge, MA: MIT Press, 2006), 5.

38. See P. N. Griunberg, *Istoriia nachala gramzapisi v Rossii* (Moscow: Iazyki slavianskoi kul'tury, 2002).

39. The Rhythm Circle was formed at the suggestion of several students, who approached Bely following one of his public lectures—whose enormous

popularity indicates the increasing prevalence, in parallel with the surge of interest in live poetry performance, of the public "performance" of scholarship during these years. For more on modernist poetry performance, see part 3.

40. It is important to remember that listening was never just a physical activity for poets during this period, and particularly for Bely, who (in his *Symphonies* and elsewhere) positioned sound, and the intuitive act of hearing it, as the bridge between the phenomenal and noumenal worlds.

41. For a detailed account of the group's work, see Grechishkin and Lavrov, "O stikhovedcheskom nasledii."

42. Mitchell, "There Are No Visual Media," 263.

43. The strange absence of the figures is emphasized by the opening sentence of this section of the essay, which reads: "Let us turn to the figures" (*Obratimsia k figuram*) (Belyi, *SS* 5:225).

44. Elsworth, "The Concept of Rhythm," 72.

45. Walter Benjamin, *The Arcades Project*, trans. Howard Eiland and Kevin McLaughlin, ed. Rolf Teidemann (Cambridge, MA: Harvard University Press, 1999), 476.

46. I am referring to "Poetry of Spells and Incantations" ("Poeziia zagovorov i zaklinanii"). Blok wrote this essay in 1906. It was originally published in E. Anichkov and D. Ovsianiko-Kulikovskii, *Istoriia russkoi literatury*, vol. 1: *Narodnaia slovesnost'* (Moscow, 1908), 81–106.

47. "The Magic of Words" closely follows Potebnya's discussion of this topic in *Iz zapisok . . .* , including borrowing specific examples. See the commentary in Belyi, *SS* 5:504.

48. The equivalent terms in the Russian are *deiatel'nost'* (activity) and *delo* (done thing).

49. Elsworth, *A Critical Study*, 32. My translation of "khodiachee slovo" (stock phrase) is playful, but intended to convey Bely's pun on the adjective "khodiachee," derived from the verb *khodit'*, "to walk." "We must be the executioners of the stock/walking word," Bely writes, "if it is already too late to breathe life back into it" (*My dolzhny byt' . . . palachami khodiachego slova, esli my uzhe ne mozhem vdokhnut' v nego zhizn'*) (Belyi, *SS* 5:320).

50. Roger Keys, *The Reluctant Modernist: Andrei Belyi and the Development of Russian Fiction, 1902–1914* (Oxford: Clarendon, 1996), 185.

51. See Bely's review of Potebnya's *Thought and Language*, "Mysl' i iazyk (Filosofiia iazyka A.A. Potebni)," *Logos* 2 (1910): 240–58.

52. Bernhard Siegert, *Cultural Techniques: Grids, Filters, Doors, and Other Articulations of the Real*, trans. Geoffrey Winthrop-Young (New York: Fordham University Press, 2015), 11.

53. David Trotter, "Modernism's Media Theory," *Critical Quarterly* 58, no. 3 (2016): 18.

54. John Durham Peters, *The Marvelous Clouds: Toward a Philosophy of Elemental Media* (Chicago: University of Chicago Press, 2015), 112.

55. This distinguishes Bely from his fellow Symbolists, who understood the significance of incantations differently. For Blok, they were a link to Russia's ancient folkloric past; for Ivanov—a route to final synthesis. Bely, by contrast, is most focused on the process of creation itself. See Shevelenko, *Modernizm kak arkhaizm* for more on the broader "archaist" tendencies into which these interests fit.

PART I. RHYTHM

1. Osip Brik, "Ritm i sintaksis," *Novyi Lef* 3–7 (1927), 3:15–16. The published study is based on two talks given at the Moscow Linguistic Circle and OPOIAZ in 1919 and 1920: "On Poetic Rhythm" ("O stikhotvornom ritme") and "On Rhythmic-Syntactical Figures" ("O ritmiko-sintaksicheskikh figurakh"), respectively. These talks were influential for Formalist studies of rhythm and were cited as a starting point by, among others, Viktor Zhirmunsky, *Composition of Lyric Poems* (*Kompozitsiia liricheskikh stikhotvorenii*, 1921); Boris Eikhenbaum, *Melodics of Russian Lyric Verse* (*Melodika russkogo liricheskogo stikha*, 1922); Roman Jakobson, *On Czech Verse, Primarily in Comparison with Russian* (*O cheshskom stikhe, preimushchestvenno v sopostavlenii s russkim*, 1923); and the later essay, "Retrospect," in Jakobson, *Selected Writings*, 5:569–601.

2. Brik, "Ritm i sintaksis," 3:16.

3. Alexander Freer, "Rhythm as Coping," *New Literary History* 46, no. 3 (Summer 2015): 550.

4. Peter Dayan and David Evans, "Rhythm in Literature after the Crisis in Verse," *Paragraph* 33, no. 2 (2010): 147.

5. As Derek Attridge argues, the perception of poetic rhythm does share some features with the perception of rhythm in other domains, in many cases involving a variety of "patterns of expectation and satisfaction." Attridge, *The Rhythms of English Poetry* (London: Longman, 1982), 309.

6. See the discussion of the relationship between poetry, "rhythm-making," and experience in Freer, "Rhythm as Coping."

7. See S. I. Gindin, "Pervyi konflikt dvukh pokolenii osnovatelei russkogo stikhovedeniia," *Novoe literaturnoe obozrenie* 4, no. 86 (2007): 64–69; and S. I. Gindin and A. V. Man'kovskii, "Kak Moskovskii lingvisticheskii kruzhok voeval s Briusovym i Potebnei," *Novoe literaturnoe obozrenie* 4, no. 86 (2007): 70–78.

8. Even the six or so "scientific" prosodists among the ranks of the Moscow Linguistic Circle (including Sergei Bobrov, Brik, Maksim Kenigsberg, Boris Tomashevsky, and Boris Iarkho), Igor Pil'shchikov notes, "came up with theories [of prosody] that differ not only in details but in their basic assumptions." "If there was such a thing as 'Moscow Formalism' as a unified historical and academic phenomenon, its unity would derive from its formulation of the 'order of the day' rather than concrete solutions and methods." Igor Pil'shchikov, "Zasedanie

Moskovskogo lingvisticheskogo kruzhka 1-go iiunia 1919 i zarozhdenie stikhovedcheskikh kontseptsii O. Brika, B. Tomashevskogo i R. Iakobsona," *Revue des Études Slaves* 88, no. 1/2 (2017): 155.

9. Thorough accounts of technical debates about prosody during this period can be found elsewhere. For a detailed look at shifting terminology during the modernist period, see Igor Pil'shchikov, "Poniatiia 'stikh', 'metr' i 'ritm' v russkoi stikhovedcheskoi traditsii," *Trudy Instituta russkogo iazyka im. V.V. Vinogradova* 11 (2017): 12–30. Maksim Shapir also provides an overview of terminological debates around meter and rhythm in *Universum versus: Iazyk—stikh—smysl v russkoi poezii XVIII–XX vekov* (Moscow: Iazyki russkoi kul'tury, 2000). The most comprehensive English-language account of Russian prosody is provided in Barry P. Scherr, *Russian Poetry: Meter, Rhythm, and Rhyme* (Berkeley: University of California Press, 1977). See also M. L. Gasparov, *Ocherk istorii russkogo stikha: Metrika, ritmika, rifma, strofika* (Moscow: Fortuna Limited, 2000).

10. Erin Kappeler, "Constructing Walt Whitman: Literary History and Histories of Rhythm," in *Critical Rhythm: The Poetics of a Literary Life Form*, ed. Jonathan Culler and Ben Glaser (New York: Fordham University Press, 2019), 130; Meredith Martin, *The Rise and Fall of Meter: Poetry and English National Culture, 1860–1930* (Princeton, NJ: Princeton University Press, 2012), 5. See also Jason David Hall, ed., *Meter Matters: Verse Cultures of the Long Nineteenth Century* (Athens: Ohio University Press, 2011); Yopie Prins, *Victorian Sappho* (Princeton, NJ: Princeton University Press, 1999); and Yopie Prins, "What Is Historical Poetics?" *Modern Language Quarterly* 77, no. 1 (2016): 13–40.

11. Susan Stanford Friedman, "Periodizing Modernism: Postcolonial Modernities and the Space/Time Borders of Modernist Studies," *Modernism/modernity* 13, no. 3 (September 2006): 434. For further detail on Russian modernist discourses around rhythm, see Svetlikova, *The Moscow Pythagoreans*, esp. 167–71.

12. Bolter and Grusin, *Remediation*, 15.

13. Gasparov, "Belyi-stikhoved i Belyi-stikhotvorets."

14. Iurii Tynianov, *Problema stikhotvornogo iazyka: Stat'i* (Moscow: Sovetskii pisatel', 1965), 18. Subsequent citations refer to this edition and are provided in text. Translations are my own.

CHAPTER TWO

1. Boris Tomashevskii, "Problema stikhotvornogo ritma," in *Izbrannye raboty o stikhe: Uchebnoe posobie*, ed. S. I. Monakhov, K. I. Tver'ianovich, and E. V. Khvorost'ianova (St. Petersburg: Filologicheskii fakul'tet SPbGU, 2007), 28–29.

2. Merrill, *Origins of Russian Literary Theory*, 104.

3. Friedman, *Planetary Modernisms*, 33–34.

4. For further discussion, see Merrill, *Origins of Russian Literary Theory*,

esp. 9–19; Erlich, *Russian Formalism*, 26–32; Iurii Shaitanov, "Formalizm kak iavlenie istoricheskoi poetiki," *Voprosy literatury* 6 (2016): 7–29; and Steiner, *Russian Formalism*, 49–64.

5. Merrill, *Origins of Russian Literary Theory*, 14–15.

6. Merrill, *Origins of Russian Literary Theory*, 19.

7. Bely's work was a formative influence for the Formalists, many of whom read *Simvolizm* at a young age. The Formalists acknowledged this debt, but critical accounts of the movement have yet to consider it at length. For a characteristic discussion, see Erlich, *Russian Formalism*, 214.

8. Daria Khitrova, "Introduction," in Yury Tynianov, *Permanent Evolution: Selected Essays on Literature, Theory and Film*, trans. and ed. Ainsley Morse and Philip Redko (Boston: Academic Studies, 2019), 11; Iurii Tynianov, *Poetika, Istoriia literatury, Kino*, ed. A. P. Chudakov, M. O. Chudakova, and E. A. Toddes (Moscow: Nauka, 1977), 502.

9. Brik, "Ritm i sintaksis," 3:18.

10. Cited in Pil'shchikov, "Zasedanie," 166.

11. Tomashevsky's use of this term differs from Brik's. For an overview of these differences, see I. A. Pil'shchikov, "Stikovedcheskaia terminologiia russkogo formalizma (fragment tezaurusnogo opisaniia)," in *Obrazy iazyka i zigzagi diskursa: Sbornik nauchnykh statei k 70-letiiu V.Z. Dem'iankova*, ed. V. V. Feshchenko (Moscow: Kult'turnaia revoliutsiia, 2018), 531–32. See also Pil'shchikov, "Poniatiia 'stikh,' 'metr' i 'ritm.'"

12. Brik, "Ritm i sintaksis," 4:27, 4:17.

13. Brik, "Ritm i sintaksis," 3:17.

14. Tomashevskii, "Problema stikhotvornogo ritma," 31.

15. Roman Jakobson, "Briusovskaia stikhologiia i nauka o stikhe," in *Selected Works, IX, Completion Volume 2: Uncollected Works, 1916–1943, Part One, 1916–1933*, by Roman Jakobson, ed. Jindrich Toman (Amsterdam: De Gruyter, 2012), 130.

16. A variety of specialized devices were contrived for this purpose. A fascinating comparative discussion of the development of these methods in the United States, Europe, and Russia can be found in Ana Hedberg Olenina, *Psychomotor Aesthetics: Movement and Affect in Modern Literature and Film* (Oxford: Oxford University Press, 2020).

17. See E. W. Scripture, *Researches in Experimental Phonetics: The Study of Speech Curves* (Washington, DC: Carnegie Institution of Washington, 1906). A special automated apparatus was used to trace the lines. Scripture also used other methods to obtain speech curves. A detailed description of these devices and the diagrams produced is given in Olenina, *Psychomotor Aesthetics*, esp. 74. For a discussion of similar trends elsewhere, see Jason David Hall, "Materializing Meter: Physiology, Psychology, Prosody," *Victorian Poetry* 49, no. 2 (2011): 179–97.

18. Tomashevskii, "Problema stikhotvornogo ritma," 39.

19. I discuss Ohrenphilologie at more length in chapter 6, where I consider it in light of debates about poetic voice.

20. Tomashevskii, "Problema stikhotvornogo ritma," 33.

21. Tomashevskii, "Problema stikhotvornogo ritma," 45–47.

22. Tynianov, *Problema stikhotvornogo iazyka*, 38–58.

23. In an otherwise skeptical review of the volume in which Tomashevsky's essay was first published, Tynianov singles it out for brief praise: "Developed on a broad theoretical (partly historical) material and coming to a number of new conclusions, the article requires special consideration." Tynianov, *Poetika, Istoriia literatury, Kino*, 141. Tynianov's *Problem of Verse Language* appears to offer just such a "consideration" of Tomashevsky's claims.

24. Tomashevskii, "Problema stikhotvornogo ritma," 49–50.

25. Elleström, "The Modalities of Media," 25.

26. Recent critical writing on rhythm has observed something similar. Mutlu Konuk Blasing, for example, argues that "biological and environmental rhythms may be givens, but social rhythms are learned. And verbal rhythm is social." In other words, as Freer comments, "all encounters with rhythmic poetry depend upon one's own history of language and language-learning as well as acquired poetic competence." "To be certain that you 'hear' a particular pattern in a poem," Derek Attridge writes, "is no guarantee that it exists beyond your idiosyncratically nurtured perceptual faculties." Mutlu Konuk Blasing, *Lyric Poetry: The Pain and the Pleasure of Words* (Princeton, NJ: Princeton Universit Press, 2008), 54; Freer, "Rhythm as Coping": 559; Derek Attridge, "Beyond Metrics: Richard Cureton's Rhythmic Phrasing in English Verse," *Poetics Today* 17, no. 1 (1996): 20.

27. Irina O. Rajewsky, "Border Talks: The Problematic Status of Media Borders in the Current Debate about Intermediality," in *Media Borders, Multimodality and Intermediality*, ed. Lars Elleström (Basingstoke, UK: Palgrave Macmillan, 2010), 62.

28. Svetlikova, *Istoki russkogo formalizma*, 99–124; Tynianov, *Poetika, Istoriia literatury, Kino*, 502.

29. Erlich, *Russian Formalism*, 213fn5.

30. On rhythm as *dominanta*, see Hansen-Löve, *Russkii formalizm*, 307–9.

31. For an alternative account of these terms, see, for example, Mikhail Gasparov, "Pervochtenie i perechtenie: K tynianovskomu poniatiiu suktsessivnosti stikhotvornoi rechi," *Tynianovskii sbornik* 3 (1988): 15–23.

32. Svetlikova, *Istoki russkogo formalizma*, 110fn1.

33. See Lev Iakubinskii, "Otkuda berut stikhi," *Knizhnyi ugol* 7 (1921): 25.

34. Merrill, *Origins of Russian Literary Theory*, 112.

35. Merrill, *Origins of Russian Literary Theory*, 112.

36. Merrill, *Origins of Russian Literary Theory*, 120.

37. This term is usually associated with Shklovsky, whose book *Unfolding of*

the Plot (*Razvertyvanie siuzheta*) came out in 1921. Svetlikova locates another potential source for this term in Herbartian psychology (*Istoki russkogo formalizma*, 123).

38. See the discussion in Ilya Kliger, "Dynamic Archeology or Distant Reading: Literary Study between Two Formalisms," *Russian Literature* 122–23 (May–July 2021): 10–11.

39. Henri Bergson, *Time and Free Will: An Essay on the Immediate Data of Consciousness*, trans. F. L. Pogson (New York: Dover, 2008), 127.

40. Marta Braun, *Picturing Time: The Work of Etienne-Jules Marey* (Chicago: University of Chicago Press, 1992), 278–79.

41. Henri Bergson, *Matter and Memory*, trans. Nancy Margaret Paul and W. Scott Palmer (New York: Dover, 2004), 259.

42. See Hansen-Löve's detailed discussion of this point in *Russkii formalizm*, 307–9.

43. David Nowell Smith, "What Is Called Rhythm?" in *Critical Rhythm: The Poetics of a Literary Life Form*, ed. Jonathan Culler and Ben Glaser (New York: Fordham University Press, 2019), 44, 46.

44. Dragan Kujundzic, *The Returns of History: Russian Nietzscheans after Modernity* (Albany: SUNY Press, 1997), 74. This definition of rhythm strikes a distinctly phenomenological note. For more on Husserl's influence on OPOIAZ, see Kujundzic, *Returns of History*; and Hansen-Löve, *Russkii formalizm*, esp. 173–80.

45. Serguei Oushakine, "Shklovsky and Things, or Why Tolstoy's Sofa Should Matter," in *Viktor Shklovsky's Heritage in Literature, Arts, and Philosophy*, ed. Slav N. Gratchev and Howard Mancing (London: Lexington Books, 2019), 96.

46. For a discussion of Tynianov's work on rhythm in relation to semantic aureoles, see Mikhail Gasparov, "Tynianov i problema semantiki metra," *Tynianovskii sbornik* 1 (1984): 105–13.

47. Oushakine, "Ne vzletevshie samolety mechty," 30.

48. Eikhenbaum cited in Lev Gudkov, "Poniatie i metafory istorii u Tynianova i opoiazovtsev," *Tynianovskie chteniia* 3 (1988): 102.

49. Erlich, *Russian Formalism*, 92.

50. Leon Trotsky, *Literature and Revolution*, trans. Rose Strunsky (Chicago: Haymarket Books, 2005), 139.

CHAPTER THREE

1. The *dol'nik* was first fully described in the 1960s, prior to which the term had been used loosely to designate a range of accentual verse; conversely, examples of what would now be referred to as *dol'nik* had often been described as combinations of binary and ternary feet. See M. L. Gasparov, "Russkii trekhudarnyi dol'nik XX veka," in *Teoriia stikha*, ed. V. M. Zhirmunskii et al. (Leningrad: Nauka, 1968), 59–106.

2. Mikhail Gasparov, "Blok v istorii russkogo stikha," in *Izbrannye trudy*, by Mikhail Gasparov, 3 vols. (Moscow: Iazyki russkoi kul'tury, 1997), 3:449–68.

3. Gasparov, "Blok v istorii russkogo stikha," 451.

4. Bolter and Grusin, *Remediation*, 38.

5. Gasparov, "Blok v istorii russkogo stikha," 455.

6. Gasparov, "Blok v istorii russkogo stikha," 454.

7. Belyi, *Sobranie sochinenii*, 4:378.

8. A. A. Blok, *Polnoe sobranie sochinenii i pisem* (henceforth *PSS*), 20 vols. (Moscow: Nauka, 1997–) 9:102. Subsequent references will be to this edition unless otherwise indicated.

9. See the discussion in Arkadii Bliumbaum, *Musica mundana i russkaia obshchestvennost': Tsikl statei o tvorchestve Aleksandra Bloka* (Moscow: Novoe literaturnoe obozrenie, 2017); and Arkadii Bliumbaum, "'Sud'ba' versus 'Sluchai' v tvorchestve Bloka epokhi 'antitezy': Neskol'ko nabliudenii," *Novoe literaturnoe obozrenie* 109 (2011): 229–52.

10. A. A. Blok, *Sobranie sochinenii*, 8 vols. (Moscow-Leningrad: Khudozestvennaia literatura, 1962), 5:52.

11. For a concise discussion of Blok's urban poetry in relation to modernist and nineteenth-century tradition as well, as exemplary contemporary responses to his work, see the excellent summary in Blok, *PSS* 2:719–22..

12. See Bliumbaum, *Musica mundana*.

13. For useful accounts, see Robert C. Williams, "The Russian Revolution and the End of Time 1900–1940," *Geschichte Osteuropas* 43, no. 3 (1995): 364–401; and Steinberg, *Petersburg Fin de Siècle*. On the influence of this trend on literature, see David Bethea, *The Shape of the Apocalypse in Modern Russian Fiction* (Princeton, NJ: Princeton University Press, 1989); Irene Masing Delic, *Abolishing Death: A Salvation Myth of Russian Twentieth-Century Literature* (Stanford, CA: Stanford University Press, 1992); and Bernice G. Rosenthal, *D. S. Merezhkovsky and the Silver Age: The Development of a Revolutionary Mentality* (The Hague: Martinus Nijhoff, 1975).

14. Blok, *PSS* 2:99. First published in *Pereval*, no. 7 (1907): 17–18. The poem was republished in Blok's collection *Earth in Snow* (*Zemlia v snegu*, 1908), where the date provided is "January 1904." The date given is that which appears in *City* in the collected works.

15. Scherr, *Russian Poetry*, 160. The term *taktovik* was coined in the 1920s. Scherr prefers the term "strict accentual verse" over *taktovik*, since the latter "derives from the temporal theories of A. P. Kviatkovsky which are no longer generally accepted by metrists." Scherr, *Russian Poetry*, 161. For more on the history of the *taktovik*, see Mikhail Gasparov, "Taktovik v poezii XX veka," in *Sovremennyi russkii stikh: Metrika i ritmika*, by Mikhail Gasparov (Moscow: Nauka, 1974), 294–351.

16. Clare Cavanagh, *Lyric Poetry and Modern Politics* (New Haven, CT: Yale University Press, 2009), 51.

17. Zara Mints, "'Poetika daty' i ranniaia lirika Al. Bloka," in *Poetika Aleksandra Bloka*, by Zara Mints (St. Petersburg: Iskusstvo-SPb, 1999), 390.

18. Zara Mints, "'Poetika daty,'" 391–92.

19. My thanks to one of this manuscript's reviewers for this observation.

20. As Blok describes in a letter to his mother on January 11, 1904, Bely, Bal'mont, and others were also present at this gathering. Blok read his poems "The Factory" ("Fabrika," 1903) and "Three Rays" ("Tri luchika," 1903). This was his first public reading in Moscow. Blok, *Sobranie sochinenii*, 8:81–82.

21. Gasparov, "Blok v istorii russkogo stikha," 458; Blok, *PSS* 2:725.

22. Valerii Briusov, *Sobranie sochinenii*, 7 vols. (Moscow: Khudozestvennaia literatura, 1973), 1:442.

23. An epigraph from the book of Revelation 6:8 ("And I looked, and behold a pale horse: and his name that sat on him was Death") make the poem's apocalyptic concerns immediately clear.

24. Blok, *PSS* 2:100–101. First published in *Belye nochi: Peterburgskii almanakh* (St. Petersburg: Vol'naia tipografiia, 1907), 11–12.

25. Kirill Taranovskii, *Russkie dvuslozhnye razmery: Stat'i o stikhe*, trans. V. V. Son'kina (Moscow: Iazyki slavianskoi kul'tury, 2010), 61.

26. Taranovskii, *Russkie dvuslozhnye razmery*, 73–76. The incidence of lines with two feet in which the stressed position is not realized is two to three times as high in the Russian trochaic line as in the iamb.

27. This is not atypical; as a general rule, the first line of the stanza tends to be more fully stressed than subsequent lines. However, the larger pattern to which this contributes makes the effect notable here. Barry Scherr, "Taranovsky's Laws: Further Observations from a Comparative Perspective," in *Poetry and Poetics: A Centennial Tribute to Kiril Taranovsky*, ed. Barry Scherr, James Bailey, and Vida Johnson (Bloomington, IN: Slavica, 2014), 361.

28. M. I. Shapir, "Metrum et rhythmus sub specie semioticae," in *Universum versus: Iazyk—stikh—smysl v russkoi poezii XVIII–XX vekov*, by M. I. Shapir (Moscow: Iazyki russkoi kul'tury, 2000), 94.

29. Iurii Lotman, *Analiz poeticheskogo teksta: Struktura stikha* (Leningrad: Prosveshchenie, 1972), 45.

30. Blok, *Sobranie sochinenii*, 8:94.

31. Roland Greene, *Post-Petrarchism: Origins and Innovations of the Western Lyric Sequence* (Princeton, NJ: Princeton University Press, 1991), 34.

32. Sharon Cameron, *Lyric Time: Emily Dickinson and the Limits of Genre* (Baltimore, MD: Johns Hopkins University Press, 1979), 165. The word "again" (*snova/opiat/vnov'*) takes on particular importance in Blok's third volume, where it is associated, less hopefully, with the Nietzschean concept of eternal return.

33. D. M. Magomedova, "Aleksandr Blok: 'Neznakomka': Vnutrenniaia struktura i kontekst prochteniia," *Vestnik PSTGU III: Filologiia* 2, no. 16 (2009): 38.

34. Blok, *PSS* 2:122. First published in Aleksandr Blok, *Nechaiannaia radost': Vtoroi sbornik stikhov* (Moscow: Skorpion, 1907), 21–23.

35. Alexander Blok, "The Stranger," trans. Frances Cornford and Esther Polianowsky Salaman. Reprinted in *The Penguin Book of Russian Poetry*, ed. Robert Chandler, Boris Dralyuk, and Irina Mashinski (London: Penguin, 2015), 183–84. Reproduced with the permission of the trustees of the Frances Crofts Cornford Will Trust. Translation modified.

36. Magomedova, "Aleksandr Blok: 'Neznakomka,'" 43.

37. For a detailed description, see Zara Mints, "Ob odnom sposobe obrazovaniia novykh znachenii slov v proizvedenii iskusstva (ironicheskoe i poeticheskoe v stikhotvorenii Al. Bloka 'Neznakomka,'" in Mints, *Poetika Aleksandra Bloka*, 532–39; and Magomedova, "Aleksandr Blok: 'Neznakomka.'"

38. Magomedova, "Aleksandr Blok: 'Neznakomka,'" 40.

39. John Bowlt, "Aleksandr Blok: The Poem 'The Unknown Lady,'" *Texas Studies in Literature and Language* 17 (1975): 356.

40. See Kirill Taranovskii, "O vzaimootnoshenii stikhotvornogo ritma i tematiki," in *O poezii i poetike*, by Kirill Taranovskii (Moscow: Iazyki russkoi kul'tury, 2000), 372–403.

41. Mikhail Gasparov, "'Po vecheram nad restoranami . . .' 4-st. iamb s okonchaniiami DMDM: Stanovlenie oreola," in *Metr i smysl: Ob odnom iz mekhanizmov kul'turnoi pamiati*, by Mikhail Gasparov (Moscow: Fortuna EL, 2012), 37–60.

42. Anna Akhmatova, "Letter to S. V. Shtein (February 1907)," *Literaturnoe nasledstvo: Aleksandr Blok: Novye materialy i issledovaniia* 92, no. 3 (1982): 271. Cited in Gasparov, *Metr i smysl*, 37.

43. Magomedova, "Aleksandr Blok: 'Neznakomka,'" 45. Compare Blok's own poem, "In the Restaurant" ("V restorane," 1910).

44. There ladies flaunt the latest fashions . . ." is the only poem in *City* to appear out of sequence (it is dated 1911), drawing the reader's attention to its status as a version of "The Unknown Woman" even after it lost its original title. Daniel Rancour-Laferriere identifies at least three other "satellite poems": "Your face is paler than it was . . ." ("Tvoe litso blednei, chem bylo . . . ," March 1906), the poem immediately before "The Unknown Woman" in *City* (*PSS* 2:121–22); "There, in the howling cold of the night . . ." ("Tam, v nochnoi zavyvaiushchei stuzhe"), in the section *Various Poems* (2:65); and "A train spattered with stars . . ." ("Shleif, zabryzgannyi zvezdami"), also in *Various Poems* (2:78). "Getting to Know Blok's 'Unknown Woman,'" in *Five Russian Poems: Exercises in a Theory of Poetry*, by Daniel Rancour-Laferriere (Englewood, NJ: Transworld, 1977), 109. I would add "In the Restaurant" to this list.

45. Mikhail Gasparov, "1905 god i metricheskaia evoliutsiia Bloka, Briusova, Belogo," in Gasparov, *Izbrannye trudy*, 3:469–75.

46. Lydia Ginzburg, *O lirike* (Leningrad: Sovetskii pisatel', 1974).

47. Cavanagh, *Lyric Poetry and Modern Politics*, 48. The classic account is given in Ginzburg, *O lirike*.

48. See the discussion in David Sloane, *Aleksandr Blok and the Dynamics of the Lyric Cycle* (Bloomington, IN: Slavica, 1988).

49. Jonathan Stone, *The Institutions of Russian Modernism: Conceptualizing, Publishing, and Reading Symbolism* (Evanston, IL: Northwestern University Press, 2017), 152.

50. Ginzburg, *O lirike*, 263.

51. Stone, *Institutions of Russian Modernism.*

52. Aleksandr Blok, letter to Bely (June 1911), in *Andrei Belyi i Aleksandr Blok: Perepiska, 1903–1919*, ed. A. V. Lavrov (Moscow: Progress-Pleiada, 2001), 406. See also Blok's 1910 essay, "On the Current State of Russian Symbolism," the guidebook to this linear journey from thesis, through antithesis, to synthesis.

53. Dmitrii Maksimov, "Ideia puti v poeticheskom soznanii A Bloka," in *Blokovskii sbornik II* (Tartu: Tartuskii gosudarstvennyi universitet, 1972), 25–121. Zara Mints develops this idea in *Poetika Aleksandra Bloka*. See also Ginzburg's discussion in *O lirike*.

54. Ginzburg, *O lirike*, 261.

55. Jacob Edmond, *Make It the Same: Poetry in the Age of Global Media* (New York: Columbia University Press, 2019). The tension between the original and the copy saturates Blok's own thought: is this the woman, or an earthly likeness? Does sharing the same date bring poem into harmony with event?

56. Gasparov, "'Po vecheram nad restoranami . . .'."

57. Edmond, *Make It the Same*, 14.

58. Edmond, *Make It the Same*, 10–15.

59. Gitelman, *Always Already New*, 148; Dworkin, *No Medium*, 32.

60. Friedman, *Planetary Modernisms*, 36.

PART II. IMAGE

1. For an overview, see discussion in Ray Frazer, "The Origin of the Term 'Image,' *ELH* 27, no. 2 (1960): 149–61.

2. For an overview, see discussion in Ray Frazer, "The Origin of the Term 'Image,' *ELH* 27, no. 2 (1960): 149–61.

W. J. T. Mitchell, *Iconology: Image, Text, Ideology* (Chicago: University of Chicago Press, 1987), 24.

3. Svetlikova, *Istoki russkogo formalizma*, 41–71.

4. See the discussion in Perloff, *Futurist Moment.*

5. Charlotte Greve, "Writing and the 'Subject': Image-Text Relations in the Early Russian Avant-Garde and Contemporary Russian Visual Poetry," PhD dissertation (University of Amsterdam, 2004, Amsterdam), 100–110.

6. Aage A. Hansen-Löve, "Intermedialität und Intertextualität: Probleme der Korrelation von Wort-und Bildkunst—Am Beispiel der russischen Moderne," in *Dialog der Texte: Hamburger Kolloquium zur Intertextualität*, ed. Wolf Schmid and Wolf-Dieter Stempel (Vienna: Wiener Slawistischer Almanach, 1983), 291–360.

7. Werner Wolf, "(Inter)mediality and the Study of Literature," *CLCWeb: Comparative Literature and Culture*, 13, no. 3 (2011): 3. See also Rajewsky, "Intermediality, Intertextuality, and Remediation."

8. Bolter and Grusin, *Remediation*, 344.

9. McLuhan, *Understanding Media*; W. J. T. Mitchell, *Picture Theory: Essays on Verbal and Visual Representation* (Chicago: University of Chicago Press, 1994), 95.

10. Mitchell, *Picture Theory*, 96. See the discussion of Greenberg in this book's introduction.

11. Rajewsky, "Border Talks," 53–54.

12. Elleström, "The Modalities of Media," 15.

13. Mitchell, "There Are No Visual Media," 257, my emphasis.

14. Ford, "Poetry's Media," 453.

15. First published in Kruchenykh's handmade book, *Pomada*, in 1913.

16. Reprinted in Perloff, *Futurist Moment*, 125.

17. Elleström, "The Modalities of Media," 30.

18. Perloff, *Futurist Moment*, 157; Ford, "Poetry's Media," 457.

19. Tihanov, *Birth and Death of Literary Theory*. A similar contradiction is inherent in the image, which claims to reproduce some part of lived reality even as it always and inevitably draws attention to its own artificiality, the conventions by which it depicts that reality. As Mitchell reminds us, an image "cannot be seen *as such* without a paradoxical trick of the consciousness, an ability to see something as 'there' and 'not there' at the same time." Mitchell, *Iconology*, 17.

20. See Ivanov, "Pasternak i OPOIAZ."

21. Andrew Kahn, Mark Lipovetsky, Irina Reyfman, and Stephanie Sandler, *A History of Russian Literature* (New York: Oxford University Press, 2018), 606–10. See also Briusov, who identifies Pasternak, Bobrov, and Aseev as *porubezhniki* ("in-betweeners") in "God russkoi poezii. Porubezhniki," *Russkaia mysl'* 6 (1914). For more on Pasternak's position in early twentieth-century culture, see V. S. Baevskii, "Lirika Pasternaka v istoriko-kul'turnom kontekste," *Izvestiia Akademii nauk: Seriia literatury i iazyka* 47, no. 2 (1988): 130–41; Lazar Fleishman, *Boris Pasternak: The Poet and His Politics* (Cambridge, MA: Harvard University Press, 1990); and Oleg Kling, "Boris Pasternak i simvolizm," *Voprosy literatury* (March–April 2002): 25–59.

22. Tihanov, *Birth and Death of Literary Theory*, 22.

23. Andrei Sinyavsky, "Boris Pasternak," in *Pasternak*, ed. Donald Davie and Angela Livingstone (London: Macmillan, 1969), 160.

24. Tihanov, *Birth and Death of Literary Theory*, 53. See also the beginning of Shklovsky's *Bowstring*, which reads almost as a prose rendering, though in a minor key, of Pasternak's "February . . ." (discussed below): "It's the end of April. The coiling snow patches in the mountains look like streams of wax on a wide candlestick. A few corpulent crows swing on treetops, balancing themselves

with their spread tails and drooped wings. They are large gray birds with black wings . . . Another page of spring . . ." Viktor Shklovsky, *Bowstring: On the Dissimilarity of the Similar*, trans. Shushan Avagyan (Champaign, IL: Dalkey Archive, 2011), 3.

CHAPTER FOUR

1. Viktor Shklovskii, "Iskusstvo, kak priem," in *O teorii prozy*, by Viktor Shklovskii (Moscow: Federatsiia, 1929), 9. Translation cited from Berlina, *Viktor Shklovsky: A Reader*, 75.

2. Shklovskii, "Iskusstvo, kak priem," 10; Berlina, *Viktor Shklovsky: A Reader*, 76–77.

3. Shklovskii, "Iskusstvo, kak priem," 13; Berlina, *Viktor Shklovsky: A Reader*, 80.

4. Cited in M. Chudakova and E. Toddes, "Stranitsy nauchnoi biografii B.M. Eikhenbauma," *Voprosy literatury* 1 (1987): 128–62.

5. Steiner, *Russian Formalism*, 44–67.

6. Cited in Steiner, *Russian Formalism*, 53.

7. See Steiner's discussion of this point and Veselovsky's ideas in *Russian Formalism*, 53–64.

8. Steiner, *Russian Formalism*, 54.

9. Steiner, *Russian Formalism*, 53.

10. Tihanov, *Birth and Death of Literary Theory*. See also the discussion in Thompson, *Russian Formalism and Anglo-American New Criticism*; and Oleg Gelikman, "Intermediality and Aesthetic Theory in Shklovsky's and Adorno's Thought," *CLCWeb: Comparative Literature and Culture* 13, no. 3 (2011), https://doi.org/10.7771/1481-4374.1791.

11. Basil Lvoff, "Viktor Shklovsky and Marshall McLuhan: Beyond Common Sense," *New Zealand Slavonic Journal* 49–50 (2015): 4.

12. Oushakine, "Tolstoy's Sofa," 95.

13. Oushakine, "Ne vzletevshie samolety mechty," 38.

14. Shklovskii, "Iskusstvo, kak priem," 21; Berlina, *Viktor Shklovsky: A Reader*, 94.

15. Alexander Potebnya, *Iz zapisok po teorii slovesnosti: Poeziia i proza, Tropy i figury, Myshlenie poeticheskoe i mificheskoe, Prilozheniia* (The Hague: Mouton, 1970), 134.

16. Osip Brik, "Zvukovye povtory," *Poetika: Sborniki po teorii poeticheskogo iazyka* (1919): 60.

17. Lev Iakubinskii, "O zvukakh stikhotvornogo iazyka," *Poetika: Sborniki po teorii poeticheskogo iazyka* (1919): 37.

18. John Fizer, *Alexander A. Potebnja's Psycholinguistic Theory of Literature* (Cambridge, MA: Harvard University Press, 1986), 117.

19. See the discussion in Thomas Seifrid, *The Word Made Self: Russian Writings on Language, 1860–1930* (Ithaca, NY: Cornell University Press, 2005), 16. For further discussion, see Fizer, *Potebnja's Psycholinguistic Theory of Literature*; and Steven Cassedy, *Flight from Eden: The Origins of Modern Literary Criticism and Theory* (Berkeley: University of California Press, 1990), 39–43.

20. For more on the influence of contemporary psychology, see Svetlikova, *Istoki russkogo formalizma*, 41–71.

21. Potebnya represents these differences via the following formulae:

myth: X ≡ a (A)
poetry: X = a < A
science: X ≡ A

—where "X stands for signification, reference, or the cognized object; a for image, attribute, or metonymic representation of X; and A for the aggregate of the previously acquired knowledge pertinent to X." Fizer, *Potebnja's Psycholinguistic Theory of Literature*, 60.

22. Oushakine, "Ne vzletevshie samolety mechty," 55.

23. Iakubinskii, "O zvukakh stikhotvornogo iazyka," 37.

24. Viktor Shklovskii, "O poezii i zaumnom iazyke," in *Gamburgskii schet: Stat'i—vospominaniia—esse*, by Viktor Shklovskii (Moscow: Sovetskii pisatel', 1990), 45; Viktor Shklovsky et al., "On Poetry and Trans-Sense Language," *October* 34 (1985): 17.

25. Shklovskii, "O poezii i zaumnom iazyke," 48; Shklovsky et al., "Poetry and Trans-Sense Language," 8, translation modified.

26. Olenina, *Psychomotor Aesthetics*, 28.

27. Shklovskii, "O poezii i zaumnom iazyke," 48; Shklovsky et al., "Poetry and Trans-Sense Language," 8.

28. Olenina, *Psychomotor Aesthetics*, 13.

29. Olenina, *Psychomotor Aesthetics*, 29–30.

30. Shklovskii, "O poezii i zaumnom iazyke," 56; Shklovsky et al., "Poetry and Trans-Sense Language," 20.

31. Svetlikova, *Istoki russkogo formalizma*, 53.

32. Shklovskii, "O poezii i zaumnom iazyke," 58; Shklovsky et al., "Poetry and Trans-Sense Language," 23, translation modified.

33. This position is to be compared with that taken by Jakobson, who saw poetic language as one of the six "functions" of language. Shklovsky and Jakobson disagreed vehemently on this point. See an overview of this argument in Ilia Kalinin, "Viktor Shklovskii versus Roman Iakobson: Voina iazykov," *Vestnik sankt-peterburgskogo universiteta* 9, no. 3 (September 2016): 55–63.

34. Ford, "Poetry's Media," 450.

35. Lars Elleström, "Transfer of Media Characteristics among Dissimilar Media," *Palabra Clave* 20, no. 3 (2017): 669.

36. For further discussion, see Iurii Lotman, "Graficheskii obraz poezii," in Lotman, *Analiz poeticheskogo teksta*, 70–74.

37. Shklovskii, "O poezii i zaumnom iazyke," 54; Shklovsky et al., "Poetry and Trans-Sense Language," 18.

38. Osip Mandel'shtam, "Slovo i kul'tura," in *Sobranie sochinenii*, by Osip Mandel'shtam, ed. A. Mets and F. Lhoest (Moscow: Progress Pleiada, 2010), 2:53–54. Translation cited from Olenina, *Psychomotor Aesthetics*, 20–21.

39. Shklovskii, "O poezii i zaumnom iazyke," 45; Shklovsky et al., "Poetry and Trans-Sense Language," 4.

40. This is one place where Potebnya and Shklovsky do briefly converge: as in Potebnya's model, which projects the tripartite structure of the word onto the poem as a whole, Shklovsky's description of the word echoes in miniature his definition of the work of art as a "relationship of materials." Shklovskii, *O teorii prozy*, 226.

41. Viktor Shklovskii, *Zoo, ili pis'ma ne o liubvi*, in *Zhily-byly*, by Viktor Shklovskii (Moscow: Sovetskii pisatel', 1966), 175. See the discussion in Oushakine, "Ne vzletevshie samolety mechty," 46; and Lvoff, "Viktor Shklovsky and Marshall McLuhan," 22–23.

42. Lvoff, "Viktor Shklovsky and Marshall McLuhan," 21.

43. McLuhan, *Understanding Media*, 66–67.

44. Michael Serres, *The Five Senses: A Philosophy of Mingled Bodies*, trans. Margaret Sankey and Peter Cowley (London: Continuum, 2008), 35.

45. Viktor Shklovskii, "Iskusstvo tsirka," in Shklovskii, *Gamburgskii schet*, 106.

46. McLuhan, *Understanding Media*, 66–67.

47. Cited in Seifrid, *Word Made Self*, 33.

48. Shklovskii, "Iskusstvo, kak priem," 20; Berlina, *Viktor Shklovsky: A Reader*, 93.

49. Oushakine, "Ne vzletevshie samolety mechty," 49, my emphasis.

50. Shklovskii, "Iskusstvo, kak priem," 23, my translation.

51. Tihanov, *Birth and Death of Literary Theory*, 53.

52. Oushakine, "Tolstoy's Sofa," 96.

53. Peters, *The Marvelous Clouds*, 33.

54. "Today we need also the will to be exceedingly informed and aware." McLuhan, *Understanding Media*, 75.

CHAPTER FIVE

1. Roman Jakobson, "Randbemerkungen zur Prosa des Dichters Pasternak," in Jakobson, *Selected Writings*, 5:426. Translation cited from Roman Jakobson, "Marginal Notes on the Prose of the Poet Pasternak," in *Language in Literature*, ed. Krystyna Pomorska and Stephen Rudy (Cambridge, MA: Harvard University Press, 1987), 311.

2. Boris Pasternak, *Polnoe sobranie sochinenii* (henceforth *PSS*), 11 vols. (Moscow: Slovo, 2005), 3:187. Further references to this edition will appear in text with volume and page number. Translation cited from Angela Livingstone, *The Marsh of Gold: Pasternak's Writings on Inspiration and Creation* (Boston: Academic Studies, 2008), 111–12.

3. Kornei Chukovskii, "Boris Pasternak," in *Sobranie sochinenii*, by Kornei Chukovskii, 15 vols. (Moscow: Terra-Knizhnyi klub, 2001), 5:456.

4. Iurii Lotman, "Stikhotvoreniia rannego Pasternaka i nekotorye voprosy strukturnogo izucheniia teksta," *Trudy po znakovym sistemam* 4 (1969): 227. Translation cited from Yury Lotman, "Language and Reality in the Early Pasternak," in *Pasternak: A Collection of Critical Essays*, ed. Victor Erlich (Englewood Cliffs, NJ: Prentice-Hall, 1978), 27.

5. Molly Thomasy Blasing, *Snapshots of the Soul: Photo-Poetic Encounters in Modern Russian Culture* (Ithaca, NY: Cornell University Press, 2021), 50.

6. Livingstone, *The Marsh of Gold*, 111.

7. Mitchell and Hansen, *Critical Terms for Media Studies*, xxi. For a helpful discussion of infrastructural media, see Peters, *The Marvelous Clouds*, 14–15.

8. Marina Tsvetaeva, "Svetovoi liven'," *Epopeia* 3 (1922): 10–33.

9. Lotman, "Stikhotvoreniia rannego Pasternaka," 226; Lotman, "Language and Reality," 26.

10. Pasternak, *PSS* 1:62.

11. Olga Hughes, *The Poetic World of Boris Pasternak* (Princeton, NJ: Princeton University Press, 1974), 17–18.

12. For this version, see Pasternak, *PSS* 1:380. I am working here with the 1929 redaction, which is the better-known.

13. Lazar Fleishman, *Boris Pasternak v dvadtsatye gody* (Munich: Wilhelm Fink Verlag, 1981), 92–112.

14. Zholkovsky has published extensively on this topic. For an overview, see "Infinitivnoe pis'mo: Tropy i siuzhety (Materialy k teme)," in *Etkindovskie chteniia*, ed. P. L. Vakhtina et al. (St. Petersburg: Evropeiskii universitet v Sankt-Peterburge, 2003), 250–71. This moment in "February . . ." stands in yet starker relief when compared with the first lines of Innokenty Annensky's "Black Spring" ("Chernaia vesna," 1906), a poem that Pasternak's own clearly reprises: "Pod guly medi—grobovoi / Tvorilsia perenos . . ." (Beneath the toll of copper, the coffin / Was being borne along its way . . .). See his related work on the motif of the window in Pasternak's work. A. K. Zholkovsky, "The Window in the Poetic World of Boris Pasternak," trans. L. M. O'Toole, *New Literary History* 9, no. 2 (1978): 279–314.

15. Other, similar networks are also established, most notably that linking writing and the rooks via the cab (*proletka*, from the verb "to fly"). F. Kh. Isparova suggests a further connection between the birds' black feathers and a quill dipped in ink. Here again, these metaphors move in both directions simultane-

ously. See Isparova, "'Smeshchenie' fevralia v stikhi v stikhotvorenii B. Pasternaka "Fevral': Dostat' chernil i plakat'!" *Vestnik RGGU, Seriia: Literaturovedenie, Iazykoznanie, Kul'turologiia* 2 (2010): 136–47.

16. Paul Ricoeur, *The Rule of Metaphor: The Creation of Meaning in Language*, trans. Robert Czerny et al. (London: Routledge, 2003), 23.

17. Andrei Sinyavskii, "Poeziia Pasternaka," in *Stikhotvoreniia i poemy*, by Boris Pasternak (Moscow: Sovetskii pisatel', 1965), 23.

18. Livingstone, *The Marsh of Gold*, 47.

19. Nikolai Aseev, "Melody or Intonation," in Davie and Livingstone, *Pasternak*, 80; Sinyavskii, "Poeziia Pasternaka," 33.

20. See Briusov's observation that "history and the present day, scientific facts and the latest news, book and life—everything, with equal rights, enters Pasternak's poetry, arranged as though on a single plane." Valerii Briusov, "Vchera, segodnia i zavtra russkoi poezii," in Briusov, *Sobranie sochinenii*, 6:518.

21. On Pasternak and visual art, see Jakobson, "Randbemerkungen zur Prosa des Dichters Pasternak"; Ludmila Lavine, "The Visual, the Epic, and Pasternak's 'Devjat'sot pjatyj god,'" *Russian Literature* 71, no. 1 (2012): 75–99; Tatiana Levina, "'Stradatel'noe bogatstvo': Pasternak i russkaia zhivopis' 1910-x—nachala 1940-x gg.," *Literaturnoe obozrenie* 2 (1990): 84–89; Lotman, "Stikhotvoreniia rannego Pasternaka"; John E. Malmstad, "Boris Pasternak—The Painter's Eye," *Russian Review* 51, no. 3 (1992): 301–18; Isobel Palmer, "Re-vision in Boris Pasternak's *City*," *Slavic and East European Journal* 66, no. 3 (2022): 411–27; F. Roziner, "Pasternak i problema vzaimovliianii iskusstv," in *Boris Pasternak 1890–1990*, ed. Lev Loseff, Norwich Symposia on Russian Literature and Culture 1 (1991), 40–51; and Dasha di Simplicio, "Pasternak i zhivopis'," in *Boris Pasternak and His Times: Selected Papers from the Second International Symposium on Pasternak*, ed. Lazar Fleishman (Oakland, CA: Berkeley Slavic Studies, 1989), 195–211.

22. Cited in E. B. Pasternak, *Boris Pasternak: Materialy dlia biografii* (Moscow: Sovetskii pisatel', 1989), 286.

23. Malmstad, "Boris Pasternak—The Painter's Eye," 301–2. Malmstad ventures that Lentulov's 1913 paintings, "Moscow" ("Moskva") and "Saint Basil" ("Vasilii Blazhennyi"), both exhibited at the Jack of Diamonds exhibition in Moscow in February–March 1914, may have been the immediate inspiration for two of Pasternak's earliest published poems, "Cupronickel" ("Mel'khior") and "On Ivan the Great" ("Ob Ivane Velikom"). These appeared in the almanac *Rukonog*, put together by Bobrov under the banner of the newly formed Futurist group, Tsentrifuga, that same year. The poems were not republished during Pasternak's lifetime.

24. Marina Tsvetaeva, *Pis'ma k A. Teskovoi* (Prague: Academia, 1969), 62, Tsvetaeva's emphasis. For more detail on the influence of Pasternak's father on his poetry, see di Simplicio, "B. Pasternak i zhivopis'."

25. Rajewsky, "Border Talks," 64.

26. Lazar Fleishman makes a similar point in "K kharakteristike rannego Pasternaka," in *Stat'i o Pasternake,* by Lazar Fleishman (Bremen: K-Presse, 1977), 4–61.

27. Pasternak, *PSS* 1:344.

28. V. V. Ivanov, "The Moscow of Pasternak," in *Vospominaniia. Issledovaniia. Stat'i,* by V. V. Ivanov (Moscow: Azbukovnik, 2015), 641; Vladimir Markov, *Russian Futurism: A History* (Berkeley: University of California Press, 1968), 244. Ivanov also attributes Pasternak's use of archaic Russian expressions during this period to the influence of Khlebnikov. V. V. Ivanov, "K istorii poetiki Pasternaka futuristicheskogo perioda," in Ivanov, *Vospominaniia*, 474.

29. Peter Middleton, "How to Read a Reading of a Written Poem," *Oral Tradition* 20, no. 1 (March 2005): 17.

30. This is literally true, given Pasternak's tendency to revise his poetry. As a result, Lazar Fleishman notes, key motifs often acquire meaning over time. In Pasternak's poetry of the 1920s, for example, winter often stands for the themes of memory, antiquity, and history—themes that are latent here, but not yet clearly defined. Fleishman, *Boris Pasternak v dvadtsatye gody*, 98.

31. As Pasternak describes the mood of the collection to Tsvetaeva, "dreariness, north, the city, prose, premonitions of revolution" (*serost', sever, gorod, proza, predchuvstvuemye predposylki revoliutsii*). E. V. Pasternak and E. B. Pasternak, eds., *Perepiska Borisa Pasternaka* (Moscow: Khudozhestvennaia literatura, 1990), 357.

32. Daniel Tiffany, *Infidel Poetics: Riddles, Nightlife, Substance* (Chicago: University of Chicago Press, 2009), 61.

33. Marina Tsvetaeva, "Epos i lirika sovremennoi Rossii," in *Sobranie sochinenii*, by M. I. Tsevtaeva, 7 vols. (Moscow: Ellis Lak, 1994), 5:386.

34. Iurii Tynianov, "Promezhutok," in *Poetika. Istoriia literatury. Kino*, by Iurii Tyninanov, ed. A.P. Chudakov, M. O. Chudakova, E.A. Toddes (Moscow: Nauka, 1977), 184..

35. Several of Pasternak's earliest poems were written before 1912, though Pasternak later appended this date to all of them. Evgenii Pasternak, "Marburge v tvorchestve Borisa Pasternaka," in *"Marburg" Borisa Pasternaka: Temy i variatsii*, ed. E. V. Pasternak (Moscow: Rossiiskii gosudarstvennyi gumanitarnyi universitet, 2009), 57.

36. Andrei Sinyavskii, "Diskussiia," in Pasternak, *"Marburg" Borisa Pasternaka*, 55. The poem was among the most frequently revisited and revised in Pasternak's oeuvre; K. M. Polivanov counts at least eight redactions. Polivanov, "Izbrannye sborniki Pasternaka i raznye redaktsii 'Marburga,'" in Pasternak, *"Marburg" Borisa Pasternaka,* 2–93.

37. Pasternak, *PSS* 1:357–58.

38. Mitchell, *Picture Theory*, 45. See also Mitchell, *Iconology*.

39. Victor Erlich, "'Strasti razriady': Zametki o 'Marburge,'" in Pasternak, *"Marburg" Borisa Pasternaka*, 25.

40. In this connection, Sinyavsky's comment that the poem represents "the birth of structure" is intriguing. Sinyavskii, "Diskussiia," in Pasternak, *"Marburg" Borisa Pasternaka*, 55.

41. Olga Peters Hasty, "Representing Ephemerality: Pasternak's 'Groza, momental'naia navek,'" in *Eternity's Hostage: Selected Papers from the Stanford International Conference on Boris Pasternak, May 2004*, ed. Lazar Fleishman (Stanford, CA: Stanford Slavic Studies, 2006), 116–32.

42. For an informative discussion of these issues, see Andrea Bachner, *The Mark of Theory: Inscriptive Figures, Poststructuralist Prehistories* (New York: Fordham University Press, 2018), 105–44.

43. Tynianov, "Promezhutok," 182.

PART III. VOICE

1. Maksimilian Voloshin, "Golosa poetov," *Rech'*, June 4, 1917.

2. Blok, *PSS* 8:55; Julie Buckler, Julie Cassiday, and Boris Wolfson, eds., *Russian Performances: Word, Object, Action* (Madison: University of Wisconsin Press, 2018), 12. See also Irina Paperno and Joan Grossman, eds., *Creating Life: The Aesthetic Utopia of Russian Modernism* (Stanford, CA: Stanford University Press, 1994).

3. Boris Eikhenbaum, "Illiuziia skaza," in *Skvoz' literaturu: Sbornik statei*, by Boris Eikhenbaum (Leningrad: Academia, 1924), 152.

4. Greene, *Post-Petrarchism*, 5.

5. Greene, *Post-Petrarchism*, 5, 8; Jonathan Culler, *Theory of the Lyric* (Cambridge, MA: Harvard University Press, 2015), 34.

6. Greene, *Post-Petrarchism*, 10; Kate Hambürger, *The Logic of Literature*, trans. Marilynn J. Rose, 2nd ed. (Bloomington: Indiana University Press, 1993).

7. Culler, *Theory of the Lyric*, 35.

8. For a typology of approaches to voice more generally, see Mladen Dolar, *A Voice and Nothing More* (Cambridge, MA: MIT Press, 2006). I do not deal in these chapters with Jacques Derrida's famous critique of the voice and the "phonocentrism" of Western metaphysics. See Derrida's extensive writings on this topic, starting with *Voice and Phenomenon: Introduction to the Problem of the Sign in Husserl's Phenomenology* (1967). For a thorough challenge to Derrida, see Adriana Cavarero, *For More Than One Voice: Toward a Philosophy of Vocal Expression*, trans. Paul A. Kottman (Palo Alto, CA: Stanford University Press, 2005).

9. See, for example, E. M. Shuvannikova, ed., *Zvuchashchii serebriannyi vek: Chitaet poet* (St. Petersburg: Nestor-istoriia, 2018); and V. Zolotukhin and V. Shmidt. eds., *Zvuchashchaia khudozhestvennaia rech': Raboty Kabineta izucheniia khudozhestvennoi rechi (1923–1930)* (Moscow: Tri kvadrata, 2018).

10. See Culler's thorough account of this history in *Theory of the Lyric*, 49–55.

11. Sylvia Huot, *From Song to Book* (Ithaca, NY: Cornell University Press, 1987).

12. On the historical motivations for and repercussions of Romanticism's entanglement of voice and poem, see Donald Wesling, *The Chances of Rhyme: Device and Modernity* (Berkeley: University of California Press, 1980). Wesling argues that Romantic poets use rhyme in order to "express the very speaking tones of the writer" and "some degree of personal meaning" (50). David Nowell Smith comments on the use of rhythm to "[impose] a single 'style,' and thereby [assure] the presence of the poet within the poem." Nowell, *On Voice in Poetry: The Work of Animation* (London: Palgrave Macmillan, 2014), 5.

13. James Longenbach, *The Resistance to Poetry* (Chicago: University of Chicago Press, 2014), 64, 61.

14. Marinetti attended one of the *samedis populaires* in 1898. These were held at the Sarah Bernhardt Theater in Paris. See Gunther Berghaus, *The Genesis of Futurism: Marinetti's Early Career and Writings 1899–1909* (Leeds, UK: Maney, 1995), 36–38; and Gunther Berghaus, *Italian Futurist Theatre, 1909–1944* (Oxford: Clarendon, 1998), 31.

15. Daria Khitrova, "Things Untimely: Death, Birth, and Poetry in Evgenii Baratynsky's 'Nedonosok,'" *Slavic and East European Journal* 64, no. 2 (2020): 293.

16. Valerii Zolotukhin, "Kolodets i kolokol: O vliianii avtorskoi deklamatsii na ispolnitel'skuiu (1905–1929)," *Voprosy teatra* 3–4 (2010): 206.

17. Five volumes of "Reader-Declaimer"—just one of a number of such anthologies—were published in total, each in multiple editions. To give a sense of their popularity, Brang provides the following figures: "Volume five came out in 1916. In the same year the overall circulation for volume one, then in its 11th edition, reached 85,000 copies; for volume two, then in its sixth edition, 32,000 copies; and for volume three (third edition), 24,000 copies." Peter Brang, *Zvuchashchee slovo: Zametki po teorii i istorii deklamatsionnogo iskusstva v Rossii*, trans. Maria Sokol'skaia and Peter Brang (Moscow: Iazyki slavianskoi kul'tury, 2010), 131.

18. On the rise of celebrity culture and the growing popularity of gramophone records, see Anna Fishzon, *Fandom, Authenticity, and Opera: Mad Acts and Letter Scenes in Fin-de-Siècle Russia* (New York: Palgrave Macmillan, 2013).

CHAPTER SIX

1. Boris Eikhenbaum, "O chtenii stikhov," *Zhizn' iskusstva* 290 (November 12, 1919).

2. Ozarovskii died in emigration in Paris. Vsevolodskii-Gerngross had been his student before the revolution. See M. P. Ossovskaia, "Sviaz vremen: Mezhdistsiplinarnaia integratsiia," *Golos i rech'* 1 (2010): 9. *Golos i rech'* is the cur-

rent journal of the Russian Academy of the Voice (Rossiiskaia obshchestvennaia akademiia golosa), established in 2007 following the publication of archival documents related to the Institute of the Living Word (also in 2007). See Ekaterina Choun and Craig Brandist, "Iz predystorii Instituta zhivogo slova: Protokoly zasedanii kursov khudozhestvennogo slova," *Novoe literaturnoe obozrenie* 4 (August 2007): 96–106.

3. The term "zhivaia rech'" (living speech) is also common in this context.

4. The term *chitka*, typically used in the theater, was also commonly used during this time to describe literary readings. See, for example, Bernshtein's comment: "Recordings of genuine readings [*zapisi podlinnoi chitki*] by poets are of great cultural and immediate artistic value." L. A. Shilov, *"Ia slyshal po radio golos Tolstogo . . .": Ocherki zvuchashchei literatury* (Moscow, 1989), 78. On the close links between modernist poetry reading and the theater, see Zolotukhin, "Kolodets i kolokol."

5. *Zapiski Instituta zhivogo slova* 1 (Petrograd, 1919), 9. See also I. Ivanova, "Razvitie poniatiia 'zhivoe slovo' v russkoi kul'ture XIX—nachala XX veka (ot slovosochetaniia k ofitsial'nomu institutu)," *Schweizerische Beiträge zum XIII. Internationalen Slavistenkongress in Ljubljana, August 2003, Slavica Helvetica* 70 (2003): 103–17.

6. For this history, see Michael S. Gorham, *Speaking in Soviet Tongues: Language Culture and the Politics of Voice in Revolutionary Russia* (DeKalb: Northern Illinois University Press, 2003); and Martha Weitzel Hickey, *The Writer in Petrograd and the House of the Arts* (Evanston, IL: Northwestern University Press, 2009).

7. Olenina, *Psychomotor Aesthetics*, 44.

8. See the discussion in Olenina, *Psychomotor Aesthetics*, 49–50 and on; Raffaella Vassena, "K rekonstruktsii deiatel'nosti Instituta Zhivogo Slova (1918–1924)," *Novoe literaturnoe obozreniie* 4 (2007): 79–95.

9. Olenina, *Psychomotor Aesthetics*, 51fn29.

10. "Opyty lingvisticheskogo tolkovaniia stikhotvorenii. 1. 'Vospominanie' Pushkina," *Russkaia rech'*, ed. L. Shcherba (Leningrad: Academia, 1923). Reprinted in L. V. Shcherba, *Izbrannye raboty po russkomu iazyku* (Moscow: Uchpedgiz, 1957), 30. Shcherba was also involved in the speech melody project at the Institute of the Living Word.

11. Eduard Sievers, "Zur Rhythmik und Melodik des neuhochdeutschen Sprechverses (1893)," in *Rhythmisch-Melodische Studien*, by Eduard Sievers (Heidelberg: Winter, 1912), 39. This book collects essays written from 1893 to 1908.

12. Eduard Sievers, "Über Sprachmelodisches in der deutschen Dichtung (1901)," in Sievers, *Rhythmisch-Melodische Studien*, 66.

13. Sievers, *Rhythmisch-Melodische Studien*, 39.

14. Eduard Sievers, "Über ein neues Hilfsmittel philologischer Kritik (1903)," in Sievers, *Rhythmisch-Melodische Studien*, 80–81.

15. The classic example of this bias in contemporary scholarship is Walter Ong, *Orality and Literacy: The Technologizing of the Word* (London: Methuen, 1982). For a critique of Ong and a helpful history of this tendency, see Jonathan Sterne, *The Audible Past: Cultural Origins of Sound Reproduction* (Durham, NC: Duke University Press, 2003), 10–19.

16. Indeed, it may be precisely due to the proliferation of new instruments for measuring and recording sound and capturing graphic traces of it that Sievers formulated this notion; there is a clear parallel with Bely's efforts to understand the essence of creativity by graphically representing rhythm in his *zapisi.* For a fascinating discussion of these technologies, see Olenina, *Psychomotor Aesthetics*. On the wider context, see Jason David Hall, "Materializing Meter: Physiology, Psychology, Prosody," *Victorian Poetry* 49, no. 2 (Summer 2011): 179–97.

17. Sievers, "Über Sprachmelodisches in der deutschen Dichtung," 62.

18. Boris Eikhenbaum, *O poezii* (Leningrad: Sovetskii pisatel', 1969), 337.

19. Eikhenbaum, *O poezii*, 336. Eikhenbaum was in a dispute with Jakobson regarding this same issue at the time of writing *Melodics*, and probably had his work particularly in mind. Tynianov and Shklovsky also insisted on the separation of poetics and linguistics. See the discussion in Hansen-Löve, *Russkii formalizm*, 283–84.

20. Eikhenbaum, *O poezii*, 340.

21. Eikhenbaum, *O poezii*, 327–29.

22. Vassena, "K rekonstruktsii deiatel'nosti Instituta zhivogo slova."

23. Vassena, "K rekonstruktsii deiatel'nosti Instituta zhivogo slova," 90.

24. Many of these recordings were severely damaged due to poor storage following the dissolution of the institute; they were restored only in the 1960s, when they were rediscovered by Lev Shilov. See L. A. Shilov, "Istoriia odnoi kollektsii," in *Zvuchashchii mir: Kniga o zvukovoi dokumentalistike*, by V. N. Vozchikov (Moscow: Iskusstvo, 1979), 121–45.

25. Sergei Bernshtein, "Stikh i deklamatsiia," in *Russkaia rech'*, ed. L. Shcherba (Leningrad: Academia, 1927), 35.

26. Bernshtein, "Stikh i deklamatsiia," 35. Bernshtein queries Sievers's assertion that it is difficult to hear an author read their own work aloud; as he notes, poetry recitation was growing in popularity in Germany during this period, too. For more information on the culture of poetry recitation in Germany, see Brang, *Zvuchashchee slovo*.

27. Bernshtein is in broad agreement with Tynianov's assessment of Ohrenphilologie in *Problem of Verse Language*, discussed above. As Tynianov summarizes, "the acoustic approach does not exhaust all elements of the artistic work, on the one hand, and introduces extraneous and unneeded elements, on the other." *Problema stikhotvornogo iazyka*, 43.

28. Bernshtein, "Stikh i deklamatsiia," 18–19.

29. Bernshtein, "Stikh i deklamatsiia," 34.

30. Bernshtein, "Stikh i deklamatsiia," 38–39.

31. See Timothy D. Sergay, "'A Music of Letters': Reconsidering Eikhenbaum's *Melodics of Verse*," *Slavic and East European Journal* 59, no. 2 (Summer 2015): 194–211. See also Bernshtein's criticisms on this point in "Stikh i deklamatsiia"; and V. M. Zhirmunskii, "Melodika stikha (po povodu knigi B.M. Eikhenbauma *Melodika stikha*, Pb., 1922)," reprinted in V. M. Zhirmunskii, *Voprosy teorii literatury: Stat'i 1916–1926* (Leningrad: Academia, 1928), 89–153.

32. Bernshtein, "Stikh i deklamatsiia," 38.

33. Eikhenbaum, *O poezii*, 338.

34. Eric Griffiths, *The Printed Voice of Victorian Poetry* (Oxford: Clarendon, 1989), 22.

35. Zhirmunskii, "Melodika stikha."

36. Eikhenbaum, *O poezii*, 335.

37. Eikhenbaum proposes these terms as alternatives to existing attempts at categorization (including by Zhirmunsky), which tend, by contrast, to distinguish between "songlike" lyric, on the one hand, and plastic or visual lyric, on the other. See the discussion in Eikhenbaum, *O poezii*, 329.

38. Zhirmunskii, "Melodika stikha," 149.

39. Zhirmunskii, "Melodika stikha," 149.

40. Boris Eikhenbaum, "O zvukakh v stikhe," in Eikhenbaum, *Skvoz' literaturu*, 204, 206. The line in question is "Shipen'e penistykh bokalov / I punsha plamen' goluboi" (from *Mednyi vsadnik*). Zhirmunsky brings up this line in his review of *Melodics*, using it to illustrate the importance of alliteration in an account of Pushkin's prosody.

41. Professional declaimers preferred the terms "expressive reading" (*vyrazitel'noe chtenie*) or "artistic reading" (*khudozhestvennoe chtenie*) to "declamation" (*deklamatsiia*), as the latter term was negatively associated with the classical style of declamation that had dominated in nineteenth-century theater but which was now considered outdated. Bernshtein, Eikhenbaum, and other researchers in this field use the term "declamation" as a neutral synonym for "reading aloud." V. Shmidt, "Zvuchashchaia khudozhestvennaia rech'," in Zolotukhin and Shmidt, *Zvuchashchaia khudozhestvennaia rech'*, 415.

42. Boris Eikhenbaum, "O kamernoi deklamatsii," in Boris Eikhenbaum, *O poezii* (Leningrad: Sovetskii pisatel', 1969), 514.

43. Eikhenbaum devotes a substantial portion of his essay to discussion of the work of the German scholar Robert Böhringer, with whom he appears broadly to agree, particularly on the importance of allowing the rhythm and sound texture of the poem to dictate the manner of recitation. While Eikhenbaum does not criticize Böhringer directly, the position he marks out in the essay is clearly at a distance from Böhringer's description of the "true declaimer" as "he who becomes a vessel for the poetic spirit, 'an intermediary between the crowd and the genius.'" Cited in Eikhenbaum, "O kamernoi deklamatsii," 533.

44. Eikhenbaum, "O kamernoi deklamatsii," 514.

45. V. E. Molodiakov, "Valerii Briusov: 'Ne po-akterski, a po-'poetski,'" in *Zvuchashchii serebriannyi vek: Chitaet poet*, ed. E. M. Shuvannikova (St. Petersburg: Nestor-istoriia, 2018), 81.

46. See the discussion in Zolotukhin, "Kolodets i kolokol," esp. 210–11. As Zolotukhin describes, Vsevolod Meyerhold took an active interest in the possibilities opened up for theatrical performance by authorial reading as early as 1905.

47. Eikhenbaum, "O kamernoi deklamatsii," 516.

48. Eikhenbaum, "O kamernoi deklamatsii," 513.

49. Cited in K. L. Rudnitsky, *Russkoe rezhisserskoe iskusstvo 1908–1917* (Moscow: Nauka, 1990), 72. This approach attracted particular criticism when his theater staged plays in verse, such as the 1915 production of Pushkin's *Little Tragedies*, when, as the Symbolist writer Fyodor Sologub commented caustically, "poetry ruined everything," getting in the way of the Art Theatre's preferred interpretation of the play as a "depiction of events and emotional experiences." Rudnitsky, *Russkoe rezhisserskoe iskusstvo*, 148.

50. Eikhenbaum, "O kamernoi deklamatsii," 536.

51. Eikhenbaum, "O kamernoi deklamatsii," 514, 541. See also Eikhenbaum's reaction to a Futurist performance in 1914: "I ran headlong for the stairs, because I felt that, a little more and I would cry out, throw myself onto the stage and begin a fight." Letter to Liubov' Gurevich of February 9, 1914, cited in Chudakova and Toddes, "Stranitsy nauchnoi biografii."

52. Eikhenbaum, "O kamernoi deklamatsii," 538.

53. Eikhenbaum, "O tragedii i tragicheskom," in Eikhenbaum, *Skvoz' literaturu*, 77.

54. Eikhenbaum, "O kamernoi deklamatsii," 514, 520.

55. Eikhenbaum, "O kamernoi deklamatsii," 539.

56. Olenina, *Psychomotor Aesthetics*, 89.

57. Eikhenbaum, "O chtenii stikhov," 1.

CHAPTER SEVEN

1. Janecek, *The Look of Russian Literature*, 216.

2. See, for example, the memoirs cited in *Poeziia russkogo futurizma*, ed. V. N. Al'fonsov and S. R. Krasitskii (St. Petersburg: Akademicheskii proekt, 1999), 658–64.

3. A facsimile of this edition can be found in Al'fonsov and Krasitskii, *Poeziia russkogo futurizma*, 129–83.

4. Nikolai Khardzhiev, *Ot Maiakovskogo do Kruchenykh: Izbrannye raboty o russkom futurizme* (Moscow: Gileia, 2006), 345.

5. Janecek, *The Look of Russian Literature*, 217.

6. Cited in Pavel Fokin and Dmitrii Timofeev, eds., *Maiakovskii bez gliantsa* (St. Petersburg: Pal'mira, 2016), 420–21.

7. A. A. Mgebrov, *Zhizn' v teatre*, 2 vols. (Moscow: Academia, 1932), 2:280.

8. A. Serditova, "Avtograf na notnoi bumage (K istorii sozdaniia tragedii *Vladimir Maiakovskii*)," *Voprosy literatury* 7 (1983): 202.

9. Aleksandra Kremer, *The Sound of Modern Polish Poetry: Performance and Recording after World War II* (Cambridge, MA: Harvard University Press, 2021), 32.

10. Charles Bernstein, ed., *Close Listening: Poetry and the Performed Word* (New York: Oxford University Press, 1998), 9.

11. The plurality of the text is demonstrated further by the extensive changes to the text and structure of the play that Mayakovsky later sketched out on a copy of the first printed edition. See the discussion in Serditova, "Avtograf na notnoi bumage."

12. For a useful discussion of these issues, see Julia Novak, "Performing the Poet, Reading (to) the Audience: Some Thoughts on Live Poetry as Literary Communication," *Journal of Literary Theory* 6, no. 2 (2012): 358–82.

13. L. A. Shilov, *Golosa, zazvuchashchie vnov'* (Moscow: Al'daon, 2004), 93.

14. V. V. Maiakovskii, *Polnoe sobranie sochinenii* (henceforth *PSS*), 13 vols. (Moscow: Gosudarstvennoe izdatel'stvo khudozhestvennoi literatury, 1955), 1:175. Further references to this edition will appear in text with volume and page numbers. Translations are my own.

15. Viktor Shklovskii, *Zhili-byli* (Moscow: Sovetskii pisatel', 1966), 296.

16. Maiakovskii, *PSS* 1:40.

17. *Trebnik troikh: Sbornik stikhov i risunok* (Moscow, 1913), 35.

18. See V. N. Terekhina, "'U iskusstva putei mnogo': Vladimir Maiakovskii i Ol'ga Rozanova," *Nashe nasledie* 126 (2018), http://www.nasledie-rus.ru/podshivka/12602.php.

19. Cited in A. Metchenko, "Rannii Maiakovskii," in *Vladimir Maiakovskii: Sbornik*, ed. A. L. Dymshitsa and O. V. Tsekhnovitsera (Moscow: AN SSSR, 1940), 31.

20. Cited in Metchenko, "Rannii Maiakovskii," 30.

21. Such events were prohibited in 1862 due to their popularity and often oppositional character. Christopher Ely, *Underground Petersburg: Radical Populism, Urban Space and the Tactics of Subversion in Reform-Era Russia* (DeKalb: Northern Illinois University Press, 2016), 45–47. See also Stephen Lovell, "*Glasnost'* in Practice: Public Speaking in the Era of Alexander II," *Past & Present* 218, no. 1 (February 2013): 127–58.

22. For further discussion of Blok and the culture of poetry readings during this period, see Iurii Lotman, "Blok i narodnaia kul'tura," in *O poetakh i poezii*, by Iurii Lotman (St. Petersburg: Iskusstvo-SPb, 1996), 659–61.

23. Livak, *In Search of Russian Modernism*, 186. See also Iurii Lotman, "Russkaia literatura poslepetrovskoi epoki i khristianskaia traditsiia," in *Iu. M. Lotman i tartusko-moskovskaia semioticheskaia shkola*, ed. A. Koshelev (Moscow: Gnosis, 1994), 365–79.

24. See the discussions in Oksana Bulgakowa, *Golos kak kul'turnyi fenomen* (Moscow: Novoe literaturnoe obozrenie, 2015), 156–64; Andy Byford, *Literary Scholarship in Late Imperial Russia: Rituals of Academic Institutionalization* (Oxford: Legenda, 2005); Louise McReynolds, *Russia at Play: Leisure Activities at the End of the Tsarist Era* (Ithaca, NY: Cornell University Press, 2003); Stephen P. Frank and Mark D. Steinberg, eds., *Cultures in Flux: Lower-Class Values, Practices, and Resistance in Late Imperial Russia* (Princeton, NJ: Princeton University Press, 1994); Jane Sharp, "The Russian Avant-Garde and Its Audience: Moscow, 1913," *Modernism/modernity* 6, no. 3 (1999): 91–116; and Sarah Warren, *Mikhail Larionov and the Cultural Politics of Late Imperial Russia* (Farnham, UK: Ashgate, 2013).

25. The relevance of Max Weber's concept of charisma in this context is discussed at more length in Gregory Freidin, *A Coat of Many Colors: Osip Mandelstam and His Mythologies of Self-Presentation* (Berkeley: University of California Press, 1987), esp. 11–19.

26. Sarah Dadswell, "The Spectacle of Russian Futurism: The Emergence and Development of Russian Futurist Performance, 1910–1914" (unpublished doctoral thesis, University of Sheffield, 2005), 19.

27. See, for example, Mgebrov's account: "When people started to talk of the two upcoming futurist performances . . . in Komissarzhevskaia's former theater, I decided firmly not to see them. Why see the full horror of humanity's fall . . . All this was all the more unpleasant given that, in this very theater, I had once had the good fortune to perform on the same stage with the unforgettable Vera Fedorovna [Komissarzhevskaia]." Mgebrov, *Zhizn' v teatre*, 2:274.

28. Marina Tsvetaeva, "Poet o kritike," *Blagonamerennyi* 2 (1926): 112–13.

29. Livak, *In Search of Russian Modernism*, 196.

30. As Livak points out, modernist anti-commercialism often served as a transparent cover for antisemitic sentiment. The favorite Stray Dog insult for non-initiates, "pharmacists," was a label that "fused two modernist mythologemes—the bourgeois and the Jews." Livak, *In Search of Russian Modernism*, 196.

31. Livak, *In Search of Russian Modernism*, 196.

32. Richard Schechner, *Performance Theory*, 2nd ed. (London: Routledge, 1988), 193–96.

33. Schechner, *Performance Theory*, 195.

34. Aleksei Beliakov, *"Tvoe Velichestvo—Politekhnicheskii!" Bol'shie liudi Bol'shoi auditorii* (Moscow: Slovo, 2022), 76–81. See the newspaper accounts of this evening gathered in V. Katanian, *Maiakovskii: Khronika zhizni i deiatel'nosti* (Moscow: Sovetskii pisatel, 1985).

35. The debate about the value of Ilya Repin, for example, organized following the vandalism of one of his paintings in Moscow's Tretyakov Gallery in 1913, was in part an attempt by the Futurist group the Jack of Diamonds to exploit this

news story in order to drum up visitors for their most recent exhibition. Beliakov, "*Tvoe Velichestvo—Politekhnicheskii!*" 76–81.

36. On Futurism and performance art, see RoseLee Goldberg, *Performance Art: From Futurism to the Present* (New York: Thames and Hudson, 2011).

37. *Futuristy: Pervyi zhurnal russkikh futuristov* 1–2 (1914): 67.

38. Mayakovsky gave a talk in early 1913 entitled "Prishedshii sam" ("He Came Himself"), a reference to Bal'mont's essay, "Griadushchii kham" ("The Coming Boor"). Bal'mont returned to Moscow in May 1913 following seven years in emigration. The incident at the train station was followed a few days later by heckling at an evening of poetry at the Society of Free Aesthetics held in Bal'mont's honor. See V. Katanian, *Maiakovskii: Literaturnaia khronika* (Moscow: Gosudarstvennoe izdatel'stvo khudozhestvennoi literatury, 1956), 47. Another such public attack took place at an evening of poetry at the Society of Free Aesthetics on November 1, 1913. As one newspaper report describes it: "The mood of the evening was somewhat spoiled by yet another appearance of the 'Futurists.' Mr. Mayakovsky declared, speaking rather coarsely, the backwardness of Bal'mont's work. Interrupted rather sharply by V. Briusov, he left the building." *Golos Moskvy*, November 2, 1913.

39. On Futurism's relationship with the carnival tradition, see Katerina Clark, *Petersburg: Crucible of Cultural Revolution* (Cambridge, MA: Harvard University Press, 1995). See also Joan Neuberger, "Culture Besieged: Hooliganism and Futurism," in *Cultures in Flux: Lower-Class Values, Practices, and Resistance in Late Imperial Russia*, ed. Stephen P. Frank and Mark D. Steinberg (Princeton, NJ: Princeton University Press, 1994), 185–203.

40. See the discussion in Pamela Davidson, "The Validation of the Writer's Prophetic Status in the Russian Literary Tradition: From Pushkin and Iazykov through Gogol to Dostoevsky," *Russian Review* 62, no. 4 (2003): 508–36.

41. "The other day, a writer (not of my generation) told me about previous literary evenings; they were very rare and always distinguished by special solemnity. There is no question that Dostoevsky was right to 'burn people's hearts' with the 'Prophets' of Pushkin and Lermontov from the stage. It was an unparalleled triumph . . . Is there anything like that now, can there be?" Blok, *PSS* 8:58.

42. *Trebnik troikh*, 35.

43. Janecek, *Zaum*, 55.

44. Clark, *Petersburg*, 84.

45. Peters, *Speaking into the Air: A History of the Idea of Communication* (Chicago: University of Chicago Press, 1999), 38.

46. As Peters has argued, the ultimate "disseminator" is Jesus, who scatters his parables over the ground in full knowledge of the fact that some of these seeds will not germinate. See his illuminating discussion of dialogue and dissemination in *Speaking into the Air*, 33–62.

47. Peters, *Speaking into the Air*, 36; Zolotukhin, "Kolodets i kolokol," 16.

48. *Pervyi zhurnal russkikh futuristov*, 4, original punctuation.

49. Edward Brown, *Mayakovsky: A Poet in Revolution* (Princeton, NJ: Princeton University Press, 1973), 94–96.

50. Bliumbaum, *Musica mundana*, 41.

51. Cited in Bliumbaum, *Musica mundana*, 41.

52. Varvara Kukushkina, Ilona Svetlikova, and Pavel Iushin, "Nauchnye konteksty 'zvezdnogo uzhasa': Kommentarii k Andreiu Belomu," *Die Welt der Slaven* 65, no. 1 (2019): 73–88.

53. Kukushkina, Svetlikova, and Iushin, "Nauchnye konteksty 'zvezdnogo uzhasa,'" 80–81.

54. Jonathan Culler, "Apostrophe," in *The Pursuit of Signs: Semiotics, Literature, Deconstruction*, by Jonathan Culler (Ithaca, NY: Cornell University Press, 1981), 135–54.

55. Iurii Annenkov, *Dnevnik moikh vstrech*, 2 vols. (Moscow: Khudozhestvennaia literatura, 1991), 1:117.

56. See Peters, *Speaking into the Air*, 33–62.

57. See the discussion in Janecek, *The Look of Russian Literature*, 236–46 ("How to Read Mayakovsky").

CONCLUSION

1. Sybille Krämer, "Kulturanthropologie der Medien: Thesen zur Einführung," in *Praktiken des Performativen*, ed. Christoph Wulf (Berlin: Akademie-Verlag Fischer-Lichte), 130–33.

2. Rajewsky, "Border Talks," 52.

3. T. J. Clark, *Farewell to an Idea: Episodes from a History of Modernism* (New Haven, CT: Yale University Press, 1999).

4. Peters, *The Marvelous Clouds*, 21.

5. Friedman, *Planetary Modernisms*.

6. Friedman, "Periodizing Modernism," 432.

7. Livak, *In Search of Russian Modernism*. On émigré modernism, see, for example, Leonid Livak, *How It Was Done in Paris: Russian Emigre Literature and French Modernism* (Madison: University of Wisconsin Press, 2003); and Maria Rubins, *Russian Montparnasse: Transnational Writing in Interwar Paris* (New York: Palgrave Macmillan, 2015).

8. Levine, *Forms*, 19.

9. Franco Moretti, "The Slaughterhouse of Literature," *Modern Language Quarterly* 61, no. 1 (March 2000): 225.

10. Tihanov, *Birth and Death of Literary Theory*, 177–82.

11. Jahan Ramazani, "Form," in *A New Vocabulary for Global Modernism*, ed. Eric Hayot and Rebecca L. Walkowitz (New York: Columbia University Press, 2016), 115.

12. Ramazani, "Form," 116.

13. Susan Stanford Friedman, "World Modernisms, World Literature, and

Comparativity," in *The Oxford Handbook of Global Modernisms*, ed. Mark Wollaeger and Matt Eatough (Oxford: Oxford University Press, 2012), 502.

14. Ramazani, "Form," 117.

15. Ram, "The Scale of Global Modernisms," 1372–73.

16. Jahan Ramazani, *A Transnational Poetics* (Chicago: University of Chicago Press, 2009).

17. See, for example, the discussion in Mikhail Gasparov, "Antinomichnost' poetiki russkogo modernizma," in Gasparov, *Izbrannye trudy*, 2:286–304.

18. See, for example, Michael Kunichika, *"Our Native Antiquity": Archaeology and Aesthetics in the Culture of Russian Modernism* (Boston: Academic Studies, 2015); and Shevelenko, *Modernizm kak arkhaizm.*

19. Merrill, *Origins of Russian Literary Theory*, esp. 9–19.

20. Perloff, *The Futurist Moment*, 6.

21. Ram, "The Scale of Global Modernisms."

22. For reflections on the relative merits of this approach, see the discussion in Jonathan Kramnick and Anahid Nersessian, "Form and Explanation," *Critical Inquiry* 43, no. 3 (2017): 650–69.

23. Friedman, "Periodizing Modernism," 428.

24. Ram, "The Scale of Global Modernisms," 1373.

Bibliography

Akhmatova, Anna. "Letter to S. V. Shtein (February 1907)." *Literaturnoe nasledstvo: Aleksandr Blok: Novye materialy i issledovaniia* 92, no. 3 (1982): 271.

Al'fonsov, V. N., and S. R. Krasitskii, eds. *Poeziia russkogo futurizma.* St. Petersburg: Akademicheskii proekt, 1999.

Annenkov, Iurii. *Dnevnik moikh vstrech*, 2 vols. Moscow: Khudozhestvennaia literatura, 1991.

Any, Carol. *Boris Eikhenbaum: Voices of a Russian Formalism.* Palo Alto, CA: Stanford University Press, 1994.

Aseev, Nikolai. "Melody or Intonation." In *Pasternak*, edited by Donald Davie and Angela Livingstone, 73–84. London: Macmillan, 1969.

Attridge, Derek. "Beyond Metrics: Richard Cureton's Rhythmic Phrasing in English Verse." *Poetics Today* 17, no. 1 (1996): 9–27.

———. *The Rhythms of English Poetry*. London: Longman, 1982.

Bachner, Andrea. *The Mark of Theory: Inscriptive Figures, Poststructuralist Prehistories.* New York: Fordham University Press, 2018.

Baevskii, V. S. "Lirika Pasternaka v istoriko-kul'turnom kontekste." *Izvestiia Akademii nauk: Seriia literatury i iazyka* 47, no. 2 (1988): 130–41.

Bailey, James. "Reviewed Work: *Alexander Blok: A Study in Rhythm and Metre* by Robin Kemball." *Slavic and East European Journal* 11, no. 1 (Spring 1967): 92–95.

Beliakov, Aleksei. *"Tvoe Velichestvo—Politekhnicheskii!" Bol'shie liudi Bol'shoi auditorii.* Moscow: Slovo, 2022.

Belyi, Andrei. *Mezhdu dvukh revoliutsii*, edited by A. Lavrov. Moscow: Khudozhestvennaia literatura, 1990.

———. "Mysl' i iazyk (Filosofiia iazyka A.A. Potebni)." *Logos* 2 (1910): 240–58.

———. *Ritm kak dialektika i "Mednyi Vsadnik."* Moscow: Federatsiia, 1929.

———. *Sobranie sochinenii.* 14 vols. Moscow: Respublika, 1994–2014.

———. *Simvolizm: Kniga statei.* Moscow: Musaget, 1910.

Benjamin, Walter. *The Arcades Project*. Translated by Howard Eiland and Kevin McLaughlin, edited by Rolf Teidemann. Cambridge, MA: Harvard University Press, 1999.

Berghaus, Gunther. *The Genesis of Futurism: Marinetti's Early Career and Writings 1899–1909*. Leeds, UK: Maney, 1995.

———. *Italian Futurist Theatre, 1909–1944*. Oxford: Clarendon, 1998.

Bergson, Henri. *Matter and Memory*. Translated by Nancy Margaret Paul and W. Scott Palmer. New York: Dover, 2004.

———. *Time and Free Will: An Essay on the Immediate Data of Consciousness*. Translated by F. L. Pogson. New York: Dover, 2001.

Berlina, Alexandra. *Viktor Shklovsky: A Reader*. London: Bloomsbury, 2016.

Bernshtein, Sergei. "Stikh i deklamatsiia." In *Russkaia rech'*, edited by L. Shcherba, 7–41. Leningrad: Academia, 1927.

Bernstein, Charles. *Close Listening: Poetry and the Performed Word*. Oxford: Oxford University Press, 1998.

Bethea, David. *The Shape of the Apocalypse in Modern Russian Fiction*. Princeton, NJ: Princeton University Press, 1989.

Blasing, Molly Thomasy. *Snapshots of the Soul: Photo-Poetic Encounters in Modern Russian Culture*. Ithaca, NY: Cornell University Press, 2021.

Blasing, Mutlu Konuk. *Lyric Poetry: The Pain and the Pleasure of Words*. Princeton, NJ: Princeton University Press, 2008.

Bliumbaum, Arkadyi. *Musica mundana i russkaia obshchestvennost': Tsikl statei o tvorchestve Aleksandra Bloka*. Moscow: Novoe literaturnoe obozrenie, 2017.

———. "'Sud'ba' versus 'Sluchai' v tvorchestve Bloka epokhi 'antitezy': Neskol'ko nabliudenii." *Novoe literaturnoe obozrenie* 109 (2011): 229–52.

Blok, A. A. *Polnoe sobranie sochinenii i pisem*. 20 vols. Moscow: Nauka, 1997– .

———. *Sobranie sochinenii*. 8 vols. Moscow-Leningrad: Khudozestvennaia literatura, 1962.

Bogatyreva, S. "Kratkoe zhizneopisanie professora Sergeia Bernshteina, uchenogo-lingvista, v vospominaniiakh i 43-kh dokumentakh." *Voprosy literatury* 6 (December 2013): 161–228.

Bolter, Jay David, and Richard Grusin. *Remediation: Understanding New Media*. Cambridge, MA: MIT Press, 1999.

Bowlt, John. "Aleksandr Blok: The Poem 'The Unknown Lady.'" *Texas Studies in Literature and Language* 17 (1975): 349–56.

Brang, Peter. *Zvuchashchee slovo: Zametki po teorii i istorii deklamatsionnogo iskusstva v Rossii*. Translated by Maria Sokol'skaia and Peter Brang. Moscow: Iazyki slavianskoi kul'tury, 2010.

Braun, Marta. *Picturing Time: The Work of Etienne-Jules Marey*. Chicago: University of Chicago Press, 1992.

Brik, Osip. "Ritm i sintaksis." *Novyi Lef* 3–7 (1927).

———. "The So-Called Formal Method." In *Formalist Theory*, translated by A. Shukman, edited by L. O'Toole and A. Shukman, 90–91. Colchester, UK: Holdman Books, 1977.

———. "Zvukovye povtory." *Poetika: Sborniki po teorii poeticheskogo iazyka* (1919): 58–98.

Briusov, Valerii. "God russkoi poezii: Porubezhniki." *Russkaia mysl'* 6 (1914).

———. "Novye techeniia v russkoi poezii: Futuristy." *Russkaia mysl'* 3 (1913).

———. "Otvet g. Andreevskomu." *Mir iskusstva* 1–6 (1901): 237–47.

———. *Sobranie sochinenii.* 7 vols. Moscow: Khudozestvennaia literatura, 1973.

Brown, Edward. *Mayakovsky: A Poet in Revolution.* Princeton, NJ: Princeton University Press, 1973.

Buckler, Julie, Julie Cassiday, and Boris Wolfson, eds. *Russian Performances: Word, Object, Action.* Madison: University of Wisconsin Press, 2018.

Bulgakowa, Oksana. *Golos kak kul'turnyi fenomen.* Moscow: Novoe literaturnoe obozrenie, 2015.

Byford, Andy. *Literary Scholarship in Late Imperial Russia: Rituals of Academic Institutionalization.* Oxford: Legenda, 2005.

Calinescu, Matei. *Five Faces of Modernity: Modernism, Avant-Garde, Decadence, Kitsch, Postmodernism.* Durham, NC: Duke University Press, 1987.

Cameron, Sharon. *Lyric Time: Emily Dickinson and the Limits of Genre.* Baltimore, MD: Johns Hopkins University Press, 1979.

Cassedy, Steven. "Bely the Thinker." In *Andrei Bely: Spirit of Symbolism*, edited by John E. Malmstad. Ithaca, NY: Cornell University Press, 1987.

———. *Flight from Eden: The Origins of Modern Literary Criticism and Theory.* Berkeley: University of California Press, 1990.

———. "*Petersburg* and Music in Theory and Literature." In *A Reader's Guide to Andrei Bely's "Petersburg,"* edited by Leonid Livak. Madison: University of Wisconsin Press, 2018.

———, ed. *Selected Essays of Andrei Bely.* Berkeley: University of California Press, 1985.

Cavanagh, Clare. *Lyric Poetry and Modern Politics.* New Haven, CT: Yale University Press, 2009.

Cavarero, Adriana. *For More Than One Voice: Toward a Philosophy of Vocal Expression.* Translated by Paul A. Kottman. Palo Alto, CA: Stanford University Press, 2005.

Chandler, Robert, Boris Dralyuk, and Irina Mashinski, eds. *The Penguin Book of Russian Poetry.* London: Penguin, 2015.

Choun, Ekaterina, and Craig Brandist. "Iz predystorii Instituta zhivogo slova: Protokoly zasedanii kursov khudozhestvennogo slova." *Novoe literaturnoe obozrenie* 4 (August 2007): 96–106.

Christa, Boris, ed. *Andrey Bely: Centenary Papers.* Amsterdam: Adolf M. Hakkert, 1980.

Chudakova, M., and E. Toddes. "Stranitsy nauchnoi biografii B.M. Eikhenbauma." *Voprosy literatury* 1 (1987): 128–62.

Chukovskii, Kornei. "Boris Pasternak." In Kornei Chukovskii, *Sobranie sochinenii*, 15 vols., 5:454–463. Moscow: Terra-Knizhnyi klub, 2001.

Clark, Katerina. *Petersburg: Crucible of Cultural Revolution.* Cambridge, MA: Harvard University Press, 1995.

Clark, T. J. *Farewell to an Idea: Episodes from a History of Modernism.* New Haven, CT: Yale University Press, 1999.

Culler, Jonathan. *The Pursuit of Signs.* London: Routledge, 2001.

———. *Theory of the Lyric.* Cambridge, MA: Harvard University Press, 2015.

———. "Why Rhythm?" In *Critical Rhythm: The Poetics of a Literary Life Form,* edited by Jonathan Culler and Ben Glaser, 21–39. New York: Fordham University Press, 2019.

Culler, Jonathan, and Ben Glaser, eds. *Critical Rhythm: The Poetics of a Literary Life Form.* New York: Fordham University Press, 2019.

Dadswell, Sarah. "The Spectacle of Russian Futurism: The Emergence and Development of Russian Futurist Performance, 1910–1914." Unpublished doctoral thesis, University of Sheffield, 2005.

Davie, Donald, and Angela Livingstone, eds. *Pasternak.* London: Macmillan, 1969.

Davidson, Pamela. "The Validation of the Writer's Prophetic Status in the Russian Literary Tradition: From Pushkin and Iazykov through Gogol to Dostoevsky." *Russian Review* 62, no. 4 (2003): 508–36.

Dayan, Peter, and David Evans. "Rhythm in Literature after the Crisis in Verse." *Paragraph* 33, no. 2 (2010): 147–57.

Delic, Irene Masing. *Abolishing Death: A Salvation Myth of Russian Twentieth-Century Literature.* Stanford, CA: Stanford University Press, 1992.

Dolar, Mladen. *A Voice and Nothing More.* Cambridge, MA: MIT Press, 2006.

Dworkin, Craig. *No Medium.* Cambridge, MA: MIT Press, 2013.

Edmond, Jacob. *Make It the Same: Poetry in the Age of Global Media.* New York: Columbia University Press, 2019.

Eikhenbaum, Boris. "O chtenii stikhov." *Zhizn' iskusstva* 290 (November 12, 1919): 1.

———. *O literature.* Moscow: Sovetskii pisatel', 1987.

———. *O poezii.* Leningrad: Sovetskii pisatel', 1969.

———. *Skvoz' literaturu: Sbornik statei.* Leningrad: Academia, 1924.

———. "Trubnyi glas." *Knizhnyi ugol* 1 (1918): 3–5.

Elleström, Lars. "The Modalities of Media: A Model for Understanding Intermedial Relations." In *Media Borders, Multimodality and Intermediality,* edited by Lars Elleström, 11–50. Basingstoke, UK: Palgrave Macmillan, 2010.

———. "Transfer of Media Characteristics among Dissimilar Media." *Palabra Clave* 20, no. 3 (2017): 663–85.

Elsworth, John. "The Concept of Rhythm in Bely's Aesthetic Thought." In *Andrey Bely: Centenary Papers,* edited by Boris Christa, 68–80. Amsterdam: Adolf M. Hakkert, 1980.

———. *Andrei Bely: A Critical Study of the Novels.* Cambridge: Cambridge University Press, 1983.

Ely, Christopher. *Underground Petersburg: Radical Populism, Urban Space, and the Tactics of Subversion in Reform-Era Russia.* DeKalb: Northern Illinois University Press, 2016.

Erlich, Victor. *Russian Formalism: History—Doctrine*. The Hague: Mouton, 1955.

Fishzon, Anna. *Fandom, Authenticity, and Opera: Mad Acts and Letter Scenes in Fin-de-Siècle Russia*. New York: Palgrave Macmillan, 2013.

Fizer, John. *Alexander A. Potebnja's Psycholinguistic Theory of Literature*. Cambridge, MA: Harvard University Press, 1986.

Fleishman, Lazar. *Boris Pasternak: The Poet and His Politics*. Cambridge, MA: Harvard University Press, 1990.

———. *Boris Pasternak v dvadtsatye gody*. Munich: Wilhelm Fink Verlag, 1982.

———. *Stat'i o Pasternake*. Bremen: K-Presse, 1977.

Fokin, Pavel, and Dmitrii Timofeev, eds. *Maiakovskii bez gliantsa*. St. Petersburg: Pal'mira, 2016.

Ford, Thomas H. "Poetry's Media." *New Literary History* 44, no. 3 (2013): 449–69.

Frank, Stephen P., and Mark D. Steinberg, eds. *Cultures in Flux: Lower-Class Values, Practices, and Resistance in Late Imperial Russia*. Princeton, NJ: Princeton University Press, 1994.

Frazer, Ray. "The Origin of the Term 'Image.'" *ELH* 27, no. 2 (1960): 149–61.

Freer, Alexander. "Rhythm as Coping." *New Literary History* 46, no. 3 (Summer 2015): 549–68.

Freidin, Gregory. *A Coat of Many Colors: Osip Mandelstam and His Mythologies of Self-Presentation*. Berkeley: University of California Press, 1987.

Fried, Michael. "How Modernism Works: A Response to T. J. Clark." *Critical Inquiry* 9, no. 1 (1982): 217–34.

Friedman, Susan Stanford. "Periodizing Modernism: Postcolonial Modernities and the Space/Time Borders of Modernist Studies." *Modernism/modernity* 13, no. 3 (September 2006): 425–43.

———. *Planetary Modernisms: Provocations on Modernity across Time*. New York: Columbia University Press, 2015.

———. "World Modernisms, World Literature, and Comparativity." In *The Oxford Handbook of Global Modernisms*, edited by Mark Wollaeger and Matt Eatough, 499–526. Oxford: Oxford University Press, 2012.

Futuristy: Pervyi zhurnal russkikh futuristov, no. 1–2 (1914).

Gasparov, M. L. *Izbrannye trudy*. 3 vols. Moscow: Iazyki russkoi kul'tury, 1997.

———. *Metr i smysl: Ob odnom iz mekhanizmov kul'turnoi pamiati*. Moscow: Fortuna EL, 2012 [1999].

———. *Ocherk istorii russkogo stikha: Metrika, ritmika, rifma, strofika*. Moscow: Fortuna Limited, 2000.

———. "Pervochtenie i perechtenie: K tynianovskomu poniatiiu suktsessivnosti stikhotvornoi rechi." *Tynianovskii sbornik* 3 (1988): 15–23.

———. "Russkii trekhudarnyi dol'nik XX veka." In *Teoriia stikha*, edited by V. M. Zhirmunsky, D. S. Likhachev, and V. E. Kholshevnikov, 59–106. Leningrad: Nauka, 1968.

———. "Taktovik v poezii XX veka." In Mikhail Gasparov, *Sovremennyi russkii stikh: Metrika i ritmika*, 294–351. Moscow: Nauka, 1974.

———. "Tynianov i problema semantiki metra." *Tynianovskii sbornik* 1 (1984): 105–13.

Gelikman, Oleg. "Intermediality and Aesthetic Theory in Shklovsky's and Adorno's Thought." *CLCWeb: Comparative Literature and Culture* 13, no. 3 (2011), https://doi.org/10.7771/1481-4374.1791.

Gindin, S. I. "Pervyi konflikt dvukh pokolenii osnovatelei russkogo stikhovedeniia." *Novoe literaturnoe obozrenie* 4, no. 86 (2007): 64–69.

Gindin, S. I., and A. V. Man'kovskii. "Kak Moskovskii lingvisticheskii kruzhok voeval s Briusovym i Potebnei." *Novoe literaturnoe obozrenie* 4, no. 86 (2007): 70–78.

Ginzburg, Lydia. *O lirike.* Leningrad: Sovetskii pisatel', 1974.

Gitelman, Lisa. *Always Already New: Media, History, and the Data of Culture.* Cambridge, MA: MIT Press, 2006.

Glaser, Ben. *Modernism's Metronome: Meter and Twentieth-Century Poetics.* Baltimore, MD: Johns Hopkins University Press, 2020.

Goble, Mark. *Beautiful Circuits: Modernism and the Mediated Life.* New York: Columbia University Press, 2010.

Goldberg, RoseLee. *Performance Art: From Futurism to the Present.* New York: Thames and Hudson, 2011.

Gorham, Michael S. *Speaking in Soviet Tongues: Language Culture and the Politics of Voice in Revolutionary Russia.* DeKalb: Northern Illinois University Press, 2003.

Grechishkin, S. S., and A. V. Lavrov. "O stikhovedcheskom nasledii Andreia Belogo." In *Struktura i semiotika khudozhestvennogo teksta: Trudy po znakovym sistemam XII*, 97–111. Tartu, 1981.

Greenberg, Clement. "Avant-Garde and Kitsch." *Partisan Review* 6, no. 5 (Fall 1939): 34–49.

———. "Modernist Painting." In *Modern Art and Modernism: A Critical Anthology*, edited by Francis Frascina and Charles Harrison, 5–10. New York, NY: Westview, 1982.

———. "Towards a Newer Laocoön." *Partisan Review* 7, no. 4 (July–August 1940): 296–310.

Greene, Roland. *Post-Petrarchism: Origins and Innovations of the Western Lyric Sequence.* Princeton, NJ: Princeton University Press, 1991.

Greve, Charlotte. "Writing and the 'Subject': Image-Text Relations in the Early Russian Avant-Garde and Contemporary Russian Visual Poetry." PhD dissertation. University of Amsterdam, 2004.

Griffiths, Eric. *The Printed Voice of Victorian Poetry*. Oxford: Clarendon, 1989.

Griunberg, P. N. *Istoriia nachala gramzapisi v Rossii.* Moscow: Iazyki slavianskoi kul'tury, 2002.

Gudkov, Lev. "Poniatie i metafory istorii u Tynianova i opoiazovtsev." *Tynianovskie chteniia* 3 (1988): 91–108.

Guillory, John. "Genesis of the Media Concept." *Critical Inquiry* 36, no. 2 (Winter 2010): 321–62.

Hambürger, Kate. *The Logic of Literature*. Translated by Marilynn J. Rose. 2nd ed. Bloomington: Indiana University Press, 1993.

Hansen-Löve, Aage. "Intermedialität und Intertextualität: Probleme der Korrelation von Wort-und Bildkunst—Am Beispiel der russischen Moderne." In *Dialog der Texte: Hamburger Kolloquium zur Intertextualität*, edited by Wolf Schmid and Wolf-Dieter Stempel, 291–360. Vienna: Wiener Slawistischer Almanach, 1983.

———. *Russkii formalizm: Metodologicheskaia rekonstruktsiia razvitiia na osnove printsipa ostraneniia*. Translated by S. A. Romashko. Moscow: Iazyki russkoi kul'tury, 2001.

Hasty, Olga Peters. "Representing Ephemerality: Pasternak's 'Groza, momental'naia navek.'" In *Eternity's Hostage: Selected Papers from the Stanford International Conference on Boris Pasternak, May 2004*, edited by Lazar Fleishman, 116–32. Stanford, CA: Stanford Slavic Studies, 2006.

Hayot, Eric, and Rebecca L. Walkowitz, eds. *A New Vocabulary for Global Modernism*. New York: Columbia University Press, 2016.

Hickey, Martha Weitzel. *The Writer in Petrograd and the House of the Arts*. Evanston, IL: Northwestern University Press, 2009.

Hughes, Olga. *The Poetic World of Boris Pasternak*. Princeton, NJ: Princeton University Press, 1974.

Hughes, Robert. "Bely's Musical Aesthetics." In *Andrey Bely: A Critical Review*, edited by Gerald Janecek, 137–45. Lexington: University Press of Kentucky, 1978.

Huot, Sylvia. *From Song to Book*. Ithaca, NY: Cornell University Press, 1987.

Iakubinskii, Lev. "O zvukakh stikhotvornogo iazyka." *Poetika: Sborniki po teorii poeticheskogo iazyka* (1919): 37–49.

———. "Otkuda berut stikhi." *Knizhnyi ugol* 7 (1921): 25.

Isparova, F. Kh. "'Smeshchenie' fevralia v stikhi v stikhotvorenii B. Pasternaka 'Fevral': Dostat' chernil i plakat'!" *Vestnik RGGU: Seriia: Literaturovedenie, Iazykoznanie, Kul'turologiia* 2 (2010): 136–47.

Ivanov, Viacheslav V. "Pasternak i OPOIAZ (K postanovke voprosa)." *Tynianovskii sbornik* 3 (1988): 70–83.

———. *Vospominaniia. Issledovaniia. Stat'i*. Moscow: Azbukovnik, 2015.

Ivanova, I. "Razvitie poniatiia 'zhivoe slovo' v russkoi kul'ture XIX—nachala XX veka (ot slovosochetaniia k ofitsial'nomu institutu)." *Schweizerische Beiträge zum XIII. Internationalen Slavistenkongress in Ljubljana, August 2003, Slavica Helvetica* 70 (2003): 103–17.

Jakobson, Roman. *Language in Literature*. Edited by Krystyna Pomorska and Stephen Rudy. Cambridge, MA: Harvard University Press, 1987.

———. "Moskovskii lingvisticheskii kruzhok." Edited by M. I. Shapir. *Philologica* 3 (1996): 361–79.

———. "Noveishaia russkaia poeziia." In Roman Jakobson, *Selected Writings, Volume V: On Verse, Its Masters and Explorers*, edited by Stephen Rudy and Martha Taylor, 299–354. Amsterdam: De Gruyter, Mouton, 1979.

———. "Randbemerkungen zur Proza des Dichters Pasternak." In Roman Jakobson. *Selected Writings, Volume V: On Verse, Its Masters and Explorers*, edited by Stephen Rudy and Martha Taylor, 416–32. Amsterdam: De Gruyter, Mouton, 1979.

———. "Retrospect." In Roman Jakobson. *Selected Writings, Volume V: On Verse, Its Masters and Explorers*, edited by Stephen Rudy and Martha Taylor, 569–601. Amsterdam: De Gruyter, Mouton, 1979.

Janecek, Gerald. "Intonation and Layout in Bely's Poetry." In *Andrey Bely: Centenary Papers*, edited by Boris Christa, 81–90. Amsterdam: Adolf M. Hakkert, 1980.

———. "Kruchenykh contra Gutenburg." In *The Russian Avant-Garde Book: 1910–1934*, edited by Margit Rowell and Deborah Wye, 41–49. New York: Museum of Modern Art, 2002.

———. *The Look of Russian Literature: Avant-Garde Visual Experiments 1900–1930.* Princeton, NJ: Princeton University Press, 1984.

———. *Zaum: The Transrational Language of Russian Futurism.* San Diego, CA: San Diego State University Press, 1996.

Kahn, Andrew, Mark Lipovetsky, Irina Reyfman, and Stephanie Sandler. *A History of Russian Literature.* New York: Oxford University Press, 2018.

Kalinin, Ilya. "Viktor Shklovskii versus Roman Iakobson: Voina iazykov." *Vestnik sankt-peterburgskogo universiteta* 9, no. 3 (September 2016): 55–63.

Kappeler, Erin. "Constructing Walt Whitman: Literary History and Histories of Rhythm." In *Critical Rhythm: The Poetics of a Literary Life Form*, edited by Jonathan Culler and Ben Glaser, 128–52. New York: Fordham University Press, 2019.

Katanian, V. *Maiakovskii: Khronika zhizni i deiatel'nosti.* Moscow: Sovetskii pisatel, 1985.

———. *Maiakovskii: Literaturnaia khronika.* Moscow: Gosudarstvennoe izdatel'stvo khudozhestvennoi literatury, 1956.

Kelly, Catriona, and Stephen Lovell, eds. *Russian Literature, Modernism and the Visual Arts.* Cambridge: Cambridge University Press, 2000.

Keys, Roger. *The Reluctant Modernist: Andrei Belyi and the Development of Russian Fiction, 1902–1914.* Oxford: Clarendon, 1996.

Khardzhiev, Nikolai. *Ot Maiakovskogo do Kruchenykh: Izbrannye raboty o russkom futurizme.* Moscow: Gileia, 2006.

Khitrova, Daria. "Things Untimely: Death, Birth, and Poetry in Evgenii Baratynsky's 'Nedonosok.'" *Slavic and East European Journal* 64, no. 2 (2020): 284–304.

Khmel'nitskaya, T. I. "Poeziia Andreia Belogo." In *Stikhotvoreniia i poemy*, by A. Belyi, 5–66. Moscow-Leningrad: Sovetskii pisatel', 1966.

Khodasevich, V. F. *Nekropol'*. In *Sobranie sochinenii*, by V. F. Khodasevich, 4 vols., 4:7–184. Moscow: Soglasie, 1996–97.

Kliger, Ilya. "Dynamic Archeology or Distant Reading: Literary Study between Two Formalisms." *Russian Literature* 122–23 (May–July 2021): 7–28.

Kliger, Ilya, and Boris Maslov, eds. *Persistent Forms: Explorations in Historical Poetics*. New York: Fordham University Press, 2015.

Kling, Oleg. "Boris Pasternak i simvolizm." *Voprosy literatury* 2 (March–April 2002): 25–59.

Koretskaia, I. V. "Literatura v krugu iskusstv." In *Russkaia literatura rubezha vekov (1890-e—nachalo 1920-x godov)*, edited by V. A. Keldysh, 2 vols., 1:131–90. Moscow: IMLI RAN, 2000.

Kornbluh, Anna. *The Order of Forms: Realism, Formalism, and Social Space*. Chicago: University of Chicago Press, 2019.

Krämer, Sybille. "Kulturanthropologie der Medien: Thesen zur Einführung." In *Praktiken des Performativen*, edited by Christoph Wulf, 130–33. Berlin: Akademie-Verlag Fischer-Lichte.

Kramnick, Jonathan, and Anahid Nersessian. "Form and Explanation." *Critical Inquiry* 43, no. 3 (Spring 2017): 650–69.

Kremer, Aleksandra. *The Sound of Modern Polish Poetry: Performance and Recording after World War II*. Cambridge, MA: Harvard University Press, 2021.

Kujundzic, Dragan. *The Returns of History: Russian Nietzscheans after Modernity*. Albany: SUNY Press, 1997.

Kukushkina, Varvara, Ilona Svetlikova, and Pavel Iushin. "Nauchnye konteksty 'zvezdnogo uzhasa': Kommentarii k Andreiu Belomu." *Die Welt der Slaven* 65, no. 1 (2019): 73–88.

Kunichika, Michael. *"Our Native Antiquity": Archaeology and Aesthetics in the Culture of Russian Modernism*. Boston: Academic Studies, 2015.

Lavine, Ludmila. "The Visual, the Epic, and Pasternak's 'Devjat'sot pjatyj god.'" *Russian Literature* 71, no. 1 (2012): 75–99.

Lavrov, A. V., ed. *Andrei Belyi i Aleksandr Blok: Perepiska: 1903–1919*. Moscow: Progress-Pleiada, 2001.

———. *Andrei Belyi v 1900-e gody: Zhizn' i literaturnaia deiatel'nost'*. Moscow: Novoe literaturnoe obozrenie, 1995.

———, ed. *Andrei Bely: Pro et contra*. St. Petersburg: Izdatel'stvo Russkogo Khristianskogo gumanitarnogo instituta, 2004.

Levchenko, Ian, and Igor Pil'shchikov, eds. *Epokha "ostraneniia": Russkii formalizm i sovremennoe gumanitarnoe znanie: Kollektivnaia monografia*. Moscow: Novoe literaturnoe obozrenie, 2017.

Levina, Tatiana. "'Stradatel'noe bogatstvo': Pasternak i russkaia zhivopis' 1910-x—nachala 1940-x gg." *Literaturnoe obozrenie* 2 (1990): 84–89.

Lewis, Cara L. *Dynamic Form: How Intermediality Made Modernism*. Ithaca, NY: Cornell University Press, 2020.

Livak, Leonid. *How It Was Done in Paris: Russian Emigre Literature and French Modernism.* Madison: University of Wisconsin Press, 2003.

———. *In Search of Russian Modernism.* Baltimore, MD: Johns Hopkins University Press, 2018.

Livingstone, Angela. *The Marsh of Gold: Pasternak's Writings on Inspiration and Creation.* Boston: Academic Studies, 2008.

Longenbach, James. *The Resistance to Poetry.* Chicago: University of Chicago Press, 2014.

Lotman, Iurii. "Graficheskii obraz poezii." In Iurii Lotman. *Analiz poeticheskogo teksta: Struktura stikha*, 70–74. Leningrad: Prosveshchenie, 1972.

———. *O poetakh i poezii.* St. Petersburg: Iskusstvo-SPb, 1996.

———. "Russkaia literatura poslepetrovskoi epoki i khristianskaia traditsiia." In *Iu. M. Lotman i tartussko-moskovskaia semioticheskaia shkola*, edited by A. Koshelev, 365–79. Moscow: Gnosis, 1994.

———. "Stikhotvoreniia rannego Pasternaka i nekotorye voprosy strukturnogo izucheniia teksta." *Trudy po znakovym sistemam* 4 (1969): 206–38.

Lotman, Yury. "Language and Reality in the Early Pasternak." In *Pasternak: A Collection of Critical Essays*, edited by Victor Erlich, 21–31. Englewood Cliffs, NJ: Prentice-Hall, 1978.

Lovell, Stephen. "*Glasnost'* in Practice: Public Speaking in the Era of Alexander II." *Past & Present* 218, no. 1 (February 2013): 127–58.

Lvoff, Basil. "Viktor Shklovsky and Marshall McLuhan: Beyond Common Sense." *New Zealand Slavonic Journal* 49/50 (2015): 1–30.

Magomedova, D. M. "Aleksandr Blok: 'Neznakomka': Vnutrenniaia struktura i kontekst prochteniia." *Vestnik PSTGU III: Filologiia* 2, no. 16 (2009): 38–46.

Maiakovskii, V. V. *Polnoe sobranie sochinenii.* 13 vols. Moscow: Gosudarstvennoe izdatel'stvo khudozhestvennoi literatury, 1955.

Maksimov, Dmitrii. "Ideia puti v poeticheskom soznanii A Bloka." In *Blokovskii sbornik II.* Tartu: Tartuskii gosudarstvennyi universitet, 1972.

Malmstad, John E., ed. *Andrei Bely: Spirit of Symbolism.* Ithaca, NY: Cornell University Press, 1987.

———. "Boris Pasternak—The Painter's Eye." *Russian Review* 51, no. 3 (July 1992): 301–18.

Mandel'shtam, Osip. *Sobranie sochinenii.* 3 vols. Moscow: Progress Pleiada, 2010.

Mao, Douglas, and Rebecca L. Walkowitz. "The New Modernist Studies." *PMLA* 123, no. 3 (2008): 737–48.

Markov, Vladimir. *Russian Futurism: A History.* Berkeley: University of California Press, 1968.

Martin, Meredith. *The Rise and Fall of Meter: Poetry and English National Culture, 1860–1930.* Princeton, NJ: Princeton University Press, 2012.

Mayakovsky, Vladimir. "A Cloud in Trousers." Translated by P. Lemke. In *Russian Poetry: The Modern Period*, edited by J. Glad and D. Weissbort. Iowa City: University of Iowa Press, 1978.

McLuhan, Marshall. *Understanding Media: The Extensions of Man.* New York: McGraw-Hill, 1964.

McReynolds, Louise. *Russia at Play: Leisure Activities at the End of the Tsarist Era.* Ithaca, NY: Cornell University Press, 2003.

Merrill, Jessica. *The Origins of Russian Literary Theory: Folklore, Philology, Form.* Evanston, IL: Northwestern University Press, 2021.

Metchenko, A. "Rannii Maiakovskii." In *Vladimir Maiakovskii: Sbornik*, edited by A. L. Dymshitsa and O. V. Tsekhnovitsera, 9–32. Moscow: AN SSSR, 1940.

Mgebrov, A. A. *Zhizn' v teatre.* 2 vols. Moscow: Academia, 1932.

Middleton, Peter. "How to Read a Reading of a Written Poem." *Oral Tradition* 20, no. 1 (March 2005): 7–34.

Mints, Zara. "Ob odnom sposobe obrazovaniia novykh znachenii slov v proizvedenii iskusstva (ironicheskoe i poeticheskoe v stikhotvorenii Al. Bloka 'Neznakomka')." In *Poetika Aleksandra Bloka*, by Zara Mints, 532–39. St. Petersburg: Iskusstvo, 1999.

———. *Poetika Aleksandra Bloka.* St. Petersburg: Iskusstvo, 1999.

Mitchell, W. J. T. *Iconology: Image, Text, Ideology.* Chicago: University of Chicago Press, 1987.

———. *Picture Theory: Essays on Verbal and Visual Representation.* Chicago: University of Chicago Press, 1994.

———. "There Are No Visual Media." *Journal of Visual Culture* 4, no. 2 (August 2005): 257–66.

Mitchell, W. J. T., and Mark B. N. Hansen, eds. *Critical Terms for Media Studies.* Chicago: University of Chicago Press, 2010.

Molodiakov, V. E. "Valerii Briusov: 'Ne po-akterski, a po-'poetski.'" In *Zvuchashchii serebriannyi vek: Chitaet poet*, edited by E. M. Shuvannikova, 78–95. St. Petersburg: Nestor-istoriia, 2018.

Moretti, Franco. *Distant Reading*. London: Verso, 2013.

———. "The Slaughterhouse of Literature." *Modern Language Quarterly* 61, no. 1 (March 2000): 207–28.

Neuberger, Joan. "Culture Besieged: Hooliganism and Futurism." In *Cultures in Flux: Lower-Class Values, Practices, and Resistance in Late Imperial Russia*, edited by Stephen P. Frank and Mark D. Steinberg, 185–203. Princeton, NJ: Princeton University Press, 1994.

Nietzsche, Friedrich. *Sämtliche Werke: Kritische Studienausgabe*, edited by Giorgio Colli and Mazzino Montinari. 15 vols. Berlin: Walter de Gruyter and Deutscher Taschenbuch, 1980.

Nilsson, N. Å. "Kručenych's Poem 'Dyr bul ščyl.'" *Scando-Slavica* 24 (1978): 139–48.

Novak, Julia. "Performing the Poet, Reading (to) the Audience: Some Thoughts on Live Poetry as Literary Communication." *Journal of Literary Theory* 6, no. 2 (2012): 358–82.

O'Brian, John, ed. *Clement Greenberg: The Collected Essays and Criticism*. 4 vols. Chicago: University of Chicago Press, 1986.

Olenina, Ana Hedberg. *Psychomotor Aesthetics: Movement and Affect in Modern Literature and Film*. Oxford: Oxford University Press, 2020.

Ong, Walter. *Orality and Literacy: The Technologizing of the Word*. London: Methuen, 1982.

Orlova, E. I. "'Mezh konturom i zapakhom tsvetka' (Iz istorii metodologicheskikh iskanii 1910-kh godov)." *Voprosy literatury* 4 (2002): 136–69.

Ossovskaia, M. P. "Sviaz vremen: Mezhdistsiplinarnaia integratsiia." *Golos i rech'* 1 (2010): 8–13.

Oushakine, Serguei. "'Ne vzletevshie samolety mechty': O pokolenii formal'nogo metoda." In *Formal'nyi metod: Antologiia russkogo modernizma*, edited by Serguei Oushakine, 3 vols., 1:9–60. Moscow: Kabinetnyi uchenyi, 2016.

———. "Shklovsky and Things, or Why Tolstoy's Sofa Should Matter." In *Viktor Shklovsky's Heritage in Literature, Arts, and Philosophy*, edited by Slav N. Gratchev and Howard Mancing, 93–108. London: Lexington Books, 2019.

Palmer, Isobel. "Re-vision in Boris Pasternak's *City*." *Slavic and East European Journal* 66, no. 3 (2022): 411–27.

Paperno, Irina, and Joan Grossman, eds. *Creating Life: The Aesthetic Utopia of Russian Modernism*. Stanford, CA: Stanford University Press, 1994.

Pasternak, B. L. *Polnoe sobranie sochinenii*. 11 vols. Moscow: Slovo, 2005.

Pasternak, E. B. *Boris Pasternak: Materialy dlia biografii*. Moscow: Sovetskii pisatel', 1989.

Pasternak, E. V., ed. *"Marburg" Borisa Pasternaka: Temy i variatsii*. Moscow: Rossiiskii gosudarstvennyi gumanitarnyi universitet, 2009.

Pasternak, E. V., and E. B. Pasternak, eds. *Perepiska Borisa Pasternaka*. Moscow: Khudozhestvennaia literatura, 1990.

Perloff, Marjorie. *The Futurist Moment: Avant-Garde, Avant Guerre, and the Language of Rupture*. Chicago: University of Chicago Press, 1986.

———. *Radical Artifice: Writing Poetry in the Age of Media*. Chicago: University of Chicago Press, 1991.

Peters, John Durham. *The Marvelous Clouds: Toward a Philosophy of Elemental Media*. Chicago: University of Chicago Press, 2015.

———. *Speaking into the Air: A History of the Idea of Communication*. Chicago: University of Chicago Press, 1999.

Pil'shchikov, Igor. "Poniatiia 'stikh,' 'metr' i 'ritm' v russkoi stikhovedcheskoi traditsii." *Trudy Instituta russkogo iazyka im. V.V. Vinogradova* 11 (2017): 12–30.

———. "Zasedanie Moskovskogo lingvisticheskogo kruzhka 1-go iiunia 1919 i zarozhdenie stikhovedcheskikh kontseptsii O. Brika, B. Tomashevskogo i R. Jakobsona." *Revue des Études Slaves* 88, no. 1/2 (2017): 151–75.

Polonskii, V. V. *Mezhdu traditsiei i modernizmom: Russkaia literatura rubezha XIX–XX vekov: Istoriia, poetika, kontekst*. Moscow: IMLI RAN, 2011.

Pomorska, Krystyna. *Russian Formalist Theory and Its Poetic Ambiance*. The Hague: Mouton, 1968.

Potebnya, Alexander. *Iz zapisok po teorii slovesnosti: Poeziia i proza: Tropy i figury: Myshlenie poeticheskoe i mificheskoe: Prilozheniia*. The Hague: Mouton, 1970.

Prins, Yopie. *Victorian Sappho*. Princeton, NJ: Princeton University Press, 1999.

———. "What Is Historical Poetics?" *Modern Language Quarterly* 77, no. 1 (2016): 13–40.

Pyman, Avril. *A History of Russian Symbolism*. Cambridge: Cambridge University Press, 1994.

Rajewsky, Irina O. "Border Talks: The Problematic Status of Media Borders in the Current Debate about Intermediality." In *Media Borders, Multimodality and Intermediality*, edited by Lars Elleström, 51–68. Basingstoke, UK: Palgrave Macmillan, 2010.

———. "Intermediality, Intertextuality, and Remediation: A Literary Perspective on Intermediality." *Intermédialités* 6 (2005): 43–64.

Ram, Harsha. "The Scale of Global Modernisms: Imperial, National, Regional, Local." *PMLA* 131, no. 5 (October 2016): 1372–85.

———. "The Sonnet and the Mukhambazi: Genre Wars on the Edges of the Russian Empire." *PMLA* 122, no. 5 (October 2007): 1548–70.

Ramazani, Jahan. "Form." In *A New Vocabulary for Global Modernism*, edited by Eric Hayot and Rebecca L. Walkowitz, 114–29. New York: Columbia University Press, 2016.

———. *A Transnational Poetics*. Chicago: University of Chicago Press, 2009.

Rancour-Laferriere, Daniel. *Five Russian Poems: Exercises in a Theory of Poetry*. Englewood, NJ: Transworld, 1977.

Ricoeur, Paul. *The Rule of Metaphor: The Creation of Meaning in Language*. Translated by Robert Czerny et al. London: Routledge, 2003.

Rosenthal, Bernice G. *D. S. Merezhkovsky and the Silver Age: The Development of a Revolutionary Mentality*. The Hague: Martinus Nijhoff, 1975.

———. "The Spirit of Music in Russian Symbolism." *Russian History* 10, no. 1 (1983): 66–76.

———. "The Transmutation of the Symbolist Ethos: Mystical Anarchism and the Revolution of 1905." *Slavic Review* 36, no. 4 (1977): 608–27.

Roziner, F. "Pasternak i problema vzaimovliianii iskusstv." In *Boris Pasternak 1890–1990*, edited by Lev Loseff, Norwich Symposia on Russian Literature and Culture 1 (1991): 40–51.

Rubins, Maria. *Russian Montparnasse: Transnational Writing in Interwar Paris*. New York: Palgrave Macmillan, 2015.

Rudnitsky, K. L. *Russkoe rezhisserskoe iskusstvo 1908–1917*. Moscow: Nauka, 1990.

Schechner, Richard. *Performance Theory*. 2nd ed. London: Routledge, 1988.

Scherr, Barry P. *Russian Poetry: Meter, Rhythm, and Rhyme.* Berkeley: University of California Press, 1977.

———. "Taranovsky's Laws: Further Observations from a Comparative Perspective." In *Poetry and Poetics: A Centennial Tribute to Kiril Taranovsky*, edited by Barry Scherr, James Bailey, and Vida Johnson, 343–66. Bloomington, IN: Slavica, 2014.

Seifrid, Thomas. *The Word Made Self: Russian Writings on Language, 1860–1930.* Ithaca, NY: Cornell University Press, 2005.

Serditova, A. "Avtograf na notnoi bumage (K istorii sozdaniia tragedii *Vladimir Maiakovskii*)." *Voprosy literatury* 7 (1983): 202–7.

Sergay, Timothy D. "'A Music of Letters': Reconsidering Eikhenbaum's *Melodics of Verse*." *Slavic and East European Journal* 59, no. 2 (Summer 2015): 194–211.

Serres, Michael. *The Five Senses: A Philosophy of Mingled Bodies*. Translated by Margaret Sankey and Peter Cowley. London: Continuum, 2008.

Shaitanov, Iurii. "Formalizm kak iavlenie istoricheskoi poetiki." *Voprosy literatury* 6 (2016): 7–29.

Shapir, M. I. "'Versus' vs 'prosa': Prostranstvo-vremia poeticheskogo teksta." *Philologica* 2, no. 3/4 (1995): 7–47.

———. *Universum versus: Iazyk—stikh—smysl v russkoi poezii XVIII–XX vekov.* Moscow: Iazyki russkoi kul'tury, 2000.

Sharp, Jane. "The Russian Avant-Garde and Its Audience: Moscow, 1913." *Modernism/modernity* 6, no. 3 (1999): 91–116.

Shcherba, L. V. *Izbrannye raboty po russkomu iazyku.* Moscow: Uchpedgiz, 1957.

Shershenevich, Vadim. *Futurizm bez maski*. Moscow: Tipografiia "Moskovskoe Izdatel'stvo," 1913.

Shevelenko, Irina. *Modernizm kak arkhaizm: Natsionalizm i poiski modernistskoi estetiki v Rossii.* Moscow: Novoe literaturnoe obozrenie, 2017.

Shilov, L. A. *Golosa, zazvuchashchie vnov'*. Moscow: Al'daon, 2004.

———. *"Ia slyshal po radio golos Tolstogo . . .": Ocherki zvuchashchei literatury*. Moscow, 1989.

———. "Istoriia odnoi kollektsii." In *Zvuchashchii mir: Kniga o zvukovoi dokumentalistike: Sbornik statei*, edited by V. M. Voznichkov. Moscow: Iskusstvo, 1979.

Shklovskii, Viktor. *Gamburgskii schet: Stat'i—vospominaniia—esse.* Moscow: Sovetskii pisatel', 1990.

———. *O teorii prozy*. Moscow: Federatsiia, 1929.

———. *Zoo, ili pis'ma ne o liubvi.* In *Zhily-byly*, by Viktor Shklovskii, 165–256. Moscow: Sovetskii pisatel', 1966.

Shklovsky, Viktor. *Bowstring: On the Dissimilarity of the Similar*. Translated by Shushan Avagyan. Champaign, IL: Dalkey Archive, 2011.

———. *Literature and Cinematography*. Translated by Irina Masinovsky. Champaign, IL: Dalkey Archive, 2008.

Shklovsky, Viktor, et al. "On Poetry and Trans-Sense Language." *October* 34 (1985): 3–24.

Shruba, Manfred. *Literaturnye ob"edineniia Moskvy i Peterburga 1890–1917 godov: Slovar'*. Moscow: Novoe literaturnoe obozrenie, 2004.

Shuvannikova, E. M., ed. *Zvuchashchii serebriannyi vek: Chitaet poet*. St. Petersburg: Nestor-istoriia, 2018.

Siegert, Bernhard. *Cultural Techniques: Grids, Filters, Doors, and Other Articulations of the Real*. Translated by Geoffrey Winthrop-Young. New York: Fordham University Press, 2015.

Sievers, Eduard. *Rhythmisch-Melodische Studien*. Heidelberg: Winter, 1912.

Simplicio, Dasha di. "B. Pasternak i zhivopis'." In *Boris Pasternak and His Times: Selected Papers from the Second International Symposium on Pasternak*, edited by Lazar Fleishman, 195–211. Berkeley, CA: Berkeley Slavic Specialties, 1989.

Sinyavskii, Andrei. "Poeziia Pasternaka." In *Stikhotvoreniia i poemy*, by Boris Pasternak, 9–62. Moscow: Sovetskii pisatel', 1965.

Siniavsky, Andrei. "Boris Pasternak." In *Pasternak*, edited by Donald Davie and Angela Livingstone, 154–219. London: Macmillan, 1969.

Sjöholm, Cecilia. "Lessing's Laocoon: Aesthetics, Affects and Embodiment." *Nordic Journal of Aesthetics* 46 (2013): 18–34.

Sloane, David. *Aleksandr Blok and the Dynamics of the Lyric Cycle*. Bloomington, IN: Slavica, 1988.

Smith, David Nowell. *On Voice in Poetry: The Work of Animation*. London: Palgrave Macmillan, 2014.

———. "What Is Called Rhythm?" In *Critical Rhythm: The Poetics of a Literary Life Form*, edited by Jonathan Culler and Ben Glaser, 40–59. New York: Fordham University Press, 2019.

Stapanian, Juliette. *Mayakovsky's Cubo-Futurist Vision*. Houston, TX: Rice University Press, 1986.

Steinberg, Mark D. *Petersburg Fin de Siècle*. New Haven, CT: Yale University Press, 2011.

Steiner, Peter. *Russian Formalism: A Metapoetics*. Ithaca, NY: Cornell University Press, 1984.

Sterne, Jonathan. *The Audible Past: Cultural Origins of Sound Reproduction*. Durham, NC: Duke University Press, 2003.

Stone, Jonathan. *The Institutions of Russian Modernism: Conceptualizing, Publishing, and Reading Symbolism*. Evanston, IL: Northwestern University Press, 2017.

Svetlikova, Ilona. *Istoki russkogo formalizma: Traditsiia psikhologizma i formal'naia shkola*. Moscow: Novoe literaturnoe obozrenie, 2005.

———. *The Moscow Pythagoreans: Mathematics, Mysticism, and Anti-Semitism in Russian Symbolism*. Basingstoke, UK: Palgrave Macmillan, 2013.

Taranovskii, Kirill. "O vzaimootnoshenii stikhotvornogo ritma i tematiki." In

O poezii i poetike, by Kirill Taranovskii, 372–403. Moscow: Iazyki russkoi kul'tury, 2000.

Terekhina, V. N. "'U iskusstva putei mnogo': Vladimir Maiakovskii i Ol'ga Rozanova." *Nashe nasledie* 126 (2018), http://www.nasledie-rus.ru/podshivka/12602.php.

Thompson, Ewa M. *Russian Formalism and Anglo-American New Criticism: A Comparative Study*. The Hague: Mouton, 1971.

Tiffany, Daniel. *Infidel Poetics: Riddles, Nightlife, Substance*. Chicago: University of Chicago Press, 2009.

Tihanov, Galin. *The Birth and Death of Literary Theory: Regimes of Relevance in Russia and Beyond*. Stanford, CA: Stanford University Press, 2019.

———. "Why Did Modern Literary Theory Originate in Central and Eastern Europe? (And Why Is It Now Dead?)." *Common Knowledge* 10, no. 1 (2004): 61–81.

Timenchik, R. D. "Tynianov i 'literaturnaia kul'tura' 1910-x godov." *Tynianovskii sbornik* 3 (1988): 159–73.

Toddes, E. A. "Mandel'shtam i opoiazovskaia filologiia." *Tynianovskii sbornik* 2 (1986): 78–102.

Tomashevskii, Boris. *O stikhe*. Leningrad: Priboi, 1929.

———. "Problema stikhotvornogo ritma." In Boris Tomashevskii, *Izbrannye raboty o stikhe: Uchebnoe posobie*, edited by S. I. Monakhov, K. I. Tver'ianovich, and E. V. Khvorost'ianova, 24–52. St. Petersburg: Filologicheskii fakul'tet SPbGU, 2007.

Tomashevsky, Boris, et al. "The New School of Literary History in Russia." *PMLA* 119, no. 1 (2004): 120–32.

Trebnik troikh: Sbornik stikhov i risunok. Moscow, 1913.

Trotsky, Leon. *Literature and Revolution*. Translated by Rose Strunsky. Chicago: Haymarket Books, 2005.

Trotter, David. "Modernism's Media Theory." *Critical Quarterly* 58, no. 3 (2016): 5–26.

Tsvetaeva, Marina. "Epos i lirika sovremennoi Rossii (Vladimir Maiakovskii i Boris Pasternak)." *Novyi grad* 6 (1933): 28–41.

———. *Pis'ma k A. Teskovoi*. Prague: Academia, 1969.

———. "Poet o kritike." *Blagonamerennyi* 2 (1926): 94–125.

———. "Svetovoi liven'." *Epopeia* 3 (1922): 10–33.

Tynianov, Iurii. *Poetika. Istoriia literatury. Kino*. Edited by A. P. Chudakov, M. O. Chudakova, and E. A. Toddes. Moscow: Nauka, 1977.

———. *Problema stikhotvornogo iazyka*. Moscow: Sovetskii pisatel', 1965.

———. "Valerii Briusov." In *Problema stikhotvornogo iazyka*, by Iurii Tynianov, 259–82. Moscow: Sovetskii pisatel', 1965.

Tynianov, Yury. *Permanent Evolution: Selected Essays on Literature, Theory and Film*. Translated by Ainsley Morse and Philip Redko. Boston: Academic Studies, 2019.

University of Chicago, Theories of Media, Keywords Glossary. "Medium specificity." https://csmt.uchicago.edu/glossary2004/specificity.htm.

Vassena, Rafaella. "K rekonstruktsii istorii deiatel'nosti Instituta zhivogo slova (1918–1924)." *Novoe literaturnoe obozrenie* 4 (August 2007): 79–95.

Voloshin, Maksimilian. "Golosa poetov." *Rech'*, June 4, 1917.

Wachtel, Michael. *The Development of Russian Verse.* Cambridge: Cambridge University Press, 1998.

Warren, Sarah. *Mikhail Larionov and the Cultural Politics of Late Imperial Russia.* Farnham, UK: Ashgate, 2013.

Wesling, Donald. *The Chances of Rhyme: Device and Modernity.* Berkeley: University of California Press, 1980.

Williams, Robert C. "The Russian Revolution and the End of Time 1900–1940." *Geschichte Osteuropas* 43, no. 3 (1995): 364–401.

Winckelmann, Johann Joachim. "On the Imitation of the Painting and Sculpture of the Greeks." In Johann Joachim Winckelmann. *Writings on Art*, edited by David Irwin, 61–85. London: Phaidon, 1972.

Wolf, Werner. "(Inter)mediality and the Study of Literature." *CLCWeb: Comparative Literature and Culture* 13, no. 3 (2011), https://doi.org/10.7771/1481-4374.1789.

Wolfson, Susan J., and Marshall Brown, eds. *Reading for Form.* Seattle: University of Washington Press, 2006.

Zapiski Instituta zhivogo slova 1. Petrograd, 1919.

Zhirmunskii, V. M. "Melodika stikha (po povodu knigi B.M. Eikhenbauma *Melodika stikha*, Pb., 1922)." In *Voprosy teorii literatury: Stat'i 1916–1926*, by V. M. Zhirmunskii, 89–153. Leningrad: Academia, 1928.

———. *Vvedenie v metriku: Teoriia stikha.* Leningrad: Academia, 1925.

Zhirmunsky, Viktor. *Introduction to Metrics: The Theory of Verse.* Translated by C. F. Brown. The Hague: Mouton, 1966.

Zholkovskii, A. K. "Infinitivnoe pis'mo: tropy i siuzhety (Materialy k teme)." In *Etkindovskie chteniia*, edited by P. L. Vakhtina et al., 250–71. St. Petersburg: Evropeiskii universitet v Sankt-Peterburge, 2003.

Zholkovsky, A. K. "The Window in the Poetic World of Boris Pasternak." Translated by L. M. O'Toole. *New Literary History* 9, no. 2 (1978): 279–314.

Zolotukhin, Valerii. "Kolodets i kolokol: O vliianii avtorskoi deklamatsii na ispolnitel'skuiu (1905–1929)." *Voprosy teatra* 3–4 (2010): 205–31.

Zolotukhin, Valerii, and Vitalii Shmidt, eds. *Zvuchashchaia khudozhestvennaia rech': Raboty Kabineta izucheniia khudozhestvennoi rechi (1923–1930).* Moscow: Tri kvadrata, 2018.

Index